SDS

SDS

ALAN ADELSON

CHARLES SCRIBNER'S SONS

NEW YORK

THIS BOOK PUBLISHED SIMULTANEOUSLY IN THE
UNITED STATES OF AMERICA AND IN CANADA—
COPYRIGHT UNDER THE BERNE CONVENTION

A—10.71 (H)

PRINTED IN THE UNITED STATES OF AMERICA
LIBRARY OF CONGRESS CATALOG CARD NUMBER 75-143913
SBN 684-12393-2

To Judy and Kerin

CONTENTS

Begin by forgetting. Very little you've heard and read about Students for a Democratic Society is true any more. Some of it never was. SDS is not the band of crazed young rowdies you probably think it is: high on some dreadful potion of ingratitude and power-lust, rampaging around the campuses and in city streets, flailing away at a society that's been too charitable with such clowns. Neither is it the underground network of arrogant bombers and arsonists whose acts of terror have been in the news so much. Nor is SDS dead, finally expired after ten years of leading violent campus rebellions, as some too quickly relieved members of the establishment have been thankfully pronouncing it lately.

It's true that for a while SDS got carried away with leading students in power tantrums. But a sense of failure and frustration set in just about when it seemed, from the outside, that SDS was reveling in marauding. Major social change, not destruction, has always been the goal for SDS. And when the desired restructuring of society wasn't actually being accomplished, disillusionment brought with it a whole new approach.

"Trashing buildings is a lot of garbage," SDS declared last year. The flashy but feeble exercise of student power that used to characterize the radicals is now ridiculed openly by the organization. It may have created the illusion of attacking the system, today's SDSers say, but in reality it rarely even posed a threat.

SDS has not grown passive or decided to co-operate in quiet efforts at reform, of course. The old tactics are still sometimes called into play, but the goals are a lot more serious now. SDS has become an amazingly dedicated cadre of college students and postgraduate (or ungraduated) hangers-on committed to battling the *systematic* evils of our society. SDS has no desire to run the universities any more. It's out to eradicate hatred between the races; the wars that it sees being brought on by the expansionist drives of the world powers; the inherent inequities of wealth and power in American society; and the degradation and abuse of women. SDS has learned from experience that it must set very rigid standards about which battles to engage in and which to avoid because victories in them won't mean much. The goals are everything. Fighting the police to prevent the eviction of a poor working family from its home is laudable, but fighting them to show you dare is child's play.

Bombing buildings is out, no matter why you do it. *SDS was never in on the bombings.* For a while a group of SDS leaders was heading the organization in that direction. But a great many of the members disagreed. A classical Left conflict developed between those who said you should build a movement by involving others and those who said forget about mass movements—we can do it ourselves. One faction wanted to link SDS' efforts with the power of industrial workers. The other said that's old hat—youth culture's the thing.

In June, 1969, after months of bitter internal bickering, SDS was torn apart by the conflicts. A small splinter of the membership, along with the most famous leaders, broke away to try to put the youth culture, go-it-alone approach into practice. In a few months they became known as the Weathermen. They were no longer organizing on the campuses, they were "underground," building bombs. They had new slogans that made those who remained in SDS cringe: "Bring the War Home" and "Smash the Glass of the Ruling Class."

The SDS they left behind moved sharply in a new direction, too. The organization started putting into effect the socialist concept of uniting militant students with a much larger and more powerful force—workers. SDS chapters began concentrating on supporting strikes and trying to defend campus workers who were being harassed or fired for organizing. SDS even launched a national effort to build protests against the skyrocketing level of unemployment.

Far from being two fraternal groups, the Weathermen and SDS were quickly at one another's throats. The Weathermen hated the radicals who were still taking the approach of educating the public to their views. They called them "chicken shits" and bureaucrats. And SDS hated the Weathermen even worse because it could hardly be effective with its proselytizing efforts if prospective allies immediately rejected it as a gang of "mad bombers." The groups brawled repeatedly and at one point SDS was actually afraid it would become one of the Weathermen's bombing targets. Each group cursed the other for being "cops." They were getting in the way of one another's program for revolution. Clearly, however slow or reluctant the news media may be in acknowledging the split that occurred two years ago, the Weathermen are no more a "faction" of SDS now than Eve was a "faction" of Adam following the rib surgery.

The split has thrown SDS into a torturous period of evolution which could conceivably lead it into extinction. Many other species of political groups have disappeared that way. It's possible that the days this book chronicles will turn out to be SDS' last. But at this point the organization is still clinging to life, though its kicking may seem peculiar compared to what one has come to expect from the famous organization of student radicals.

Unlike the Weathermen, SDS is an amazingly open organization. It has to be since its whole strategy is to reach thousands of new people and "win them over" to joining the long-term battle against the system. Pity the foolish police agents who bother to infiltrate their way into the endless series of tedious meetings and utterly legal demonstrations by which the organization now exists. Other than some embarrassing internal rivalries, SDS has nothing to hide. If there are lots of strange faces at a meeting, the members feel more secure. It means their ideas are catching on. I came to them from the "belly of the beast," as the Black Panthers say: straight from three years with the *Wall Street Journal*. I was welcomed. Some helped me enthusiastically with this book. Others were a little afraid of it—cynical that it would "tell the truth about SDS," since so little has.

The book that follows does tell the truth. But "objective journalism," when it actually exists, is often a waste and I make no pretense of it here. It would be foolish to have to seem dispassionate about the vital challenges SDS is posing to the structure of contemporary American society. But this is not a manifesto either. It couldn't be since I have no right to speak for SDS.

This is a profile of SDS by someone who went through college six years ago, when there were "teach-ins" about Vietnam and a lot of people were actually rising to defend the war. It is by someone who has experienced the same limitations of liberal reform politics that have frustrated SDS as an organization. By someone who used to say: "I support those student radicals. I believe in their cause, and if I were still a student I'd be one of them." But by someone who has since come to understand that if you do believe strongly in a cause, there's no excuse for only giving it that kind of lip-service support.

Alan Adelson
New York, 1971

PART ONE

CAMBODIA SPRING

CHAPTER ONE

COLUMBIA:
CONFRONTATION IN
LEFT FIELD

SDS would never stage a phony dog burning nowadays. It has become too politically mature to resort to such stunts. But a few years back, in what they call "the old SDS," there was a whole rash of them. Once in a while now when a chapter is overwhelmed with frustration because it can't arouse an apathetic campus, some member is likely to advise everyone to have patience. He'll remind the radicals that it takes a long-range perspective to build a really durable movement. And he may describe how several chapters in 1966 and '67 got so frustrated they destroyed themselves with desperation dog burnings.

The ploy was created by a chapter at a big university in New England. It had a core of excellent leaders, but SDS had only been on the campus for a little over a year and hadn't yet built up much of a following. Over the summer the leaders vowed to make SDS a powerful force in the coming year. They met repeatedly to analyze how SDS could be really effective in fighting the system. They spent long hours discussing their university's role in society. And they concluded that despite its pretenses of accumulating knowledge and inspiring scholarship, the school was really an integral part of the system's corruption. So they decided to battle it fiercely.

They launched their struggle on the day school opened in September. SDSers welcomed freshmen with leaflets describing how oppressive the school they were entering really was. And from that day on the SDS members continued to arm themselves with leaflets and proselytized among the swarms of students. At first they demanded the firing of professors on the campus who were being paid by the government to devise lethal weapons systems that would rain down death on millions of people. Later they exposed how the university's program in international affairs was training CIA agents to undermine the liberation fights of impoverished and embittered people around the world. When Dow Chemical came to the school recruiting new executives and technicians, the SDSers deplored the company's manufacturing of napalm and paraded around the campus chanting "DOW SHALT NOT KILL."

With each new phase in the year's effort they wrote carefully reasoned leaflets trying to show why it was necessary to protest and how the university's corruption was bolstering society's corruption. Each time, they scraped together enough money to buy reams of paper and mimeographed thousands of copies of the leaflets. Then they blanketed the campus with them, always calling on the other students to join SDS in militant demonstrations.

But the students never seemed to come. SDS would gather alone for the pitifully small demonstrations and then would have to meet later to try to figure out why the rest of the students hadn't responded. Usually the chapter would decide it simply hadn't made clear enough how completely necessary it was for everyone to join SDS in the struggle.

So the radicals would sharpen their explanations the next time around, and they'd redouble their efforts to persuade everyone to join them. Every time it seemed they couldn't fail to bring out at least several hundred students. But when the demonstration time came around there would only be the same twenty or so SDSers who'd come to the planning meetings, who'd written the leaflets, run them off, and given them out. One or two would make a final effort to bring a few more people over by giving rousing speeches through a bullhorn, but the only ones listening to them were their fellow radicals, and they already knew what had to be fought.

Finally May came and SDS still had no active support. Students the radicals talked to agreed about banning the war research and said napalm was shameful. But they didn't seem to feel compelled to do anything about it. And by May if you haven't actually got people moving, you probably aren't going to get them moving. SDS met once more and the demoralization that everyone had been fighting off all year finally got the best of them. "We've been talking about killing and maiming, about imperialism and the oppression of half the world, and these kids just keep goofing with their Frisbees and smoking their marijuana," despaired one of the SDS women who'd worked indefatigably for months. "They won't come out for anything."

And then the funky, slouched-in-a-corner guy no one had noticed much during the year said: "I'll bet they'll come out for a dog burning."

So the leaflet was written. They left out all of the scholarly analysis of how society works. Just a big headline: "DOG IMMO-LATION." And a sketch of a dog going up in flames. They went out into the walkways and dormitories to hand them out and the students, who were sick of SDS leaflets, tried to shun them. But the leafleters would say: "Hey, no! This one is different. We're gonna immolate a dog."

"Oh, yeah? Wow, man! Wild! When?"

They came in droves. The SDS speaker, nearly sick with rage, climbed up the steps and shouted: "We've been talking to you all year about how this rotten institution is helping the government hold people down all over the world. How supposedly moral men here are running computers and playing with deadly germs to help set up a military threat that might be used to kill millions of people. How this university tries to look clean and liberal but helps to maintain the system that holds people down and forces them to live in anguish and deprivation so that the fat cats on the board of trustees can get rich through their billion dollar corporations. We asked you to join us to fight this university and those guys, but you never gave a shit. And now when we tell you we're going to burn up some poor dog, all of you come pouring out here to see it happen. Man, that's sick. You'd probably let us do it, like you let the U.S. burn Vietnamese with napalm. Now, listen! Listen, will you all, because we're trying to tell you how this shitty system can be fought."

And as he began to outline a program of massive demonstrations against war research and the CIA and ROTC and the draft, the people who'd come out to see the dog burned drifted away.

Dog burnings and all other ploys that sucker students out without first persuading them why they really ought to be demonstrating are disparaged as "opportunism" in SDS now. You just build even greater cynicism toward radical politics that way, the radicals say.

But every SDS chapter in the country still has to fight to overcome the same kind of agonizing isolation that plagued the ill-fated (and in the end, suicidal) New England group. Despite all you've heard about the explosive impatience of college students, they simply aren't easily mobilized to lay down their Frisbees and their joints to take up a fight based on somewhat distant moral and political judgments. The *radicals* are by their very nature way out in Left field. All the present authorities have to do to preserve their power and the existing order of society is keep the radicals from breaking out of that isolation and avoid any blunders that will knock the moderates out of their comfortable insulation and send them to join the radicals who would lead them in the attack.

The radicals will get nowhere as long as students believe there's no need for change (which few accept any longer), or that there's no hope for change (which is especially widespread now and accounts for a lot of the patronage of pot), or that the change that anyone wants can be brought about within the system (which is called "liberalism").

So SDS works its hardest to persuade more moderate students that sweeping change is a must and can only come by attacking the system. The young radicals are always criticized for being too impatient; for not listening but just ranting; for seeing everything as either all good or all bad; and for trying to wreck the institutions instead of reforming them. But they've tried the other tack, and they've decided that dealing politely with people you want to overthrow risks leading your following back into the system's clutches. They've found that the men in charge may, when they are really threatened, make some concessions to preserve the basic structure on which their power rests. But none will give up anything without a fight. So SDS is out there all the time, trying to get that fight going.

The job is a good deal harder than it seems on television. The radicals carry on a constant search for "issues." There is plenty they'd like to fight about, but it takes some very careful research and some very judicious choosing to find something that might, if put forward expertly, kindle the interest of the rest of the students who, unlike SDSers, aren't in college to shut it down. It needs something very concrete that they can't ignore; and, if at all possible, something that will finally produce moral indignation in people who, for the most part, try to spare themselves such inconvenient feelings. Even once SDS has something like that going, it takes almost brilliant strategic leadership to win anything. Unless, of course, it's up against an unusually clumsy team of administrators.

A radical following can get lost very quickly. And radical leadership has an annoying tendency to wander off by itself. In 1968, SDS at Columbia led students and a good many campus workers and instructors in the most militant and violent fight ever waged against an American university. But by the spring of 1970, though SDS was even more dedicated to shutting the place down and was a good deal more astute politically, it was back in relative isolation.

It had been a frustrating year. Like a ghetto that had risen in rebellion and had been crushed back into quiescence, Columbia felt it had had its battle for a while. And though a few new students had deliberately come there after the '68 affair hoping things would stay hot, most of the upper classmen were cooling it.

It wasn't as if the great rebellion had all been for naught. In fact nearly all of SDS' 1968 demands had been won. (Which is something of a defeat, say most doctrinaire radicals, since by their analysis a successful campaign will demand more than the power structure can afford to concede and still preserve itself). The chief issue, a sprawling gymnasium that the university had quietly begun constructing on a patch of Harlem's only open space, had been blocked. All that remained of it by 1970 was a fenced-in hole in the ground where the excavation had begun.

And the Institute for Defense Analysis (IDA), a multi-campus war research conglomerate that evaluates the Pentagon's strategic weapons systems, had been formally severed as a university affiliate. Some papers were rewritten and though IDA continued doing the same work, Columbia was no longer officially to blame for it.

The strikers' demands for amnesty had largely been won as well. The charges against the 712 students arrested during the revolt had been dropped. But the university had gone ahead with the prosecution of the many community blacks who had been arrested in the big bust and one of the last cases was just winding up. It was being directed by Frank S. Hogan, the District Attorney of New York, and one of Columbia's trustees. Mr. Hogan was the most unpopular man on campus that spring since he was also charging twenty-one Black Panthers with conspiracy. So a round-the-clock police guard was positioned in front of the house where the D.A. lives, a few blocks from the university. (A year later the students' anger over the charges was upheld when a jury found the Panthers innocent.)

Grayson Kirk, who had understood the growth of the university chiefly in terms of its owning more and more real estate, had been replaced in the president's office by Andrew W. Cordier. It was a temporary appointment. Soon a younger man, William J. McGill, was to take over. But the task of cooling Columbia had fallen to Cordier—a shrewd move in the eyes of many. Cordier had worked for years as a trouble-shooter for the State Department and the United Nations and had been very versatile in handling brewing national revolts. People were betting that in times of campus strife, "the old fox" would fake them out.

The president's office had changed too. Its big glass windows had been replaced with rock-proof plastic, and the word was that all the embarrassing correspondence between the president and various corporation, military and government officials had been stashed in some secret and less vulnerable place.

A herd of campus police had been mobilized on motor-scooters, equipped with walkie-talkies and empowered to make arrests. It hadn't looked very good in 1968 when New York's riot squad, the Tactical Patrol Force, had swarmed on campus and beaten everyone, including clergymen, women, professors and a whole lot of students. So it struck people as a slick move when Columbia put together its own police force. Ed Connelly, the grand old radical of Columbia SDS, who'd been around since 1962, nicknamed the process "Columbiaization" because it seemed akin to President Nixon's Vietnamization program, by which the people of Vietnam would fight one another instead of the U.S.

And the university had spent a tremendous but as yet unannounced amount to install highly sensitive electronic security systems in certain important buildings where delicate technical machinery and documents were located. This was undertaken despite the fact that the university had been publicizing that it had a budget deficit which it estimated at $15 million.

But any changes the university had instituted since the '68 strike were minor compared with the massive redirectioning that the Columbia-Barnard SDS chapter had undertaken.

Since the split in the organization in the summer of '69, when the Weathermen broke away, the Columbia chapter, along with most others in the country that still considered themselves part of national SDS, had lined up behind the intensely committed and extremely hard-line leadership of the Progressive Labor Party. It had been an astounding victory for PL, which had been baited mercilessly by SDS' previous leadership for several years. PL wanted to do a lot more than just purify some questionable or even inhumane practices that were going on at American universities. The Party's avowed purpose is to smash the entire American power structure which it feels those universities serve, and then to replace it with a socialist state run by the workers.

By 1970, radicals in all factions of the movement were beginning to conclude that to be really effective, student revolutionaries would have to attack the entire American system rather than just one outgrowth of it that was considered sacrosanct— academe. PL's program was for SDS to ally itself with American workers. A revolution is very much a possibility in this country, PL reasons, if the tremendous industrial work force can be united in struggle with the legions of students. That powerful worker-student alliance would be enough to run out the entrenched "rulers" here just as the fusion of workers and peasants had established "a dictatorship of the proletariat" in China. Being disciples of Lenin as well as Marx, PL saw the need for a cadre of highly disciplined revolutionary leaders to carry all this out. That was the role the Party had chosen to play.

For a while the pro-PL faction in SDS had worked at building a Worker-Student Alliance caucus within the organization. But after the Weathermen-to-be broke away in 1969, what was left of SDS was basically sympathetic to the idea of the alliance and it became the major thrust of the entire organization. As a primary focus for the effort, PL proposed that SDS members undertake a concerted program to reach the thousands of workers on the campuses. By taking part-time jobs the students could get to know them, and by supporting them in their wage demands and any other grievances, they could show the workers that both groups had a common interest in fighting the administration. In time, according to the strategy, the Campus Worker-Student Alliance would become a model for fighting the national power structure on what would truly be a revolutionary basis.

The Columbia chapter had done quite well at it, really. But that didn't much impress an awful lot of students.

"What the hell have you lousy ranting bastards done all year?" an envigorated member of the rival December 4th Movement contemptuously demanded of SDS leaders one April night. His group was formed and named after the day Chicago police killed Panther leader Fred Hampton in his bed. It had just come in from an evening of old style student rage, breaking windows around the campus to add muscle to its demand that Columbia put up the bail for the twenty-one Panthers trustee Hogan was prosecuting for conspiracy.

"We've won back the jobs of two cafeteria workers," an SDS girl shot back. "That's a lot better than breaking windows."

It may well have been. But for less ideologically committed students, it certainly didn't seem like as much fun. They wanted action. (A very violence-prone group in the old SDS had actually come to be known as "the Action Faction.") Even if the Campus Worker-Student Alliance was going to lead toward a revolution, some students weren't exactly up for waiting. The "Do It!" ethic was making the long-term approach seem silly. SDS, which still used the slogan "Less Talk, More Action" in its newspaper, *New Left Notes*, was getting workers into its alliance more readily than it was getting students.

But there had been moments of inspiration. At Columbia, SDS had teamed up with the black, Asian and Latin American students of the Third World Coalition to call a solid boycott of campus cafeterias. The goals were to win back the job of a very militant shop steward, James Colbert, and to force out Jane Phair, Colbert's boss, a woman who workers considered unfair. Mrs. Phair had held her own, but Colbert was rehired.

"People are coming around and telling me 'you've got to break off with those SDS radicals', Bill Lyons, an electrical worker, told Colbert's "Partial Victory" meeting. "They're trying to break us up. But I tell them, I'm glad to be working with those radical SDS students." And everyone applauded.

"There's a real alliance there," Alan Egelman noted when he relayed the comment to an SDS chapter meeting that night. That didn't solve all the chapter's problems though. Members were pretty worried. Things were by no means as desperate as they had been for the chapter that had planned the dog burning, but SDS at Columbia was faced with grave challenges. The chapter hadn't even been fighting back when it was under attack—and that can really hurt.

Alan and Mike Golash had been selling the Progressive Labor newspaper on the campus a few evenings before when the newly mobilized campus cops swept down on them, dragged them off to the campus security office and roughed them up. Though quite a group of SDSers had seen the incident, no one really sprang to their comrades' aid. The members were upset about that at the meeting and were trying to work it out.

"I was there and I saw them moving on Mike and Alan and I knew I should do something, but I just stood there," admitted a far from wilting flower girl, who soon proved her readiness to fight. "I wasn't intellectualizing over whether it was exactly the right time to move or not. I was just scared and I don't know what to do about it."

Hand-to-hand combat with policemen, even the relative cream-puffs Columbia gets for its security force, doesn't come naturally to a white middle class college kid, however rampant campus violence may seem. The student has to groom himself for it.

"Man, now is the time to teach ourselves that we can take it. I mean if we don't do that now, we're going to be useless in a few years. Those guys out there don't have guns, only clubs. So the worst that's going to happen is you'll get your head busted. Anything but fighting back is just bullshit," lectured Eddie Goldman, a wrestler in his high school days who had established his credential as a political fighter. He'd already gone to court for smashing a dean in the face.

"I can take it all right," said another guy. "But I'm not so sure I can dish it out."

"That's all a hangover of the pacifism they've been teaching us all of our lives so we wouldn't fight back," said someone else. "We really have to confront it and get rid of it or we can forget the whole thing. I mean if I ever get busted and there's thirty people around and they're supposed to be with me and they don't help, then that's it. You won't see me around this group any more under any circumstances. And hell, remember what Mao says: 'One person fighting for the working class is as good as ten fighting for the capitalists'."

And everyone laughed because it wasn't Mao that said that at all. It was Eddie Goldman.

But there's still the problem of getting a massive struggle going on the campus before the year ends. Someone suggests the chapter begin building for a "huge confrontation" with President Cordier to demand the firing of Mrs. Phair. Others add that the chapter should "respond militantly" to the roughing-up the campus cops gave Mike and Alan.

The demands have to be put forward a lot more militantly, Steve Cohen insists. "We've been overly moralistic all year and we get worse and worse with each new struggle. It's like the New York Times' 100 Neediest Cases charity. We've got to keep this politics and not a charity.

"And what about those campus cops? I'd like to force the bosses of the university to fire them. Then the next time those goons are busting our heads under orders from the top, they'll have to worry that they might end up losing their jobs." (Trade union terminology had become very common in SDS since the Worker-Student Alliance was put forward. Authorities are "bosses." Their police are "goons." And about the worst thing an SDSer can call anyone is a "scab.")

Then comes piecing together a strategy for bringing off the confrontation. Just announcing there will be one no longer brings anyone out. Someone suggests there should be a small rally to build for the big one, but someone else says you'll wear people out that way. "You can't make grandiose gestures and not make good on them. And if you make it seem like there'll be violence, then there better be some or people won't come the next time."

There's also the problem of making sure there will be someone to confront. "Someone could make an appointment with Cordier under a fake name to make sure he'll be there for us."

"Don't worry, if we've got enough people, he'll be there."

"How militant should we be?"

"Well, it depends. We can figure if we've only got about . . . "

"Cut that shit out. The last time around we spent hours

figuring out a different contingency plan for every additional twenty-five people we might get out. And we spent so much time planning we didn't get anyone."

Finally people are sent off to write three different leaflets, and to "build like mad" for this one. "Remember, the mood on this campus now is to really do something. We just have to show them this is what has to be done."

The leaflets come out. "CONFRONT CORDIER. RALLY-SUNDIAL-NOON-THURS. We Will Not Be Intimidated. JAMES COLBERT WON. LET'S STEP UP THE FIGHT!" And then several detailed paragraphs on how the university is attacking its militant workers and radical students for the same reason the government is attacking the Panthers. "JOIN US." SDSers canvas the dormitories at night. "We're going over to confront Cordier tomorrow about the hassling of the workers and the beatings the security guards gave two of our members. We think it's important and we hope you'll come." Some people shoo them away and others argue that you can't fight the administration over "little things." A few say they'll come.

Thursday noon turns out to be a dismal scene on Low Plaza. The bright spring weather has been replaced with gloomy chill. No one is sitting on the palatial steps that lead slowly, in several tiers, to pillared Low Library, the administration building. Lonely Alan Egelman is rasping through SDS' battery-powered bullhorn down at the Sundial, which has become the launching pad for radical protests.

People from a few other political groups are milling nearby, waiting to feed off the crowd which hasn't come. Some women's lib people hold up a banner big enough for a demonstration of thousands and several Panther women wait with shopping bags full of the Party's newspaper. Alan talks on, bouncing his words around the vacant campus, and then hands the bullhorn over to a speaker from the Third World Coalition, which had been working very closely with the almost totally white SDS in support of campus workers.

"All right now man, we're all gonna gather around and rap about how this university is just part and parcel of a nationwide campaign to wipe out the Black Panthers and how its racist, sexist employment policies are keeping black women in the lowest paid jobs on this university." He tells how Columbia is refusing to give adequate compensation to the family of a man named Charles Johnson who'd been killed while working in one of the buildings. An elevator had cut his head off and co-workers blamed the accident on the university's negligence. A few people start coming in but there are still only about ten confronters—hardly an impressive force. Someone tells Alan to keep it going because there will be a lot more people passing by when classes get out at 12:15. So he mounts the fat wedding cake levels of the sundial platform and keeps the rap up.

By 12:20 there are about twenty-five people and Alan cuts into the call for action. "O.K. now we're going to head up there and confront big boss Andy Cordier to hear what he has to say about the atrocities of this racist university." And he begins climbing the steps toward Low. With a few hundred people, that can be an impressive sight: like a scene in an Eisenstein movie with the people storming up the endless steps toward the Czar's palace. But this day it looks too much like a few SDSers going to confront Cordier. For a while things are phased out of dramatic battle and into guerrilla theater.

Proctor Kahn is there. The university pays him a substantial salary to hang around Low Plaza and go along on all the demonstrations, to be the students' friend and to "reason" with them. He wears sport jackets and slacks, slaps backs and seems friendly enough. But he has testified at various judicial proceedings against SDSers and to them he's known as "Proctor Clown, a well-dressed pig."

His legs are kind of short and he has to scamper to keep up. "But President Cordier's in Washington," he says at the top of the first tier. "That figures," someone says and all keep climbing. A few more people have come along on the chance something might happen, but the front entrance to the building is opportunely locked. A sign says *Please use the Southeast Entrance.* People caucus. Proctor Kahn repeats that the president is in Washington and no one responds. It's agreed to go over to Livingston Hall, where the administrative offices for dormitories, cafeterias and such are located. But the group decides to first try the Southeast Entrance.

SDS marches down the stairs again, swings around the building, all the while chanting "SAME STRUGGLE, SAME FIGHT, WORKERS AND STUDENTS MUST UNITE," and wheels up in front of the Southeast Entrance. A dozen more people have joined and Alan is starting to groove on the whole thing. Naturally, the Southeast Entrance is locked too. The guys that run the security force are there on the inside, looking out defiantly through their unbreakable window.

Alan puts the bell of the bullhorn right against the window and booms out: "IS THIS THE SOUTHEAST ENTRANCE?" Everyone laughs except Proctor Kahn and the security men. Then Alan roars out another one-liner: "CAN ANDY COME OUT AND PLAY?" and since no one can imagine grumpy old Andrew Cordier playing with SDS, even Proctor Kahn laughs at that one.

Then Alan turns and announces: "The administration as usual has been afraid to confront us and we're going over to Livingston Hall to engage the bosses over there." And the group swings around, maybe fifty strong now, and heads back across campus. They pass one of the head security guards and the bullhorn barks out: "Good afternoon, sir. Hope you're feeling well this fine day." And someone else howls: "Hang 'em high . . . sir."

It's important to understand that these campus "confrontations" are usually more battles of ideas than of force. So while the SDSers certainly savor any success they may have in actually intimidating a school official, their basic goal is just to bring along as many spectators as possible and "expose" him. Not in the sexual sense, of course, though that's often joked about, but just to show him for what he really is. In part that means being rude because he doesn't deserve respect. It's been called "de-mystification."

The ritual is relished on both sides since both deans and demonstrators see themselves as invincible. The radicals go in saying: "Watch us strip this pig of his good-guy cover and reveal his sinister commitments to the corrupt system." And the school officials think: "Ah, here they come again. Fresh bastards. I'll really stand up to them and people will see how they're just working out their neurotic maladjustments on dedicated, honest people."

The radicals had staged a really good one a few weeks before when William J. McGill, the psychologist who'd just been chosen as the next president of Columbia, cruised into a "welcoming" reception, ready to give a preview exhibition on how to handle student radicals. He mostly pleaded ignorance when SDS demanded to know why campus workers were paid so poorly, why the expanding university, as slumlord in the surrounding community, kept kicking working people out of their homes, why it wouldn't accept its responsibility to the widow and children of the slain worker, Charles Johnson.

"Do you support the vicious war of repression that's being waged against the Black Panthers?" came one of the rapid-fire questions.

"You might as well ask me whether I beat my wife," he snapped back.

"Oh? And are you a male chauvinist?" an SDS woman responded.

Finally seeing he wasn't getting any mileage out of the session, McGill tried to change the ground rules—which is itself an integral stage in the ritual. "You people aren't asking questions. You're giving speeches."

"What's wrong with speeches?" came another question.

"Go and give them somewhere else," McGill ordered. But it was the president-elect who finally left.

Anticipating just such a victory again, SDS and friends poured into oak-paneled Livingston Hall to confront any authority figure who could be found. Into the lounge to meet them stepped one Paul Gangi, a young middle-manager, wearing an iridescent sharkskin suit and an orange shirt that didn't go at all well with his red face once things got rolling. The first thing people demand to know is his title. That's important because he's bound to start saying that things aren't under his purview and to combat that they have to know what his purview is.

He gives a long title; something like assistant director of financial affairs for dormitories. Then he goofs and says: "What do you want to know?" Half the fifty people squeezed into the small lounge fire questions at once. Something gets through to him about the Johnson family not being able to live on what the University is paying them as compensation for Mr. Johnson's death.

So Mr. Gangi starts to *reason* with them. "You have to look at this thing historically. Not just Columbia's history, but everyone's. Now after the unfortunate accident Mr. Johnson's pay check was never cut off. We kept sending it to his family. And what company would do that?"

"How much was that check?"

"What?"

"How much was the check for?"

"Well, I don't know exactly. I think he was taking home about $80 a week."

"Do you think that's enough?"

"Well, now. That isn't for me to decide. I haven't any control over the whole labor market."

"No, but you'd like to." Laughter.

"I do understand there was a Workmen's Compensation settlement for the family though."

The students have figures on that. "It was $60 a week. Do you think that's enough?"

"Well, that's for Workmen's Compensation to determine."

"How much do you make?" "Does anyone even make you punch in?" "We hear you're going to lay off all the black and Latin maids?"

"Now one question at a time. Just give them to me and I'll get you the answers."

"Yeah. Just like you've been doing."

Any doubts that may be plaguing the SDSers about the value of their campaign to help the campus workers quickly pass when they come up against the enraging run-arounds they get from the campus bosses. There's nothing more reassuring in radical politics than meeting your enemy head on. Susie Boehm shouts at the man: "Don't give us that. We were here a week ago and two weeks before that and we still haven't gotten any answers from you guys."

Neil Mullin, an amazingly good leader in these situations, sticks his head right in front of Gangi's and says: "Listen. These are our demands. We want $15,000 a year for the Johnson family. Do you think that's fair?" Gangi doesn't answer. "And we want a guarantee that the maids won't be fired. And we want Mrs. Phair fired because she's a racist who brutalizes her workers."

Then the questions start coming again. "Why is it that the maids are all either black or Latin Americans and why do they get the lowest salaries the university pays when they work as hard or harder than anyone?" "Why does a janitor in one of the dormitories get harassing letters all the time because he refused to wipe out toilets with his hand instead of a brush?"

And Mr. Gangi says: "I thought that one was all settled. I

don't know what letters you're talking about. I've never seen one.
Show them to me."

That was a mistake. People start offering to go into his office
to get out the copies to show him. Then Carole Martin, who'd
been following the Johnson case very closely for SDS, stands up,
furious, to really give it to Gangi:

"We're sick as hell of these lies. Lies like the university
Newsletter claiming the Johnsons were getting a lot more than
they are. And lies like when the university got up in court and
made these racist claims that the Johnsons weren't really entitled
to much money because only two of the kids in the family are
actually Charles Johnson's kids. So Charles' elderly mother has to
fly all the way up from the South to testify that there are five kids
in the family, and that her son was the father of all of them."

And Gangi asks: "What would you kids do to change
things?" That's a question a lot of people ask of SDS. Steve Cohen
jumps on it: "Why, man, we'd have a revolution, and kick all your
bosses' asses the hell out."

Neil figures that's a pretty good note to sum up on. "O.K.
Mangy or Gangi or whatever your name is. You've got our demands now. We'll be back here Tuesday at noon to hear your
answers. And you'd better realize we're not just screwing around
here. There's going to be hell to pay at this university if we aren't
given these demands." Might as well shoot for a little intimidation
too.

As people turn to leave, they find Dean William Stuart, just
standing in the back, smoking his pipe and looking quite smart; a
little man in a bright checked sports jacket and bow tie. He'd just
strolled out to see if maybe anyone had any questions for him.
They have, of course. This round is centered around trustee
Hogan's charges against the Panthers. One of the SDS women has
been doing a thesis study on the case and she rattles off about five
minutes' worth of facts showing how it is all a fantastic frame-up.
A bearded black West Indian, speaking very slowly and cautiously,
reminds the dean that the university always insisted it had to be
neutral on all political issues. If it's to remain true to that,
shouldn't it drop Hogan from the board since he's obviously not
neutral on the issue of the Panthers?

The dean compliments him: "That's a good point."

Eddie Goldman had been in court that morning, fighting

charges by the university that he had taken part in the window breaking episode staged by Ed's arch enemies in the December 4th Movement. It wasn't just being accused falsely that enraged Ed. It was being accused of doing something he felt was so politically destructive with such politically "reactionary" companions. Ed sidles over to the dean, who must know what's coming because he starts gripping his pipe so tightly the knuckle on his thumb whitens.

"Listen, Dean Stuart. You scumbags in the administration (they like that one and laugh) are trying to frame me for the D4M thing when you know damned right well that I have nothing to do with any of those guys and neither does anyone else in PL or SDS. I wasn't there that night at all."

And the dean, very calmly to contrast with Eddie's fury, comes back: "Now, Eddie. I saw you that night myself and you smiled at me and we said hello."

Susie Boehm defends Eddie against that slander: "Now, Dean, just wait a minute because I was with Eddie that night and I never remember seeing you at all."

The dean tells Eddie that this is all something "the courts will determine." And he reminds him, by way of reassuring everyone in the American system of justice, "Don't forget, Ed, you've been acquitted by the courts before." The dean is really smiling now and it almost sounds as though he's already getting ready to tell the story that night over cocktails.

People start yelling things like: "Why do you guys keep harassing Eddie and dragging him down to court all the time anyway?" And someone else asks if the dean saw Eddie throw a brick as he had been accused. Dean Stuart kindly admits, "No, when I saw Eddie he was acting like a perfect gentleman." So everyone declares that he should be a witness in Ed's behalf. And they say he should come to next Tuesday's confrontation too, and that he should bring along trustee Hogan, who must be a good friend of the dean's, because people have a lot of questions for Hogan.

"My goodness. I can't even get my wife to come somewhere when I want her to. What makes you think I can bring the District Attorney?" And everyone howls about the dean's being a male chauvinist for bossing his wife around.

Then one more shot at Gangi, who'd been relaxing too much

while the dean was getting it: "Do you think it's a coincidence that the worst paid workers on this campus are all black females?"

"Ah, no, it isn't a coincidence . . . "

"Wow, he admits it. What about you, Dean. Is it a coincidence?"

"I don't speak for the university on these matters."

"Who do you speak for?"

"He speaks for his wife."

"You're both fired!"

And the crowd, which by then had grown to one hundred, pours out into the campus. Many are already reliving the event. " 'What would you kids do to change things?' " Steve Cohen was mimicking. "Wow!"

CHAPTER TWO

"FREE BOBBY! FREE THE UNIVERSITIES!"

Columbia SDS never made good on its vow to come back the next Tuesday for Mr. Gangi's answers. President Nixon invaded Cambodia a few hours after the Livingston Hall confrontation, successfully diverting the radicals. "Those guys all work together," someone in the chapter observed.

Perhaps the President could have gotten away with invading Cambodia. More flagrant acts of American militarism have gone unhindered by public protest. But coincidentally, the Left was planning an invasion of its own for the very next day. It wasn't going to be the usual picnic-for-peace thing with lots of songs and speeches and then the bus rides home. The usual Moratorium-Mobilization-Women's Strike for Peace coalition, which had organized most of the massive but painfully ineffective anti-war demonstrations, wasn't calling this gathering. And it wasn't even going to be about peace.

The Black Panthers were getting it together in New Haven to show the government that revolutionaries weren't intimidated by its attempts at repression—and maybe even to do a little counter-intimidating. Chairman Bobby Seale and eight other Panthers were going on trial for a new string of conspiracy charges and the Party wanted to show that it had mass support.

The persistent gunning down and jailing of Panthers was making many liberals, who'd once been hostile to the black revolutionaries, suddenly very sympathetic. Far from weakening the Party, the police pogroms were building a massive base of support for it. It was such a bewildering development that some Leftists, especially those that agreed with Progressive Labor's criticisms of the Panthers' program, began to think that John Mitchell's mysterious gang down at the Justice Department was deliberately martyring the Panthers to divert the movement away from a direct attack on the system and into Panther support instead.

A lot of peace people had probably considered coming to New Haven, but there had been several unfounded scares in the news about people buying up guns to bring to the New Haven shoot-out. The National Guard had been called out with a flourish and lumber yards were selling out their entire stocks of plywood so stores and banks could board up for the siege. So most of the people who turned out for the May Day Panther weekend were radical enough not to believe the news or radical enough to want to be there just in case it turned out to be the beginning of an armed revolution after all.

SDS organized in force for its own splinter rally on the New Haven Green across from the courthouse. SDS' very particular political standards have led it of late to distinguish itself from the rest of the movement at such gatherings. And since the split in 1969, SDS hasn't been very comfortable with the Panthers. Progressive Labor has always maintained that the Panthers fail to address themselves to the problems of workers on a *class* basis. Others in SDS strongly disagree and support the Party whole-heartedly. PL applies the traditional dialectical approach: either you're part of the solution or part of the problem, as the Panthers themselves say. And since PL doesn't feel the Panthers are working to solve the problems of the entire working class, black and white, they conclude that the Panthers are helping to hold down the workers instead by dividing them on the basis of race.

It's another case of political groups wanting to fight the same system, but having such totally different approaches that they can't help but get in one another's way. PL reflected the working class disdain for the *lumpen proletariat*—the unemployed "street people" of the ghetto—who the Panthers were seeking to organize as their base. Quite bitter disputes were breaking out between the groups. In Boston, the Panthers had run several PL members out of a black neighborhood, telling them to leave ghetto organizing to ghetto people. And later in the summer of 1970, the Panthers were to accuse PL angrily of staging a "provocateur's" march which could have resulted in breaking up their tense People's Constitutional Convention in Philadelphia.

The two parties labeled one another "cops" in their newspapers and continually baited each other as racists. It was a very difficult situation for the typical independent SDSer to inherit. Not nearly as finicky as the PL members about what is and isn't a "progressive" group, the independents felt the same affinity for the Panthers that many other politically concerned people did. But because of SDS' association with PL, they inevitably were caught in the rivalry between the two political parties. SDS found itself suspected and resented on campuses where a great deal of political activity was centering around supporting the Panthers.

Yale University was very uptight about the Panther trial. Originally, Panther leaders thought they would target Yale, a symbol of white elitism, as their enemy, along with the New Haven courts. But Yale President Kingman Brewster, probably the shrewdest of all the academic co-opters, kept heading the radicals off at the pass. He braved the wrath of Agnew to voice his doubt that the Panthers could get a fair trial; and rather than try to protect the university against the onslaught of migratory radicals swarming into town for the weekend, he threw it open to them. Huge barrels of cereal were ladled out free at lunch, and rice, corn and salad was given away at dinner time. Housing was open at the school and all its facilities made available for "rational discussion." The idea was to show that Yale was on the Panthers' side—thereby saving Yale from attack as the foe.

It worked. The Panthers, somewhat bewildered by such overwhelming hospitality from the university that at best had ignored them in the past, laid off Yale. But SDS didn't.

Standing on a stump at the SDS rally, a speaker tried to expose Kingman Brewster:

"Look around. All this used to be housing for workers and poor people until Kingman Brewster and his boys started plowing it down. They evicted hundreds of blacks for the Social Science Center over there. Down there where the superhighway comes through, thousands of people were cleared out so the rich people from the suburbs, the bosses and their families, could come into the city real fast without having to look at any of the squalid effects of the oppressive system that's making them fat. They just zip right downtown to shop for all their expensive shit and then zip right back to their posh homes."

A chant builds up:

> Support the Workers,
> Fight Yale,
> Keep Bobby
> Out of Jail

Nothing gels in the weekend affair though. There is a really militant spirit. Lots and lots of people yelling things like "Free Bobby!" and "Off the Pig!" Real storm-the-Bastille, get-the-revolution-going rhetoric. But the Panthers are afraid that stuff might be taken too seriously. What they really want is a peaceful show of strength. Somewhat sheepishly, they start cautioning people to "Cool It for the Revolution." And that obviously disappoints quite a lot of the radicals. Things are getting too volatile nowadays to get big militant protests together without chancing tremendous eruptions. It's like gathering a critical mass of uranium. Get enough of it, and get it close enough together and it will blow. That is something that is probably going to change the whole idea of public demonstrations soon. It's increasingly risky for a group to have huge rallies unless it's willing to "let it happen." New Haven showed how hard it is to keep things down. The *action freaks*, provocateurs without serious political goals who SDS hates and fears, are threatening to dominate the streets.

The people who have come to New Haven for violence are confused by the Panthers' turnabout in tone and all the "love Yale" talk they're getting during the first day. A lot of them are grumbling about how it looks like this one is going to turn out to be just another picnic after all. But the roaming tribes of urban guerrillas, who disdain SDS and almost every other political organization, spot one another, see fellow contingents in army jackets and motorcycle helmets, carrying gas masks and bags of rocks and bottles, and say: "Wait until tonight. Don't worry. Just wait."

The Yale organizers knew the action freaks would come.

They had a night full of programed gatherings laid out, hoping to keep people out of the streets. For its part, SDS, which had no interest in what was to happen in the streets, called for workshops and serious political discussion. The whole Chicago Conspiracy was there to support Bobby Seale, its most vocal member until Judge Julius Hoffman ordered him gagged, lashed to a chair and finally severed from the trial. So the celebrities were each assigned to hold a rap session at the university. And the action freaks, knowing their own kind, left the more rational types like Dellinger and Hayden and Davis in peace, patronizing Yippie leaders Jerry Rubin and Abbie Hoffman.

The weather fit into the whole scene beautifully. It was a pitch black, cool night that could have passed for Halloween. The weird Yippies, wearing painted faces and black capes stenciled with glowing marijuana leaves, were giving Indian war calls and freaking out before the rap sessions started. Abbie Hoffman was, as usual, into innuendo. "We all know what I mean but I can't say it 'cause they've got these spooks with me all the time," he explains at the outset. A couple of war whoopers answer that they dig it. Then Abbie slips into this dream he's got about the day New Haven will become New Heaven; how in New Heaven the kids will run things: "*AND THERE WON'T BE ANY COURT HOUSES ... AND THERE WON'T BE ANY BANKS ... AND THERE WON'T BE ANY YALES.*" With each new thing that there won't be any more of, Abbie's Yippies go wild, wailing from up in the trees and in the crowd and on the ledges above the plaza where everyone is crowded. They scream "DO IT!" and "Let it Happen!" And they give their war cries. Dozens of joints are being passed around and pretty soon some saner people let out their own first amateur war whoops. Abbie starts talking about "President Agnew" and "General Mitchell" for a while, and then it's question time.

"What about tonight, Abbie?" What about Macy's Department Store?" a Yippie calls out.

"Macy's?" Abbie comes back. "I hear they're having a *FIRE SALE.*"

And all of a sudden there's this tremendous explosion that reverberates right through a person's chest, and people gasp and a few scream. People think: "One of those crazy clowns has bombed us." A huge gray cloud of smoke rises to hang over one side of the terraced plaza. But it was only a superfirecracker to let on what's supposed to be coming later. Right on cue all the Yippie lieutenants send down a skyful of leaflets; maps of downtown New Haven with the main streets marked out and fifteen little numbers in circles dotted around at various locations. Down below is the key:

Big fat shivering number one points to the location of the courthouse where the trial is to be held. Two is juvenile court. Three, adult probation. And on down: army recruiting, navy recruiting, the phone company, IBM, G.E., N.Y. Life Insurance, three different banks, the university bursar's office. Last comes an animal shelter. At the bottom of the map is a sketch of a very delicate hand holding a flaming match to the edge of the downtown area.

"Man, look at this," one guy says to his companion. "I told you it was going to happen. I told you it was." And the crowd pours out into the street. While that was going on—exactly at the same time so it couldn't have been an accident—someone rushed into Jerry Rubin's packed session next door and called out: "The pigs are busting the Panthers!" sending that mob rushing out into the street too. Kids with their chains and bottles start tramping down the street toward the courthouse, bellowing in rhythm, "FREE BOBBY SEALE! FREE BOBBY SEALE!" It sounds very much like they're going to try to do it.

But the loyalists are ready. Dozens and dozens of Yalies—the most athletic and straight looking the school has to offer—are blocking the way as marshals. They tell the troupe to turn around. "Go back to Yale. The Panthers don't want this. Bobby doesn't want this." The kids don't believe these Yalies give a shit about the Panthers and some of them ask how people are supposed to "Free Bobby Seale" just by milling around on the campus. First the marshals try to keep everyone off the New Haven Green but soon there's a change of strategy and they let everyone onto the Green. The kids run around in the dark between the trees, lighting fires in barrels and tearing off "gas masks" for themselves from a huge silk parachute some quartermaster type has brought along for the crowd.

The police and the National Guard are lined up opposite the

Green in front of the stores along the main street and in front of the courthouse. The kids sneak forward in the dark, lob their bottles and dash back. A few tear gas canisters are fired into the park and the guerrillas dash off in panic but the veterans calm them, chanting, "Walk! Walk! Walk!" Pretty soon everyone's happily scampering away when the gas comes and rushing in again when it clears. Then the police and the Guard put on gas masks, which give them the snouted looks of real pigs. A weird whining noise starts up. The kids think at first that the police are using some newfangled machine to drive them wild with its sonics. But it's a machine for laying down gas. A contingent of police are running it up toward the crowd, which scurries to get out of the way of its white cloud. One stalwart stands his ground: "Hey. Hey. Its only smoke. They aren't using gas." The cloud envelops him for a moment and then suddenly he's gasping and choking and he comes groping out, clawing at his eyes, gagging and wheezing for breath. In between seizures, he's laughing and shaking his head, trying to say something. When he can finally get it out, he hollers: "Well, hell. I never claimed to be a scientist."

They play urban guerrilla like that for hours. All the while, Yale marshals and dignitaries like Chaplain William Sloane Coffin are pleading with them to "go back to the old campus. Go to the Ingalls Rink. There's a program going on at Ingalls Rink." It turns out that the program includes the explosion of a bomb, which blows out the rink's windows, somehow injuring only one person. But despite all the Yippies' inciting, New Haven doesn't burn that night. None of the targets on the map is hit.

While those few hundred kids were pretending that the revolution was in full swing on the New Haven Town Green that night, a group of seriously political people from many different organizations began discussing how the gathering could accomplish something beyond the shouting of speeches and the throwing of a few more bottles. They called a big open meeting for the next morning to find a way for the thousands of students who had come to New Haven to take the struggle back home with them. Because they were of a more radical bent than the organizers of the huge peace demonstrations, they were intent on having more than a massive and cathartic demonstration that wouldn't have any impact beyond the actual event.

They decided to call a "National Student Strike." The universities around the country would be struck around three central demands:

1. An end to the "systematic oppression of political dissidents" such as Bobby Seale and the Black Panthers.

2. The immediate, unilateral withdrawal of American forces from Southeast Asia and a permanent end to U.S. aggression in Vietnam, Laos and Cambodia.

3. An end to the complicity of the universities in the war effort to be achieved through the suspension of defense research on campus and the elimination of ROTC programs.

These three national demands were to give focus and cohesion to what was hoped would be the greatest series of political struggles ever launched on the campuses. The people who met and called for the strike assumed that each individual school would attack the specific manifestations of what was wrong with the system as they appeared on that campus.

A few schools had already started to move before the national call came and were on strike even prior to the New Haven meeting. But at most campuses, this was the opportunity everyone was looking for. And although the strike call was given only passing attention in the media's coverage of the Panther rally, strike organizing was already underway on the campuses by the time the buses returned from New Haven.

The National Student Strike began out of the radicals' drive to deliver a sharp blow to the American system. It ended out of the liberals' compulsion to ward off such attacks and to preserve the system. When Spiro Agnew's campaign rhetoric lumps radicals and liberals into "radiclibs," both groups feel abused. They are arch rivals. Their assumptions are totally opposite and their approaches to political work can't help but obstruct one another. Cambodia made the differences between radicalism and liberalism strikingly clear. And it showed how the system itself makes use of those differences to defuse dissidence.

The liberals were aghast when word came of the invasion. In the dormitories they sat in front of television sets and cursed and raved and said they couldn't believe it. How could Nixon be so stupid? Now it was his war, not Johnson's. But the radicals who are always ready to think the worst weren't at all surprised.

At Princeton, SDS leader Dan Lichty said: "Of course he invaded Cambodia," and went to bed. The rest of the university stayed up most of the night discussing the invasion.

Because the anti-war movement had become so broad-based and in the process progressively more mild and ineffective, SDS had begun to think it was "a dead issue." So chapters all around the country were surprised that after the Cambodian invasion the great masses of usually quiescent students were suddenly ready to start fighting. In the face of the storm, SDS began a last minute attempt to assert leadership in the strike. Columbia-Barnard SDS seized the initiative Sunday, the day after the strike was called, and issued a brilliant gold leaflet screamingly mocking the President's challenge to campus protestors: "ATTENTION ALL *BUMS!* PEOPLE'S STRIKE MEETING TONIGHT."

But at the same time the radicals were gathering, a much more moderate group of professors, student government types and various unaffiliated liberals met to analyze what the university's response ought to be to the expansion of the war. They were years behind the radicals politically even if they were decades older. "I'd never done anything about the war before this at all," admits English professor and former department chairman Quentin Anderson. "Lots of us saw this as the first chance we had to be against the war on immediate public grounds." They decided to have acting University President Cordier call a day of "Moratorium" for Columbia on Monday. A massive convocation could be held and members of the "university community" could speak their minds about the war.

The radicals had no doubt what their response to Cambodia should be: Columbia should be shut down, and shut tight. But the administration's Moratorium had the effect of a lock-out in the face of a strike. They couldn't shut the school down if it was shutting itself down. So from the start the situation for the radicals was one of rivalry with the liberals. SDS didn't want Cordier to speak at a convocation. Members accused him of complicity in the murder of Congolese revolutionary Patrice Lumumba because Dr. Cordier had been the U.N. representative in the Congo and had taken Lumumba into his "protective custody" when Lumumba was eventually killed. (SDS even published a pamphlet nationally with Cordier on the cover and the caption: "WANTED FOR MURDER.") SDS wanted to heckle the president off the podium at the least, or preferably take him off it. "He's a pig just like Nixon's a pig. When the workers go on strike at a factory they don't ask their bosses to come and address them, do they?" But others didn't want to risk alienating all the students who would feel the president had a "right" to speak. The moderate radicals finally prevailed with the argument that there was nothing to fear in letting Cordier speak, since he would "show himself for what he is anyway."

The threat of liberal co-optation of the strike was enough to encourage the various radical groups to forget their mutual hatreds for each other for a while and at midnight Sunday they met in a newly formed "Radical Caucus" to plot strike strategy. As people kept noting nervously, it was like a reunion of the various groups on the Columbia campus that in the previous year or two had considered themselves part of SDS but had since left in the strain of political controversies. The present SDS, with its heavy orientation toward allying with campus workers, was the strongest group in the caucus. Then came the D4M, with basically an anti-repression, Panther-support outlook, and then a string of lesser groups along with quite a flock of unaligned radicals.

There were two clearly different ways the students could go on strike: they could strike *against* the university, placing specific demands upon the administration. Or they could strike *with* the university and not make any Columbia-oriented demands at all but simply act in repudiation of the Cambodian invasion. Striking against the school would be less popular with the mass of liberal students, but might be the only way really to accomplish anything, most of the participants agreed. As one SDSer put it: "It's institutions like Columbia that are carrying out Nixon's shit. We shouldn't even bother to call it a strike. We should say we're taking this fucking place over—and do it."

But then there was the thorny question of what you're doing it for. SDS wanted to use the strike to win the campus worker demands it had been building around all year. Others, who hadn't especially related to those politics, remained unenthusiastic: they wanted something more direct and active. Andy Kaslow, a scholarly sophomore SDSer who has a very precise understanding of socialist theory and history and is extremely enthusiastic about the idea of a worker-student alliance, argued for such a strategy.

"We want to point out that the whole nature of Columbia is to exploit the black and Latin workers. That it's part of the same exploitative system that produces these imperialistic adventures in Southeast Asia. The capitalists have got to keep fighting to control cheap labor and raw materials to keep themselves expanding, so they start wars in Asia just as naturally as they screw workers here. We've got to attack Columbia as a ruling class institution. That way we won't only be bringing thousands of workers into our fight, we'll also be taking a giant step forward in the student movement. We'll be showing that student radicals don't just care about themselves; we'll be readdressing the student movement to the struggle against the entire system. If we have that kind of a long-range perspective, we'll end up making Nixon shake in his boots and shit bricks."

The culmination of an ideological argument in such promising colloquialism has people chuckling. But there's still a lot of resistance to the SDS-proposed demands. "This demand for $15,000 a year for the family of Charles Johnson is ridiculous. My old man doesn't even make that," says one of the independent types.

Another student speaks up then: "You're losing perspective when you start concentrating on things like compensation for the Johnson family. Hell, there's more suffering from this war in Cambodia in one day than the Johnson family will have to bear in their whole lives."

Carole Martin, an articulate SDS advocate of supporting the workers, tries to lay down a challenge. "I was talking to a black campus worker and he told me that if we strike against the university, we'll really be showing the workers here that we are against their oppressor. That means we can't stand up there with Cordier and claim we're against the war. And it means that we can't be condescending any more and say the workers aren't progressive—it's a question of whether we'll be as sharp on oppression as they are."

SDS decides on six specific demands: an end to all war research on campus; the firing of D.A. Hogan from the board of trustees; abolishing various courses in business and foreign affairs which are oriented toward increasing American influence in peasant lands; supporting the workers' fight for job security; and better compensation for Charles Johnson's family. A kid sitting on a window sill introduces himself to everyone's delight as "a typical bourgeois pig student," and says even he endorses the six demands SDS is proposing.

After a speech about how the whole country watches what happens at Columbia so it can tell which way the student movement is going, and another which implores radicals to prevent the liberals from "co-opting the strike and making it an auxilliary to the peace politicians," the SDS demands are finally voted in by the radicals—which of course has no sway with the liberals. "The kids," Professor Anderson later interpreted it, "were feeling sort of feisty and they were applying their broad brush to everything. What a void there was! What a gap!"

Andrew Cordier, "the peacekeeper," was up against it this time. There he was, kid-gloving Columbia University through two years of quiet. Not even Kingman Brewster at Yale, who was getting better write-ups, was doing so well. Then suddenly Cordier is facing a crippling strike just when he's about to ship out the year's production of degree holders. It must have been strange for Cordier, after spending all his life making and defending American foreign policy, to become the head of a university where there were perhaps only a dozen people who would condone what the U.S. was up to in Southeast Asia.

Andrew Cordier carefully placed himself on the side of the majority at his convocation Monday. Low Plaza was thronged with all the people of the university community but the workers, who were the only ones not given the day off. Chunky little Dr. Cordier came slowly to the podium with its nest of radio and television microphones and in a tortuously halting, quaking way, he delivered a condemnation of the war. "I join with millions of Americans, including students and faculty on this campus, in expressing shock over further American involvement in the Vietnam War. . ." Agonizing pauses would come right in the middle of words. It was hard to tell if the president was stage struck, or sick, or whether he was having a hard time saying such things. "What the hell's wrong with him?" one student whispered. Another thought Cordier was "going to croak." But the president made his way slowly through the speech.

". . . American military effort in Vietnam is and will remain futile." ("Typically liberal," a radical mutters. "It'd be all right if we were winning.") "It is a quagmire from which we should free ourselves. The conflict is for the Vietnamese a disaster, and the expenditure of American lives and resources in that conflict is totally unwarranted. Our men must be brought home. The squandering of their lives in Vietnam and Cambodia must stop." It brought some applause and there was almost no heckling. And after one or two other faculty speeches, the radicals moved forward.

Rich Reed, a black from the Third World Coalition, who later joined SDS, seized the microphone and declared that such peace talk wouldn't mean a thing unless people moved "to build a mass movement against the source of imperialism and racism which is closest to us—COLUMBIA UNIVERSITY." He denounced Cordier's own School of International Affairs at Columbia for training the henchmen of imperialism and for concocting its oppressive strategy. And he condemned Andrew Cordier as the dean of that school and as the murderer of Lumumba.

When Reed began describing how black and Latin workers on campus are inevitably consigned to the lowest paying and dirtiest jobs, the peace people out on the plaza jeered at him to "talk about the war." When he responded that the war is based on the very same racist assumptions—that non-whites are worthless and can be freely slaughtered and oppressed—they jeered at him again. That absolutely horrified the SDSers out on the plaza and the ones up on the platform who had helped Reed seize the podium. It was blatantly racist, they thought, to tell a black man not to talk about his own oppression and to "talk about the war instead."

In bitter dismay, the microphone was finally returned to the faculty speakers. And William Leuchtenburg, a historian, brought the whole thing to a head. Woefully he warned that Americans "are losing faith in their democracy." But the radicals throughout the crowd cheered and called out things like "It's about time." Leuchtenburg said: "Our hope lies in the ballot box." "BULLSHIT!" cried the radicals. Through the electoral process we can be freed from the war, the professor said, and he mentioned he'd been talking to politicians in Washington and had been informed that several of them planned to introduce bills that would get us out of Vietnam. One of the radicals called out, "Three cheers for Congress." When the professor finished by saying what radicals hate to hear the most—that it's not the system's fault but only the fault of the people who happen to be running the system at the present time—an angry black student started scuffling with him and they had to be separated by others.

CHAPTER THREE

UP AGAINST LIBERALISM

The whole radical-liberal feud was bound up in Dr. Leuchtenburg's plea for reform through the ballot box. SDS was delighted with the fact that the whole country was losing faith in its system of government. That is exactly what should be happening, according to the radicals. And since they are convinced that the faith was never deserved in the first place, they want to make very sure that men like Leuchtenburg don't succeed in restoring it.

SDSers can't be accused of not having tried it inside the system first. Though a rare few can say proudly that they were never fooled, almost all of the radicals were previously ultra-committed liberals. They slaved in crusades like Eugene McCarthy's and they are bitter now that they ever wasted their efforts. It isn't so much because McCarthy lost, but because they are now quite certain nothing could have changed even if he had won. So it's enraging to them when someone like Professor Leuchtenburg comes along to try to pull the lousy system out of the fire just when people are beginning to believe it should burn. American democracy is a "hoax," as far as SDS is concerned, and anyone who tries to hold it out as a solution is just misleading people into perpetuating the sham.

Dr. Leuchtenburg was saying that if Congress brought the boys home it would prove that the same system that started such a war had the capacity to end it. And so he was urging the students to work their hearts out for the Cooper-Church and Hatfield-McGovern amendments to limit the scope and duration of the war.

It was a "Band-Aid" approach that SDS dubbed *McGovernment.*"
SDS never doubted that the war could be called off, but it was
certain that many more wars of the same kind would follow, just
as others had preceded it.

In a very carefully documented fifty-page pamphlet, published at the time of the strike, SDS argues convincingly that the
Vietnam war was not a "tragic mistake," as liberal politicians
describe it. Instead, it explains in detail, the war was an inevitable
outgrowth of our economic system and was typical of our many
military efforts. We needed control of the land and people of
Southeast Asia not for any military advantage but for our own
economic well-being. If it had just been a mistake, we'd have
corrected it decades ago.

But why have we been so intent on holding onto Vietnam?
The media's liberal pundits have ignored the problem of determin-
ing the "motive" behind our "mistaken" Vietnam venture. The
SDS pamphlet quotes *U.S. News and World Report* from way back
in 1954, in an article headlined: Why the U.S. Risks War in
Indochina: It's the Key to Control of all of Asia."

"One of the world's richest areas is open to the winner in
Indochina. That's behind the growing U.S. concern . . . tin, rubber,
rice, key strategic materials are what the war is really all about.
The U.S. sees it as a place to hold at any cost."

The troops are there in Vietnam, then, to pave the way for
the corporations. A whole spectrum of quotations from the businessman's press is used to prove the point:

Guy Francis Stark, chief industrial development advisor for
the U.S. Foreign Service in Saigon, wrote in the *Wall Street
Journal* in 1967:

> Let me use your pages to make this proposal: a massive
> invasion of South Vietnam by American industry . . . In
> the modest development that presently exists, a num-
> ber of American-sponsored enterprises have been im-
> mensely successful.

Nation's Business, in 1969:

> The best thinkers on the subject in business and govern-
> ment agree that magnificent business opportunities
> await in Vietnam, Thailand, Indonesia, Malaysia and

Singapore. As the military situation in Vietnam improves, they expect the flow of business to double, triple and quadruple.

Henry Cabot Lodge, in a speech in 1965 to the Middlesex Club of Cambridge:

Geographically, Vietnam stands at the hub of a vast area of the world—Southeast Asia—an area with a population of 249 million persons ... He who holds or has influence in Vietnam can affect the future of the Philippines and Formosa to the east, Thailand and Burma with their huge rice surpluses to the west, and Malaysia and Indonesia with their rubber, ore and tin to the south.

This is what SDS means when it uses the label "imperialism." It means the normal, supposedly "healthy" growth of American business in overseas areas. Every successful corporation does it unabashedly through a vast network which it calls its "international" operations. For our economic system to survive, business has to keep growing. In order to keep growing, we have to keep reaching further and further out into the "underdeveloped" world, partly to find new markets for American goods, but more often to take advantage of the cheap native resources and labor to make products that can be brought back and sold at greater profits. That's what SDS means by "exploitation." The money goes to the American stockholders from all these "ventures."

All over the world, the people in the countries we've come to as saviors—"economic uplifters"—keep trying to run us out because we're robbing them. Usually we have to kill to establish our "footholds" in the new areas. When there's trouble, as there was in the Dominican Republic in 1965, American troops are sent in to "protect" the few American citizens who are already there—doing business for American corporations. And since the system keeps using imperialism and exploitation to get along, SDS says the system has no right to survive—and, in fact, must be smashed.

Which gets back to Professor Leuchtenburg and the liberals. They don't say that. A few of them probably agree with SDS's explanation of why we're in Vietnam in the first place, but they resist discussing such questions since they would never think of abolishing capitalism, which is what the whole thing really comes down to. Each side thinks the other is naive, really.

The more politically sophisticated liberals may admit that a massive overhauling of nearly revolutionary proportions would do us some good, but they say it's naive to think you'll ever get a revolution going in this country. So they limit their goals and hope for the best with politicians they'll admit they really haven't that much faith in. And for their part, the radicals say the liberals are naive to think politicians whose very prosperity and power is linked to the system will ever weaken themselves by changing that system. The radicals may not have much certainty that they'll get the revolution, but they're convinced something must be done and that revolution is the only hope.

Since the 1969 split, SDS has made a major effort to "expose" liberal politicians. During a Moratorium peace rally in New York City, a large contingent of SDSers fought through the crowd and took the platform to try to make clear what lay beneath Mayor John V. Lindsay's liberal facade. Mike Golash from Columbia decried Lindsay's efforts to break strikes, even through the use of troops; his increases in the subway fares, which hit poor people directly; the brutality of his police in the ghettos. This super-liberal has shown that when it has really come to a question of whose side he's on, he hasn't been for the poor and working people, Golash shouted. During the 1970 state and Congressional elections, SDS had two major slogans: "Rely on the people, not the politicians," and "Elections are a hoax."

The liberals can afford to be a little tolerant of such disruptions and accusations. They are pushing an alluring concept—two-minute ballot-box change. Even though liberal politicians, along with all other politicians, almost never deliver what they promise, people tend to be awfully accepting of the shortcomings. So the radicals don't pose much of an initial threat. But the radical alternative can't be nearly as tolerant of competition from the liberals because it's so much more demanding and difficult to sell. The radical is trying to convince people to make an infinitely higher level of commitment: to dedicate—perhaps even risk—their lives to build a revolution. And very few people will do that if they think there's an easier way. So it can stymie the radical's cause when there's a liberal around saying: "Nonsense. We'll get you what you want, and believe me, it will be a lot less messy."

There's absolutely no confusing a radical program with a liberal one. No serious candidate for political office in America would run on the pledge to scrap the system. No foreign policy statement of a major party would include the vow to bring American troops *and businessmen* home and keep them home. No civil rights program would call for the jailing of racists. And no economic policies would pay the workers in a factory as much as their bosses in the offices get. Few of the anti-war senators have even called for the *immediate* withdrawal of all U.S. troops. Gene McCarthy even criticized President Johnson for saying he'd bring the troops home within six months of the start of serious negotiations. "I'd put the limit at about five years," he said.

A contingent of liberal Eastern senators really had SDSers chuckling last summer. The same guys who'd been saying the U.S. will have to stop being the "cops of the world" issued a joint statement urging Nixon to arm Israel better "to protect America's interests in the Middle East." The radicals want to eliminate America's interest in the Middle East.

As far as SDS is concerned, you either think the system works or it doesn't. And anyone who's governing the system obviously believes in it. Back in 1964, SDS had the election slogan: "Part of the Way with LBJ." The organization vows now that it won't be fooled again.

Instead of uniting the Columbia University community in a mutual deploring of the war, Dr. Cordier's peace convocation just exacerbated the difference between the radical and liberal approaches. The radicals came away more determined than ever to prevent the liberals from misleading dissenters into another useless effort to make change through the "hoax" of democracy. The liberals became equally certain that the radicals were just totally and destructively belligerent. The radicals saw the convocation with utter cynicism. It was just a meaningless charade aimed at making the students think they'd done something to condemn and even halt the war when they hadn't at all. But most liberals, who have to believe that reason will prevail in the end, came away that much more bolstered in the conviction that the "illogical and mistaken war" would soon end.

Professor Anderson, who had dealt closely with Dr. Cordier in arranging the convocation, saw the university president's condemnation of the Cambodian invasion as a "magnificent and difficult gesture which questioned some of the basic premises of his own long career as a diplomat." SDSers were persuaded that Cordier's speech couldn't mean a thing since he was still the dean of a school that unashamedly trained State Department and CIA men, and since Cordier himself had been responsible for policies quite parallel to those that led to Vietnam. "If he's upset about Cambodia at all," one SDS leader said that afternoon, "it's because he thinks that, strategically, the Cambodian invasion will weaken our military position in Vietnam."

The students had not formally voted to strike yet. So late Monday afternoon the ad hoc mechanism for taking that action was assembled—and a more bizarre and chaotic gathering has never pretended to function.

Two thousand people crammed into Wollman Auditorium in the Columbia student center building and immediately began making an air force of paper gliders out of the ream of leaflets they'd gotten as they ran the gauntlet of organizations at the entrance. The meeting never quite came to order and couldn't have functioned at all if half the crowd hadn't left early in bewilderment. Two self-designated chairmen were to try to choreograph the calling of the strike. They were Faris Bouhafa, a very melodramatic senior whose politics were unclear but who had resigned earlier in the year from the Student Senate, calling it "a damn body" and a "hoax," and Robert Stulberg, a former editorial chairman of the Columbia *Spectator*, a somewhat walrusy looking guy who appears, from his sedate manner, easily ten years older than he is. Bouhafa, as he is wont to do, takes most of the limelight at the start.

Immediately the Third World Coalition, formed through the tentative fusion of the Student Afro-American Society, the Asian American Political Alliance and the Latin American Student Association, demands that it be given the chair since the whole strike should be directed at ending the oppession of Third World people. But Faris doesn't especially want to yield his podium. An Asian girl calls him a racist and most SDSers applaud the epithet, but the crowd votes about two to one to keep Faris. The girl then turns and begins to shout at the crowd that they are almost all white and are acting in a typically racist way. A youth leaps up in the middle of the hall and calls out: "It's not our fault if we're white." And people are just getting going on a laugh at that when SDS's Steve Cohen stands and turns the tide with a smoke-lifting "FUCK YOU!"

Somehow the thing's got to be held together at least long enough to get the strike called. So the chair starts the crucial process of declaring the shut-down that's already a foregone conclusion. "The three national demands are immediate withdrawal from Southeast Asia, end of the repression of dissidents and end of the university's complicity in the war. All those in favor of an indefinite strike around these basic demands?" And a roaring "STEERIKE" rocks the hall. A fluttering squall of paper airplanes takes flight and people go crazy celebrating their liberation. A chant that was to boom around the campus repeatedly for days picks up steam and for a while at least unifies the fist-raising meeting: "STRIKE! STRIKE! STRIKE! STRIKE! STRIKE!"

There are still a great many different reasons for striking that have to be merged, and the factions begin functioning again. The Third World Coalition, which obviously has doubts about the whole mass strike circus, announces that Columbia should endorse the ten-point program of the National Liberation Front of South Vietnam. People want to know what the hell difference the endorsement would make, and what the hell the program is. So the ten points are fetched up slowly from some resourceful guy's document pile and are read in their entirety. The program is adopted rubber-stamp style, to keep things moving.

The "peace action" groups, as the peace groups have seen fit to call themselves after the radicals baited them for inertia, want the university to become an anti-war center and build for another huge mobilization in Washington for the end of the week. That's voted up. People bellowingly agree with the Radical Caucus' proposal that D.A. Hogan either drop the charges against the Panthers or that he be dropped by the university. And all agree that the court injunction outlawing "disruption of the normal functions of the university" immediately be lifted since, among other things, it would render the strike illegal and might be the basis for a police bust.

The Third World Coalition is bitterly convinced that racism should be the primary issue on the campus, and the chief target of the strike. They call again for leadership of the meeting, but are denied by the group. "The real fight is against our own factionalism," says a moderate. Things are coming apart. Frantz Derencourt of TWC threatens that his group will walk out of the meeting if it insists on maintaining its racism. And the crowd doesn't want that. SDS and the Coalition begin to caucus at a side of the hall, and Faris Bouhafa announces at the podium: "I get the feeling that there is personal hostility toward me and that it is dividing this meeting. I'm turning the chair over to Stulberg."

And then sensing the time to move, someone from the Radical Caucus proposes that Stulberg be joined as chairman by representatives of the three member-factions of the Third World Coalition. The chant "Share the Chair" begins and the idea is quickly adopted. A black, a Latin and an Asian mount the stage to join Stulberg, a Jew. It's like a little U.N. meeting. Derencourt, the black, begins again. He tries to explain that the strike should be against racism and that the victims of racism should lead it.

But the liberals in the audience don't want to hear that. They want various organizations to submit proposals for policy positions and actions, and they want to vote them up or down. Clearly they don't think racism is the primary issue. Derencourt, finding himself the leader of a racist meeting, bails out. "This token leadership doesn't mean a thing," he announces, and the Third World people walk out of the meeting.

Bonnie Britt, a journalism student and a very powerful SDS speaker, rushes to a microphone, but it's dead. It clicks on only to catch Bonnie, a very handsome woman, laying into some guy: "Don't you call me 'honey,' you fucking male chauvinist pig." And then it dies again. The crowd cheers.

Stulberg tries to get the meeting together and someone yells at him: "Hey, Stollworth, this is the God damned worst meeting I've ever seen," and a squadron of paper gliders takes off in agreement. Then a masked kid in a cowboy hat suddenly leaps onto the stage with a gun and squirts water into the chairman's face. And still Stulberg tries to hang in there.

Alan Egelman from SDS gets the floor and announces: "The main thing wrong with this meeting is there isn't enough political discussion." The crowd obviously thinks there are other problems and more leaflets sail. Alan hands off to Bonnie, who was angry when she tried to speak the first time and is raging by now. "You've got to see what the hell you all are. A black was up there on the steps this morning talking about how blacks and Latins are getting the blood sucked out of them by this university, and you heckled him. That was incredibly racist of you. And now this afternoon you've driven the Third World people out of this meeting because you insist on maintaining that racism. You've got to look at yourselves critically and cut that shit out or we aren't going to get anywhere." She is about to read the Third World Coalition's demands, which are very much like SDS' original ones and which have now been adopted, for solidarity's sake, by SDS. But there are only about a hundred "strikers" left in the once-packed auditorium and, under the assurance that SDS would get a lead speaking spot at a second "mass meeting" that night, Bonnie holds off.

Three thousand leaflet glider-makers jam into Wollman Auditorium that night. Stulberg is the sole chairman, with Bouhafa conspicuously inconspicuous in the background. Things are even crazier as a swarm of compulsive parliamentarians actually outnumbers the factionalists this time around. Points of order, points of information and points of procedure virtually overwhelm the good intentions to decide anything. If it hadn't been for the Great Political Paper Airplane Contest which was going on in the hall while Columbia was placing itself on strike, there wouldn't have been any reason for anyone to be there.

The solemn pledge to give SDS the lead speaking position is broken immediately. The New University Conference, a moderate Left-leaning group of professors and graduate students was called on instead to outline how the strike's "co-ordinating committee" could be formed to sustain the strike and administer it. The group would be made up of any organization that wanted to send a representative. It was a crucial move. It meant the radicals would either isolate themselves by refusing to work with the broad-based group, or co-opt themselves by joining it. Once again there was the chore of actually declaring the strike. Somehow the afternoon's vote was being considered "unofficial" and the action had to be validated by the evening crowd.

So Stulberg states the three national demands once again and calls out: "All those in favor of a strike around these basic demands?" And again the word roars out of thousands of chests and the auditorium is white with flying leaflets. "Any opposed?" Two, maybe three, ruggedly individualistic but softly spoken faculty "nays" emerge, to be greeted with exhuberant booing. "THIS UNIVERSITY IS NOW ON STRIKE!" shouts Stulberg and still another squadron takes flight on the roar of the crowd.

But one of the parliamentarians starts going crazy. He's yelling, "Point of procedure, Mr. Chairman. Point of procedure," over on the left side of the hall. Stulberg heaves a sigh and finally calls on him and the poor guy announces why he's so consternated: "That vote said we were in favor of a strike *around* those demands, but it didn't actually *declare* a strike!" The kids can't believe it and they start swearing and yelling at this fool who's got to bug the groovy strike meeting with such nit-picking. A lot of delta-winged jobs swoop down near the guy but none hit him. Stulberg must have figured it would be fun for people to do over again anyway, so he inquires of the assembly: "Are we on strike?" And an even more resounding "SSTEEERRIIIKE" is bellowed and another cloud of paper takes flight but it's not so heavy this time because people just can't fold anything that will fly without a little time to do it in.

Of course President Cordier wasn't idle all this time. The last thing he wanted was for Columbia University to be closed by a strike. While all those students and faculty members were declaring the university on strike, Dr. Cordier had convened an "emergency session" of the University Senate under its presiding officer, Dr. Cordier. It was a closed meeting—the first time in its history that the Senate had found it necessary to shield itself from its constituency. Knowing full well there would be no way to get classes together the next day, the lock-out was extended by the Senate. Classes were suspended for two more days. Some other concessions were made: students who wanted to spend the rest of the semester in anti-war activities could do so and take "incompletes" provided they made up their work by the next fall. And seniors about to graduate were given the right to take pass-fail grades instead of letter ones.

But while the people in Wollman were organizing picket lines and talking about "shutting the place down," their senate was over in Low Library stating in a "scab" resolution: "We recognize the right of those who wish to attend classes and pursue other scheduled academic activities, and the obligation of the faculties of the university to provide instruction. A denial of this principle will only contribute to the attacks on the integrity of the university and on the rights of each individual within it." Dr. Cordier told the group that a general strike "would not contribute to the winning of the ends we want to achieve. It would weaken those ends."

Initiative was everything and Cordier knew it. He couldn't keep canceling classes indefinitely, but he needed time and he was counting on a quick return of student apathy to keep the university functioning. If he had kept classes on for Tuesday, they never would have happened and people would have declared the strike completely successful. By extending the Moratorium he was at least holding off that victory. There was no opposition to Cordier at the Senate, though he'd have been attacked if he'd shown up across the campus and tried to read his resolution to the crowd in Wollman.

In Dr. Cordier's absence, the Wollman people proceeded to attack one another. The Third World Coalition made one last attempt to lead the strike by proposing that half the seats on the Strike Co-ordinating Committee be given to Third World delegates. When the proposal was defeated a Coalition representative accused the group of racism and then declared: "We will not participate in your strike but we will honor it."

Finally, with easily half the original evening crowd departed with meeting-fatigue, SDS gets its promised turn to speak. Neil Mullin, who is beginning to take a leadership role in the chapter, begins in a quiet, restrained tone: "The one thing that has to be made clear is that while we all say we want to smash racism in this society, some of us have been acting racist ourselves. We've got to be a little self-critical. We've got to open our minds. Now SDS *supports* the demands of the nationwide strike." (That brings applause. The moderates are surprised that SDS is joining them on anything.) "But in addition, SDS supports the Third World Coalition's four demands which are aimed at specifically smashing the racism that exists right here at Columbia."

And he reads the newly constituted demands. They closely parallel SDS' original demands, but give particular emphasis to abolishing the East Asian Institute at Columbia where professors have been accused of working out a strategy to hold back the rush to communism in Southeast Asia. All defense contracts and all "imperialistic business" courses would also be barred. And the buildings Columbia has been holding vacant in the area to be cleared for new university construction would be opened up again to community residents badly in need of additional housing.

"Racism is not abstract," Neil continues, "and it has to be fought on a very concrete basis. These things are what racism is all about and we have got to commit ourselves to fighting it."

The "Strike Circus Meeting," as it had already been labeled, ended some time after midnight when someone set off a fire alarm and the building was cleared. The radicals returned to the basement of Carman Hall, the biggest men's dormitory, for still another meeting—this time of the Radical Caucus.

"If that meeting had been at the University of Alabama at least the people would have been a lot more honest about their racism," an SDSer said. Hundreds of radical students are there, sprawled all over the tile floor and the cushionless furniture (the cushions having been confiscated or stolen earlier in the year), smoking like mad, and pretty much agreeing that the "mass" meeting had been a mess. But the unity ends there.

SDSers insist the only way to sharpen the strike is really to push on support for the workers' demands. Leaders want a mass rally on Low Plaza the next day to confront Cordier. The D4Mers don't much care for that idea, but they're still hot on their one issue: Columbia putting up bail money for the Panthers—which doesn't really appeal at all to SDS. "I've got an idea," one of the unity types says sarcastically. "Why don't we just split back into different organizations and do our own thing?" His point makes a pretty good impression and people settle down to looking for a common strategy again.

Jay Facciola, a burly, radical jester who was one of the organizers of D4M, makes his way out into the middle of the circle and slips into a semi-facetious rap tone, dancing around like a bear. "God damn! These are all great demands! God damn it, let's free the Panthers! And God damn it, let's help Charlie Johnson's family. Sure. I'm not sectarian. I've never fought for Charlie Johnson's family before, but O.K., let's. I'm a very simple man. But let's remember, what we've really got to do is OFF AMERI-CAN IMPERIALISM."

Steve Cohen is turned on to the idea of confronting Cordier. He's always liked the idea. "We'll ask him about money for the Johnsons and he'll fumble around and say he hasn't got it and we'll tell him to sell his yacht. And maybe we ought to take that racist American flag down and run up, say, a red flag."

Bonnie Britt, her patience gone, cuts through the talk. "I'm sick as hell of rallies and posting demands. Let's seize a fucking building and hold it." And people agree that's a great idea, once there's enough of a following to do it.

CHAPTER FOUR

"SHUT IT DOWN!"

There was no precedent in the frenzied history of student activism in America for the nationwide strike that followed the invasion of Cambodia. Campus rebellions had always been relatively isolated from events at other schools and were somewhat vague in how they related to the state of the world. Each protest had grown out of catalyzing incidents right at the schools involved. And while several universities were often under siege simultaneously during the spring uprising seasons of the late Sixties, there was never much sense of unity or co-ordination among the rebellions, though their issues were very closely connected. At Berkeley, Columbia, San Francisco State and Harvard, local protest actions had brought on busts by the police, and the busts had brought on huge strikes.

But Cambodia catalyzed hundreds of campus strikes called in unison all over the country, and its remoteness to campus issues left most radicals with the task of leading actions at their own schools to forge connecting links. Sentiment to "do something" in response to the expansion of the war was prevalent with broad ranks of students. But it was left to the radicals to provide a strategy that would concretize the campus strikes into specific demands that could be made against the universities themselves.

Ostensibly Columbia was on strike by Tuesday morning. The trappings were all there. Sheets hung from windows, flapping out the declaration: ON STRIKE! Fists were being spray-stenciled in

red onto the university's granite, often over the whiter, sand-
blasted patches where the same declarations of militance had been
emblazoned and then removed after the 1968 rebellion. Crowds
were already milling out in the central campus plaza, waiting to do
something more than just be on strike.

By then everyone had heard or read that four straight, white,
hardly political kids had been killed by the National Guard at
Kent State University the day before, and a grim sobriety had
settled over the initial strike exuberance. It was obvious that
Nixon and the men who run this country were playing for keeps.
(The President hadn't yet backed off from his hard-line, "campus
protesters are bums" posture but he soon would, to avoid looking
like a smug murderer.) While the radicals were already talking
about "avenging" the Kent State killings, whimsical joking about
violent action was no longer very funny.

Kent State wasn't really that much of a shock for the
radicals, any more than Cambodia had been. Though white middle
class America hadn't especially taken note of it, three black
student protesters had been shot in the back and killed in a
demonstration in Orangeburg, South Carolina, two years before.
(Even while the uproar over Kent State was going on, police
opened fire on a black dormitory at Jackson State College in
Mississippi in an even more astounding "unprovoked" incident and
killed two more black students, but that also somehow went
relatively unnoticed by the white media.) SDS had always maintained that if radicals are really posing an effective threat, the
powers they are threatening are bound to attack them. Mao
Tse-tung wrote that it is a victory for revolutionaries to be attacked by their enemies. It is often quoted by SDSers.

Kent State did make it clear that the already narrow range of
tactical options available to radical protesters was getting even
narrower as the conflict in the country sharpened. Since it has
become axiomatic to them that *co-operation leads to co-optation*,
the radicals always have to take a combative approach. But unlike
the Weathermen, SDS ruled out bombings and other acts of
terrorism. Small groups of invisible bombers with little or no
popular support can't accomplish the building of a revolution and
might even prevent it, SDS maintains. What was left in between
co-operation and terrorism was "mass action." That is, demonstrating with as many people as can be mustered and as militantly

as possible. After Kent State it appeared that even when such demonstrating is relatively peaceful, it might bring down massive violence from the government's unrestrained fear. SDS never changed its course after Kent State, but a lot of other campus radicals decided to either go underground or to drop out of the movement altogether.

"We've got to remember that there's nothing in between violence and non-violence and any time you move at all you might end up getting what they got at Kent State," one of the unaffiliated people warned at a Radical Caucus meeting Tuesday afternoon. It was a principle many of the radicals had already fully realized. While he spoke, several caucus members began taping up a poster-size blowup of the picture of a Kent State girl, her arms out in supplicating disbelief, screaming over the bleeding body of a fellow student. Across the scene in dripping red letters was printed the word "AVENGE."

The meeting was searching for an "action" that would solidify the strike, but nothing much was being suggested. Talk of occupying buildings was generally derided as old hat. The 1968 Columbia rebellion had largely consisted of "occupations." The police had been called in that time to clear the kids out and had been brutal enough to create a lot of sympathy for the radicals, so in the end the tactic more or less worked. But college administrations were acting a lot smarter now and were ignoring the building seizures until the occupiers finally tired and slinked out. SDS tried it at Columbia again in 1969, but this time the radicals were almost totally ignored by the rest of the students and the administration. They finally came out voluntarily. "It's ridiculous. You hang around for a few days and no one cares you're in there and then you either come out or you stay forever. Big deal! We've got to find a way to build an on-going movement," one of the wizened veterans lectured.

Drop building occupations and the radicals are left with very little in the way of tactical options—except for the old standby, the confrontation. So that's more or less what people settled on for that night's action. After an assembly to be given by Chicago Conspiracy lawyer William Kunstler and his colleague, Gerald Lefcourt, who was defending the New York Panther "conspirators," the Radical Caucus would lead a march to President Cordier's house where it was rumored a dinner party would be going on. The radicals' demands would be nailed Martin Luther-style to his door, and then everyone would march another thirty blocks north to City College to support the students who were trying to seize that campus.

The march would lead up through Harlem bringing the students into contact with the "community people." But there was some doubt about whether the police would allow those two volatile groups to come together and possibly pool their militancy. "If we hit the streets we've got to be ready for what the pigs are going to do. They aren't going to let us march through that community without a fight first," a guy named Josh declared from one of the window sill perches. And that more or less clinched the idea for everyone.

There had been reports all day that the campus workers wanted to take the "Moratorium" day off to protest the war, just as students and professors had done. Now word came back from two scouts the Radical Caucus had sent out from its meeting to check on the situation (one was an SDSer, the other a D4Mer, just so one of the conflicting political perspectives wouldn't be allowed to manipulate the united group). About 150 workers were massing in the lobby of the Low Library. They were going to confront the administration with their own desire to protest the war. Any student support they could get would be really appreciated. It was the sort of call to action SDS, with its Worker-Student Alliance program, dreams of getting.

The hundred radicals, suddenly provided with a political action to take, pour out of their basement lounge and sweep across the campus, heading for Low. The SDS chant, "SAME STRUGGLE, SAME FIGHT, WORKERS AND STUDENTS MUST UNITE," booms out and a lot of Frisbee players out on South Field join up to see what's happening. Up the steps of Low again, past the surrogate-mother statue, "Alma Mater," which has sat peacefully through dozens of radical assaults on her administration headquarters, and up to the front doors of Low, which are open this time. The workers are massed in the lobby and Judy Lacoff, a leader of militant rank and file campus workers, is announcing through a bullhorn that the administration is only willing to let the workers use their "floating holiday" if they want to take the day off. There would be no Moratorium for non-teaching employes.

Andy Kaslow out on the steps begins a rap to let the rest of the campus know, through the facilities of the SDS bullhorn, exactly what's going on. "The workers of this university are massed in Low right now confronting the administration for their own right to protest the war, and they want all the student support they can get. When the workers move, this place is really threatened. When students and workers shut down the cafeterias here to get rid of a racist boss, this place lost a lot of money and it didn't like it. Now they're trying to kick a lot of the students who supported those workers out of school."

Andy reads the letter that he and five other SDSers just received, notifying him that he'll be brought up before a university "tribunal" for breaking the school's new rules barring protests that block access to facilities. Then he moves into the broader political picture to try to explain why student support for workers grievances is so necessary:

"The families of these workers are kept isolated and hungry. The university pays these people peanuts: $80 a week for cleaning toilets. You can't feed your babies on that. These people have hungry babies just like all the people of Harlem have hungry babies, and they need our support if they're going to fight for what they need to live and what they deserve."

A lot more people begin gathering around to lend their support. Then over to the left of the Low steps a skirmish begins. Some of the nonaligned radicals get into a tug-of-war with a lone university cop over the flagpole rope. The students win. The American flag is brought down, to cheers, and handed over to several people who insist on folding it respectfully. To more applause, a somewhat skimpy North Vietnamese flag is produced, tied to the halyard, and run up the high pole. One of the guys puts the rope in his teeth, runs over to a nearby tree, and shinnies and squirms and hauls his way up to the highest, thinnest branch where he ties the rope securely. He returns to earth and the congratulations of all. Then several of the campus cops who want that "enemy" flag down try quite futilely to climb up themselves but they can't get to even the lowest branches. "Pigs can't climb trees," one of the radicals tells them. "No, but guerrillas can," someone adds.

The workers suddenly pour out of Low and gather with the students on the steps. They have been turned down by the administration in their demand for the right to participate in the Moratorium. *So they are going ON STRIKE! along with the students*. People go wild cheering, and Judy Lacoff announces that the workers are going to march around the university to pass the word to all other workers. She says student support would still help. The merged group of several hundred workers and students pours back down past Alma Mater and heads directly for huge Butler Library across the way.

Up through the pillars of that building under the names of Aristotle, Plato and six other Greeks, and into the vaulted hallways, rhythmic chanting rocks the usually hushed sanctuary.

> The bosses can't profit
> When the workers fight.
> Shut it down
> And make it TIGHT!

Up to the circulation desk on the second floor where the chanting quiets down so the workers there can be told what's happened. And with the word that the workers have called a wildcat, most of the clerks who man the library complex pour over and around their counters to join the march as it heads on down the corridor shouting, "STRIKE! STRIKE! STRIKE!"

Outdoors again and over to the big oak-paneled cafeteria in John Jay Hall. All the food is laid out, ready for dinner, and leaders caution the brigade to keep its hands off. "No trashing." Again the workers are given the word and more join up. Then out again to head for the bookstore. Alan Egelman is thrilled. All year long SDS has been offering itself to the workers for whatever support was needed. And now the SDS strategy everyone had scorned as a pipe dream was coming true. The workers were leading the students, marching around Columbia, shutting it down. "This is great," Alan declares. "I love it." And he slaps a fist hard into his other hand. Andy Kaslow is also elated. "We've been talking about this all year and it's finally happening. I can hardly believe it. Man, we've been telling everyone it's the workers that have the power. Now we've just got to keep it going. We've got to make sure we can keep control away from the liberals."

Such exuberance over the walkout of a few hundred campus workers might seem like outlandish over-reaction and optimism on

SDS' part. But radicals don't see it as optimism; it's "fighting defeatism." The task of recasting society is oppressively mammoth to begin with, even if it's going fantastically well. Pessimists would never stick to such a long-term effort. So radical organizations have got to sustain the conviction that they are winning. They have to fight bitterly against the slightest signs of cynicism and demoralization. That often means placing such minor victories into the symbolic context of the larger struggle—which makes the victories themselves larger.

The Left has a chronic problem just trying to determine what the country's political situation is. Factions and personalities are constantly fighting over how close or remote "the revolution" is. The radicals have no poll takers; there's very little feedback really. And while committed radicals are perfectly willing to work for months without any concrete signs of success, when such indications come it's reason for euphoria.

"We have all been told a lot of lies in the press about how workers are fascists and racists and how they support the war. But this gives the lie to that," Andy announced through the bullhorn. "These people are risking their jobs to oppose the war."

SDS was quite convinced that the support it had given earlier in the year to those workers had helped to bring them out for the strike. SDS National Headquarters in Boston rejoiced when told of the Columbia development that night. A sign went up declaring that a great step forward had been taken and the word was passed to contacts on campuses all over the country. *New Left Notes* later heralded the joint worker-student strike at Columbia as one of the few successful campus strikes in the country that spring because it had effectively hampered the university's operations.

When workers strike for a political goal like ending the war in Southeast Asia, the Left savors the event. It's a sign that they are recognizing their power and using it for more than just better wages—which, of course, is an absolute necessity if workers are eventually to lead a revolution. The march at Columbia and similar walkouts at two other campuses were publicized by SDS as the first *political* strikes in decades, clear evidence that when workers and students ally, they not only wield tremendous power but wield it in the right direction.

While not enough workers actually went on strike at Columbia to shut the entire university down effectively, many did go out and that was an awfully good sign. Next time the wildcat would be larger and would hold out longer. Eventually there would be no holding it back. It's the natural way to see things when you're engaged in a very difficult effort. The Pentagon keeps boasting about how it's winning the war in Vietnam and always sees victory just around the corner. The generals seize the data they need to convince themselves so that they can go ahead and convince everyone else. And if the Pentagon's allowed to do it, SDS ought to be. The radicals even jokingly compete with one another to be the greatest optimist. "How many people did we have at our last demo?" one SDSer asks another. "Oh, about a hundred." "A hundred? It was easily a thousand," chimes in a third.

The role of radical student leadership that SDS has sought for itself is an incredibly tricky affair. Fed up with the way the system is structuring their lives, the students come looking to SDS for anarchy. It gives them discipline and organization instead. They want to tear down buildings but somehow end up writing leaflets. SDS has to provide a program of action and must somehow rally the masses needed to implement it. But it also has to hold them back from their own desire to act when it feels the time isn't right. The hardest task of all, and the one SDS chapters were confronted with all over the country during the National Student Strike, is finding a way to lead the masses when they're already on the move by themselves.

Any mistakes will leave the organization hopelessly isolated. If SDS says wait and the students want to move, SDS will be left behind. And if SDS moves and the students don't follow, it leaves them behind. All these judgments have to be made without much evidence of what the whimsical student population is ready to do. So in the end SDS leaders just have to figure out the strategy with the greatest potential and hope their own leadership is strong enough to execute it. At Columbia, on the second night of the strike, it wasn't.

Easily two thousand students queued up for ten blocks on the sidewalk that runs along Broadway in front of the Columbia campus, all hoping to get into the auditorium where William Kunstler was going to speak. SDS had leaflets for them announcing:

"MARCH TONIGHT."

"The liberal leadership of the Columbia strike has shown no real ability to lead a struggle at Columbia against racism and imperialism. By consuming student energy in endless non-productive meetings and symbolic actions they are accomplishing nothing toward the three national demands. They are rapidly selling the people out. The Radical Caucus seeks an alternative to this liberal leadership. We see that a struggle against this government's policies must encompass a struggle against Columbia and that it must include a struggle against racism. We recognize that the Third World people best understand the issues and the need for this struggle. We support, therefore, the Third World Coalition's demands. We call on all Columbia students to *ACT* with us in this nationwide struggle. FIGHT RACISM!"

Kunstler made his speech a call to united action on the Left. He likened the situation in the U.S. to Germany just as Hitler was consolidating his power. Factionalism kept the Left from uniting to fight Hitler, he said, and "the gas covered all. The bodies were united, but the union of dead bodies did no good." He said the National Student Strike could be the beginning of shutting the country down, and he said students must be absolutely solid in the strike. "If there is one university which is not on strike by this time next week, then we have failed. You must make sure there are no commencements anywhere this spring. What good is a degree in a world like this?"

Kunstler passed the mike over to his colleague, Gerald Lefcourt, who challenged the liberal claims that the strike should only be directed against the war and not against the university: "When I came to this campus tonight some people told me this was a one-issue strike. They said they are against the war and that's all. And I thought: 'This can't be the same Columbia University that was the first to call for an end to university complicity in the war, the first university to recognize the community around it.' War, racism, poverty—it's all related in the same oppressive system."

It was a terrific boost and the radicals cheered enthusiastically. Then a representative from the Third World Coalition dramatically announced that things were already on the move. The Coalition had taken over the fifth floor of Kent Hall, where the university ran its East Asian Institute. And he picked up Lefcourt's theme: "We support the national demands 100 per cent.

But you can't isolate the racist war in Vietnam and Cambodia from racism right here at home."

By that time the crowd's fighting spirit was really up. To cap it, several students who had been evacuated from the Kent State campus described the killings: "Ours was a peaceful demonstration," said one. "If you can imagine what it's like shooting wooden ducks, that's what the National Guard had going on the Kent Green yesterday," another said, on the verge of tears. "But you can't imagine what it's like to see a guy carrying his girl with her guts spilling out." Finally someone from the Radical Caucus was given the microphone on Lefcourt's urging. He announced that students were holding the whole southern portion of City College and that the assembly should march up to the college to support them.

Most of the SDSers never got close to the assembly. They were busy getting out leaflets and painting huge banners in anticipation of the march. When the crowd came pouring out of the auditorium, to SDS' amazement, it flowed up right behind the SDS banner and began moving out—a crowd of thousands. SDS is in the lead and it's almost too good to be true. The entire campus hasn't moved together this way since the 1968 rebellion. Alan Egelman has the SDS bullhorn and skipping backwards to stay at the head of the line, he announces: "We are going to post our demands on Andy Cordier's door, and then we're going up to City College where they've taken over the ROTC building and a lot of the campus." He doesn't know that the crowd has already been mobilized for the march uptown.

The SDS banner, a huge strip of cloth declaring: "NO MORE RACIST ATTACKS ON THIRD WORLD PEOPLE. U.S. OUT OF SOUTHEAST ASIA; FREE ALL POLITICAL PRISONERS NOW," reaches Amsterdam Avenue at the other end of the campus, while the great crowd is still pouring into the line of march way back on the Broadway side.

Then the first crisis over SDS' leadership hits and is silently but quickly resolved. To get to the presidential mansion for the posting of the demands, the march must keep going straight for another block. But as soon as the SDS contingent begins to cross Amsterdam Avenue and head for Cordier's house, the line breaks and the crowd under its own leadership wheels left and begins the hike northward. "Hey! . . . We're . . . We're going directly to City

College!" Alan announces to himself, SDS, and the crowd that is already headed that way. The SDSers have to really hustle to make it back to the head of the march.

Straight uphill under Harlem's open windows, the crowd from Columbia University, one of the most expensive and elitist schools in the country, marches to rally with its comrades-in-struggle at the City College of New York, one of the country's only tuition-free and fully open schools. Past 125th Street, Harlem's main drag, a blazing plaza of white-owned furniture stores boasting easy credit, honky-tonks and pawn shops. Then past the dark, crowded tenements where hundreds of kids hang out the windows to see who's in the streets. The crowd chants the Panther slogan:

> Po-Wer to the Pee-Pal
> OFF THE PIG!

And the "pig himself," half a dozen strong in several cruisers, swings into the lead of the march.

When the Panther chant begins to falter a bit, SDS gets the crowd going on its own line:

> Workers and Students
> Gonna Shut it Down!

Lots of Harlem's blacks raise their fists in support of the march below them in the street. The farther the students march, the bigger the crowd swells as young black kids, who live late into the night in Harlem's streets, happily join up.

City College is finally reached and the Columbia contingent sweeps through the gates and up into the campus. A girl with soaking wet hair comes running over and asks one of the invaders: "Who the hell are you all?"

"We're from Columbia. We've come to support you."

"Wild! We liberated the swimming pool. We've all been in." People are herded together on a hillside, with the Columbia people easily outnumbering the City College liberators they've come to reinforce. Kunstler is about to address the group when the tail end of the Columbia march arrives with urgent word that the Third World students in Kent Hall have been served with a restraining order barring them from taking over the facility. They need legal advice and want Lefcourt back. So the speeches at City are extremely brief. Kunstler tells the crowd to "Do it! For God's sake, DO IT!" And though SDS' Alan Egelman gives him the Third World-SDS demands to read, Kunstler doesn't.

Then like a receding wave, the Columbia group rushes down out of City College and heads again for the Morningside campus. Again the SDSers have to hurry to stay in the lead. They still have their demands to nail up and try to head the group back down Amsterdam. But people in the crowd just behind them think it would be more fun to take over Broadway. This time there's a mid-intersection discussion and SDS prevails. But by the time everyone reaches Columbia again the demands-posting has been given up in favor of rallying in support of the Third World people "in occupation" at Kent Hall. So the entire group, easily two thousand, pours back onto campus, up to the dark lawn in front of Kent and then begins waiting for something to do.

The tremendous crowd is itching to act. A voice calls out, "Let's seize the campus." And another answers, "We have the campus." Still a third responds, "We do?" SDS announces that the Third World Coalition is preparing a statement of its demands and people should wait to find out what support is wanted. Frightening rumors begin circulating that Weathermen nurtured in the earlier years of strife at Columbia are lurking in the crowd, waiting for action. But no one sees a Weatherman they know is a Weatherman.

Neil Mullin takes up the SDS bullhorn and ties in the march to City College with what's to come. "We've marched through black and Latin working class neighborhoods that are being exploited by this institution which claims it's value-free. And we say these oppressive, exploitative institutions that run people out of their homes and pay people slave wages have got to come down."

Finally, members of the Coalition come down from their fifth floor sanctuary with a somewhat legalistic statement of their purposes and demands. But it's almost pitch dark in the quadrangle in front of the building and they can't see the statement well enough to read it. They try holding a match, but it's too dim and it blows out almost immediately. Then they try to make a torch out of sheets of paper and that's only good for a sentence or two. Finally the whole crowd shifts over toward the entrance to

Philosophy Hall where two big globes give off more than enough reading light.

The occupation of the East Asian Institute, it was announced, was "non-obstructive"—meaning its perpetrators didn't want to be held in violation of the university's "interim rules" against campus disruptions. They said that injustice in America is the product of our society's "inherent racism," and that same racism is the cause of the genocide of hundreds of thousands of Southeast Asians whose lives were being casually eradicated because they were not "white" lives. The Coalition's demands were reiterated.

Then the Third World Coalition went back into Kent Hall to continue its occupation. No word was given about how the huge mob of students outside could help. So SDS picked up the ball again. The leaders desperately wanted to go as far as the crowd would to back up the coalition with massive strength.

"Do you support these demands?" Alan Egelman bellowed. And the crowd, *the whole crowd*, roared "Yes!" Alan left it to them. "How?" And people everywhere started yelling, "Take Low. Seize the administration building." More and more people picked up the call "Seize Low! Seize Low!" Quckly five or six SDS leaders caucused. "They want to do it. They want to do it. They want Low." When you've worked all year to rally a campus, and you've finally got a couple of thousand students ready to fight, it's suicide to hold them back. SDS moved.

"All right. We all know what Low Library is to this university," Neil announces. "Let's go over and open it up!"

For still another time in that crazy night SDS races to the head of the crowd. This time the SDS leaders have to rush clear through the massive crowd to lead the way to Low, and in doing that they may have made their first tactical error. The militants who were the most ready for the action were scattered all through the swarm and hadn't been rallied together into a fighting core. Not everyone is as good at fighting their way to the head of a moving mass of people as SDSers are because not everyone has had the experience.

Once again they rush past old Alma Mater and up to the Low main door. It's sealed again and the "Please Use the Southeast Entrance" sign is out. A few people advise the group to take one of the side doors to avoid the "pigs in the lobby," but the rest are for the direct approach. Four, then six SDSers lift the big sign up and turn its weighty base toward the heavy wooden doors of Low.

Hundreds of people are mobbed around on the steps. The SDSers, led by several members who a week or so before had been chastising themselves for being too pacifistic, smash the heavy block into the locked doors. There are a lot of grunts, and someone calls for each big lunge. One, two, three charges with the ram and the doors buckle open. You can see deep into the rotunda where a wide semicircle of panicked campus policemen in full riot gear is waiting for the onslaught. Visions of Kent State come to many people who dodge to either side of the doorway to be out of the line of any fire. But the SDSers begin going to work on the first of two sets of glass doors inside.

Way in back, behind the cordon of police, is a cluster of deans. Though none of the radicals saw him—it would have been an incredible inspiration if they had—it was later reported that President Cordier was among them.

Over at the Southeast Entrance a very worried security officer called to an SDSer and offered to negotiate. Call off the attack and several representatives would be let in to discuss the demands. But the attack was already underway, and besides SDS doesn't negotiate with people it wants to overthrow. The first set of glass doors are broken easily. Then the campus police take the offensive and charge the second set, smashing their clubs down through the glass, cutting Alan Egelman on the face. It's the radicals' moment of truth: time to rush in to Low and battle the police. They have the numbers to force the police out. The SDSers pause for a moment to rally themselves. And way, way down at the bottom of the steps, down near the sundial in the center of the plaza, a liberal chant begins. "Don't Do It! Save Our Strike! Don't Do It! SAVE OUR STRIKE!"

The radicals look around. About 150 people are up there on the steps with them, but many hundreds more are down below, begging them to call off the attack. "Shit. They're not with us," one of the SDS women mutters. They could win the battle—but the rest of the campus is against it. Slowly the battering ram is dropped and the radicals stumble down the steps. Those anonymous voices that called for the seizure are nowhere now. Some of the D4Mers who had been up for taking the administration building are now bailing out of the whole fiasco. "You owe us an apology," one of them screams at Alan. "No one authorized violent action. What the hell were you doing up there?"

Alan stares blankly at the guy, not aware of the blood that's running down his cheek. "I don't owe any apologies; not to you. We all owe our apologies to those Third World people who've been jeered and mocked in utter racism. We were up there trying to support them. Where were you?"

"Wollman!" people from the strike steering committee start announcing. "Meeting in Wollman." And though it's very tired of always being steered to meetings, the crowd figures that the action out on the plaza is done, so it slowly filters into the auditorium.

"We had a beautiful thing going tonight until those trouble-makers got out of hand," a black declares from the stage. Some-one calls out: "Who are you anyway? What group are you with?" And he smiles and says: "I'm myself, man. I'm not with any group." And the crowd roars in applause. They are sick of all the various factions and organizations, each with its own specialized program for action and each putting the others down as mis-leaders. It's a chronic problem in Left politics. The unaligned people who are needed to make up a mass capable of a strong, long campaign are very cynical about the organizations that offer them proposals for action. But the unaligned people themselves are notoriously reluctant to come up with their own programs— and if perchance a few do, they are likely to just become still another special-interest faction. In the end, a lot gets proposed to the people and almost nothing is taken up.

A tall bearded youth takes the stage and says: "As far as the workers are concerned, the trashing up there at Low that just happened was BULLSHIT."

Andy Rotstein from SDS responds. "About the only thing that has really become apparent this week is that a strike like this one is a fairly complex situation." People chuckle agreement with the understatement. "But it seems to us that it is absolutely vital for this strike to come to life through an attack on the origins of the social evils the strike is supposed to be combating. The attack here should be against the university. At Yale they've tried to say there's no need to attack the administration. But the student movement has got to see that these universities are controlled by the same small group of men who own and control the means of production in this country. They are pushing all the racism and exploitation and oppression for the sake of profits and power. You know all these trustees are corporation presidents and bosses of one kind or another. The Third World Coalition sees the necessity to attack the university and fight it for our demands until we win. They see it because Third World people are the ones who have the oppression of institutions like Columbia coming down heaviest on them.

"Now I also agree that senseless trashing and individual acts of violence are useless. SDS condemns such acts. But the attempted seizure of Low just now was a worthwhile step. We weren't just throwing rocks and running. We wanted to take a concrete step with the hundreds of people out there to support the Third World people in their fight against this racist university. And we *still* recognize the leadership of the Third World Coalition."

But the SDS-TWC alliance was in trouble. Throughout the strike's development, emissaries from the white Radical Caucus had been sent to sit in on Third World Coalition meetings, and people from the Third World Coalition had been sent over to co-ordinate things with the Radical Caucus. But when it finally came time for action, neither group knew what the other was going to do or what it could do to help. And the breakdown ended in catastrophe for the Columbia radicals. "We thought everyone was going to sit down in front of Kent Hall while we were inside," one of the Coalition members recalled weeks later. "We thought a bust was coming and we wanted support."

SDS never knew that and, in the pressure of the moment, tried to find its own way to back the Third Worlders. Its action, the assault on Low, came as an astonishing surprise to the Coalition. Many TWC members, who were already extremely worried about being arrested for occupying the building, were enraged that an even more flagrant provocation to the police had been made by SDS in their name. So a Coalition representative rose at the Wollman meeting and repudiated the attack on Low. "We don't want violent, destructive support. We want a serious, long, hard struggle, not an overnight flash in the pan."

The Coalition had been under extremely severe strain because its several nationality factions were viewing the strike from different perspectives. The Asian students resented any domestic focus that would take attention away from the American killing, maiming and pillaging in their homelands. Cambodia and Vietnam, the

American imperialist atrocities, should be what the strike was all about, they felt. They wanted to attack the East Asian Institute where scholars developed the theories that sent in the troops. One member from the Asian-American Political Alliance cried because of the decimation of her people and pleaded that the occupiers destroy the institute which she held responsible. But the blacks and Latins were against any direct action that would jeopardize the fights they thought were absolutely necessary to wage against the university's racist treatment of its workers, the community and, through trustee Hogan, the Black Panthers.

After the attack on Low the Asians split from the Coalition, in effect scuttling it. Han Hua Chang later told a rally regretfully that the Low assault could have been a very progressive step. "Any act of violence directed against Nixon's policy of escalating the war against Asian people is a just and constructive act. Peaceful protest is bullshit!" Many non-Asian members of the Coalition agreed, once they could look back on that night without the incredible paranoia that comes with being isolated in a grim university building at night, convinced the police are about to come to drag you away. "The very next day we knew we'd blown it," recalls Warren Tull, a black ex-Marine who later became one of several Third Worlders who decided to join Columbia SDS, breaking down the usual radical racial separation. "We started to think: here were more than 1,500 students ready to do whatever the Coalition wanted them to—whatever we thought would help. And we cooled it with them when we could have said, 'Tear this place apart.' Who knows when another chance like that will come along."

As it happened, it was the SDSers who were dragged away by the police. The bust didn't come right away. But early on a Saturday morning several weeks later, when the campus was deserted by all but the most politically committed students, police invaded the Columbia dorms. Alan Egelman was awakened by the proverbial pounding on his door. He jumped out of bed, hauled on his pants and yanked open the door to cuss out the rowdy dormmates he thought had roused him. Instead he found about a dozen detectives and deputies from trustee Hogan's District Attorney's office. He tried to go back to bed, but they wouldn't let him. Without telling him what he was being arrested for, they slapped handcuffs on him and led him off to the waiting elevator which was also full of policemen—"just in case you think of making trouble." Alan had been expecting to have to "spend some time in the clink during the summer" because of the abortive Low assault and took it all in good spirits. At the booking, when they asked him his mother's maiden name, he said "Raft." And when they couldn't understand him he finally explained: "Raft. Raft. You know—rhymes with *graft.*"

They didn't knock on Steve Cohen's door. They just barged in, dragged him out of bed and handcuffed him without even saying they were police. Then they started to search his room. Minutes later he was a political prisoner, en route to police headquarters in an unmarked but heavily populated police car.

Susie Boehm was an earlier riser. She was in the lobby of her dorm when she spotted Warren Monroe, known to SDS as "Boss" Monroe, the head of campus security. There were an awful lot of men with him, but Susie didn't find out why because some parents were in the lobby and Monroe wanted to avoid an incident in front of them. The strong-arm approach wouldn't go very well with Barnard College's tea sipping tradition. A squad of police had blown past the shocked dormitory desk attendant and was waiting for Sue when she appeared at her room. One of them casually inquired if she lived there. When she said she did, they seized her.

The university seemed quite pleased with the arrests. The next day two high Columbia officials spoke proudly of the move in a somewhat unusual story the *New York Times* squeezed into its Sunday edition. (Columbia was certainly well enough connected to "place" the story in the *Times*. Arthur Sulzberger, the president and publisher of the *Times*, is another of the university's trustees.)

The SDSers (the *Times* conspicuously neglected to say they were SDSers) had been charged with two felonies, criminal mischief and criminal contempt, which could net each one of them five years in prison. That seemed to impress the *Times* reporter the most. "This is the severest sort of action that has been taken by the university," an official "who asked not to be identified" was quoted as saying. It was the first time, according to the *Times*, that the university had lodged felony charges against students involved in a campus demonstration as a result of its own investigation."

But there was much to indicate that Columbia's trustee, New

York District Attorney Frank Hogan, had something to do with the events leading up to the arrests by his plainclothesmen. The university said it had begun its investigation the morning after the incident, and that it presented its complaints to Hogan's office five days after the assault, on May 11. But the D.A. didn't move his men in for the arrest until May 23—either because he was co-operating with the university in delaying the bust until it would cause the least trouble, or because he wanted a more complete case himself.

Bail was originally set at $5,000 a piece, but when Jane Moorman, a special assistant to Barnard College President Martha Peterson, came to the jail to vouch for Sue Boehm, all three were freed without bail. Andy Kaslow was also charged in the incident, but he was not around when the police came looking for him. He "surrendered himself" the next Wednesday. Quite a number of other SDSers who also "were on the ram" during the Low assault went through some anxious hours as well after word of the bust spread, but the arrests were held to four. By February of the next year the SDS Four were still mired in the plodding judicial system and had neither been to jail nor stood a trial, though Steve, Andy and Alan were suspended from school.

Columbia had accomplished its purpose. Finding the radicals at an unusually weak point, the university had moved, as its own officials admitted, more severely than ever before.

None of this either crushed SDS or broke the strike, however. The day after the Low assault SDSers were ready on campus with a leaflet admitting: "We are self-critical about our abortive seizure of Low Library last night. The time was not politically right for our leadership. This mistake stemmed from an overestimation of white student support for the Third World Coalition's demands." But SDS held steadfastly to its call for a fight against Columbia.

Recriminations mixed with strategy when the Radical Caucus, still somehow holding together in the aftermath of the Low fiasco, gathered in its basement meeting place. (Someone suggested that the Caucus "go underground" since all its meetings were subterranean anyway.) Alan Egelman said three major factors blocked SDS' success in the Low assault just as they had undermined the group's work all year: "Racism, liberalism and pacifism." Banks were burning in California and students were seizing city halls in the Midwest, but Columbia people had fought two years ago and they weren't that enthusiastic about doing it again.

"Last night we took over this movement and an hour later we lost it. Even the liberals had been saying, 'Seize Low.' I heard them," one of the D4Mers recalled. "But they wouldn't move when the time came. Down there singing their fucking 'Save our Strike.' What strike? If we don't get something going, people are going to start straggling back and having classes on the lawn and all that bullshit, and then they'll have their final exams and graduation and it'll all be flushed into nothing."

Bonnie Britt again summed it up: "Those pacifist bastards fucked us last night. If we had done it, it would have been out of sight. Since we didn't, I guess we made a mistake moving in the first place."

CHAPTER FIVE

"WAR MAKER, STRIKE BREAKER!"

Dr. Cordier's string of "Moratorium days" ran out that evening. Starting Thursday there could be no confusing the Columbia strike with an officially sanctioned respite in the university's usual business. Professors were directed to hold their classes and students were told that if they wanted to go to them, they had every right to do so. The radicals sharply disagreed, of course. As the week had progressed the whole logic of a strike against the university had been crystallizing for the radicals, even as it was dissolving for the liberals. The university was producing strategy and technology for the war, and for the exportation of American "influence," which leads to such wars, the radicals maintained. It was abusing its workers, and it was training people at its business school to become the lieutenants of American industry. They would go on to abuse and exploit the entire working class of this country and every other country they sought to expand into.

SDS said, look at the trustees of this university and you'll see what the institution's real interests are: the trustees are defense moguls, international business lords, repressive politicians and media magnates. The radicals said, look at the careers the university is piping its students into and you'll see whose interests it's really serving: students were graduating to become businessmen, government advisors, military and industrial researchers. And so it was reasoned that if IBM and Dow Chemical and the CIA were depending on schools like Columbia for their manpower, they'd be severely hurt if suddenly, because of a prolonged shut-down of the universities, their supply of new blood was cut off. For the radicals, especially groups like SDS with a strongly socialist analysis, the strategy of the strike was summed up in the slogan: "NO CLASS TODAY, NO RULING CLASS TOMORROW."

Admittedly some of the university's graduates would not share so directly in wealth and power. There would also be teachers, social workers, and pure academicians. But as long as the system itself was putting all the power and wealth of the country into a few hands, SDS and others maintained, whatever good intentions these more innocuous people might have would never really be accomplished and their work would just serve to mask the real problems and solutions. The schools and the country as a whole had to be totally shut down. Then, with power redistributed, the universities would be opened up again to teach what people really needed to better not just their own lives but everyone's.

At the outset of the Columbia strike there were three clearly opposing strategies being put forward on campus: the "radical" strike; a "liberal" plan which said university facilities should be used more directly to oppose the war but ignored any assistance the school was providing the military; and a third which said there should be no strike, the university was an excellent institution and should defend itself and its role against any attack or shut-down.

At first the liberals more or less endorsed the idea of a strike, though their reasoning for doing so wasn't that clear. They were sincerely outraged at the expansion of the war into Cambodia and wanted, as one professor explained, "to show we were against the war." But as the official Moratorium on classes expired and the lockout became a strike, they began to also want to show they were "for the university." And there the conflict rested for them. Because they have great faith invested in the idea that America and its institutions are largely good, they were frightened to see the system threatened by the radicals' efforts to close those institutions down. So they began to move in cautious and at first even unaware steps toward joining with the conservative opponents of the strike. In the end, the liberals were fighting the radicals to defend the university. "When it comes down to choosing sides, they always go with the establishment. They're worse than the open conservatives because they fight us all the while they claim they support our goals," an SDSer had warned in the beginning.

To sustain the strike, the radicals had to physically prevent classes from resuming. Like workers shutting down production at a factory, the militant students threw up picket lines to seal off all classroom buildings. And the Third World Coalition finally gained leadership of the strike by organizing those picket lines. Students who hadn't gotten up for an early morning class in months kept a 7:00 A.M. telephone chain unbroken, waking one another for the lines. Even varsity football players hepled with the picketing. The lines would gather slowly at the entrances to the major classroom buildings and wait to be challenged. For several days there were few attempts to enter the buildings. Many "moderates" even joined the picket lines. Once in a while a professor would become incensed at being shut out of his office. Several doorway scuffles occurred when the students insisted no one had the right to be carrying on their work—to scab. Several members of the faculty complained furiously to President Cordier that they had been struck or otherwise abused by the students. "Civil liberties" for scabs weren't as important as freedom for the Vietnamese, the students insisted.

For the most part the strike held. The Senate's moves to allow students to end the semester early in order to do "political work" (or whatever else they wished) did a lot to evacuate the campus. Most of the people who remained were there either to keep the strike going, or to play Frisbee, or to organize drives for signatures on anti-war petitions. Very few people remained to catch the tail end of their courses.

For a few days the debate among the politically active students was over whether it was best to go off campus and reach workers and community people to explain why the students were protesting the war, or to stay on campus to fight the war through its "academic" support such as war research. SDS did both. On Thursday of strike week, SDS led hundreds of workers and students down to the garment center for a massive rally against the war and the corporations that profit from it. Seventy-seven long blocks of marching, straight through midtown Manhattan with its towering corporate headquarters, bellowing chants:

SMASH THE RULERS   ONE TWO, THREE, FOUR,
    KICK THEIR ASS   VIETNAM'S A BOSS' WAR
POWER TO   FIVE, SIX, SEVEN, EIGHT,
    THE WORKING CLASS   NOTHING TO NEGOTIATE

As the brigade passed Lincoln Center, its white terrazzo being admired by lots of Midwestern ladies in hats and gloves:

ONE, TWO, THREE, FOUR,
WE DON'T WANT YOUR FUCKING WAR

At Times Square they were chanting: "Pig firms get rich while GIs die," when a construction worker, easily twenty stories high on the skeleton of a new corporate home, leaned way out from his I-beam and majestically gave the students the finger. It would have hurt morale a bit, coming from one of the students' hoped-for allies as it did, if the march just then hadn't come in range of the news sign that flickers on the old *New York Times* (now Allied Chemical) Tower: "WASHINGTON AUTHORIZES STATES TO USE NATIONAL GUARD TO PREVENT VIO-LENCE. STUDENT PROTESTS COMBINED WITH FIRE-BOMBINGS AT FOUR CAMPUSES." Using the National Guard to "prevent violence" seemed like a pretty ironic idea after Kent State, but what really perked people up was having this great revolutionary tote board give the blow by blow on the battle even as it was being fought.

SDS kept up its work on campus too. About $300 was raised to help support the campus workers who had virtually crippled operations at the library and the university's computer center by staying out in support of the strike. The rank and file leaders of the strike were later severely reprimanded by their unions for "taking an SDS bribe" during the wildcat. But a number of the workers themselves were heartily pleased with the students' act of generosity and solidarity.

With the weekend came what might be one of the last of this country's massive "peace" rallies. Almost with a resigned, one-last-time approach, the liberal peace groups called for another gathering in Washington to protest the war. President Nixon made a last minute gesture of tolerance and granted the protesters access to the Ellipse behind the White House. He spoke somewhat sympathetically for the first time about student protesters. He had outraged a lot of parents with his "bums" hyperbole about their children by this time and had to change tack simply to wash the blood of Kent State from his hands. And he claimed that because of "the safety valve" of dissent, "you're not going to have revolutions," which is why the radicals resent such ineffective demonstrations.

It was a blazing hot day. A relatively hardcore of peace stalwarts turned out. There were hardly any songs, and few speeches. Folksinger Phil Ochs parodied the last Moratorium's theme song, "All we are saying, is give peace a chance," by hardening the line: "All we are saying, is give *revolution* a chance." There was a sense that America, *somehow*, might be on the verge of combining political and economic struggles in a great general strike. It had happened in France in May, 1968, bringing that country as close as a highly industrial state has come to having a revolution. David Dellinger announced to the lackadaisical crowd that a draft board had gone on strike in New Jersey and that he foresaw even GIs striking. While this theme got passing mention at the mass gathering, it was what an SDS rally afterwards was all about.

Mobilization for Peace people with bullhorns spread out through the crowd as it poured off the Ellipse, barking to everyone that the SDS rally was not "official" and begging them to stay away from it. "Go instead to George Washington University for workshops." But their vague intimations of the violence that might come from an "SDS thing" didn't prevent a tremendous group from turning out in front of the Labor Department, where SDS has lately found it most symbolically appropriate to hold its rallies. Across the street at the fountains of the Smithsonian Institution, hippies began skinny dipping. SDS never noticed them and they never noticed SDS.

A contingent of campus workers from Columbia bused to Washington for the SDS rally—a proud display of the force that, once mobilized, really can shut universities down. Judy Lacoff, the rank and file workers' leader, told the delighted crowd: "The workers at Columbia this week have been doing a lot of marching and chanting. The administration called a Moratorium for the students and we said, 'What about us?' We didn't go back to work on Tuesday after lunch, and we stayed out Wednesday, Thursday and Friday. We know we have the power now, and we know we can do it under our own leadership."

Gregg O'Bryant of Boston State College, a black, warned the students not to trust college administrators—"wolves who dress in sheep's clothing"—and to reject the "Trojan horses" that their deans and presidents would be giving them in the way of apolitical concessions like the canceling of final exams. What the radicals should push for, he said, was an end to racism in all its forms on the campus. And then Bob Leonhardt, the student organizer of the Progressive Labor Party, sent the students back to their campuses with a call for militancy:

"Let's be clear on who our enemy is. It's the bankers and politicians and big businessmen who run this country. This guy Nixon may seem like he's in hot water, but it's the Fords and the Rockefellers who are milking the profits from Vietnams and Cambodias and they're out to save Nixon—their class brother. They're the ruling class in this country and they've got to be overrun. There is only one voice that must be heard in this country, and that's the MAJESTIC, OMNIPOTENT VOICE OF WORKING CLASS REVOLUTION. *POWER TO THE WORKERS!* Do you think a liberal politician in this country today is for that program? Do you think Henry Ford is, or Cyrus Eaton, the millionaire industrialist who gives his money to the peace movement? Do you think Abbie Hoffman is for it? Or David Dellinger? Do you think the liberal Cordiers and the fascist Hayakawas are for it? They're all together and they're all against it.

"So we've got to lead the strike ourselves. The students and workers have to lead this strike around the country, not the college administrators. GO BACK TO YOUR CAMPUSES, FORM MILITANT PICKET LINES, AND SHUT THOSE UNIVERSITIES DOWN TIGHT!"

There was an astounding difference in spirit between the peace demonstration on the Ellipse and the SDS rally which followed it. Neither gathering was violent. But the SDS rally culminated in the conviction that militancy would bring victory, while the peace gathering had sort of slowly let itself down without much hope at all. The SDS crowd poured away chanting and ripe for furthering the fight. But people drifted quite wearily out of the peace rally and one could hear a great many members of the demonstration crowd vowing that "this one" would be their last. The peace-in-Vietnam movement has nearly been crippled by such demoralization.

The peace movement was once a hopeful surge of popular protest, but with each successive peace demonstration, the crowds became larger and larger and so did the war. The movement might eventually be responsible for finally getting the war to ebb, but all the while it has nurtured cynicism and frustration and fatigue. This was to be reflected in an overall abstaining by collegians from campaigning for "peace candidates" for Congress in the wake of Cambodia. They didn't crusade even though many colleges adopted the "Princeton Plan" to let school out so the students could work in the campaign. The trend is bound to continue. Unless peace demonstrations can somehow be made more potent than they have been in the past, it seems quite clear that they are doomed to greater and greater cynicism. Even a massive escalation in the war, though it could temporarily recharge the movement, would at the same time show how futile it had been.

Back in the mid-Sixties, before the peace movement became so massive, radicals were protesting the war by trying to block weapons trains and shut down napalm plants. But there wasn't the numerical strength to make that kind of militancy work and it was eventually replaced with the huge Moratorium-Mobilization gatherings in parks. There's every reason to believe that now things are getting ready to shift back to the militant action level, but this time on a massive scale. The threat of violence was really mongered by the press at the series of peace demonstrations in the fall and spring of 1969-70. But if anything, the scare lured people out from the main rallies to the splinter actions at the Justice and Labor Departments where it was warned the violence might occur. The same people with their picnic baskets and babies on their backs went out looking for more action and braved tear gas to see it. It's a phenomenon no one has been doing much talking about, but something the liberals, the radicals and the government are all quietly taking into account. The prospect of a crowd of half a million (and peace rallies have drawn many more than that) actually assaulting the government because of its war policy is enough to give people of any political bent a good deal to think about. The Mayday, 1971, assault on Washington, which resulted in mass arrests and jailings of 13,500 youths sworn to "shut down the government," was a clear emergence of this new militance on a broad scale. It's a pattern that's sure to escalate.

It seemed either terribly naive of the university president or terribly audacious. Right in the middle of the first week of the militant strike, with not a class in session on the Columbia campus, Andrew Cordier said in an unusual live television news interview (also not difficult for his Public Relations people to arrange, since William S. Paley, chairman of Columbia Broadcasting System, is still another Columbia trustee):

"It seems entirely likely to me that we'll end the year just as we hope to, with commencement exercises and all the rest."

The radicals vowed Cordier would eat his words, but they didn't know then that the machinery was already in operation to carry out Cordier's amazing coup. Even before the end of the first week of the strike, several groups on the strike steering committee began steering the strike to an end. They were chiefly from a coalition of peace groups that wanted to get going full tilt on a campaign to build support for the Hatfield-McGovern and Cooper-Church amendments, and for the various pro-peace candidates running for Congress. And heading them was the Student Mobilization Committee, under the leadership of the Young Socialist Alliance. Their overall strategy was to "open the university up" for peace activity. Although the committee had been established to lead the strike, these members actually opposed a strike because it would shut the university down—peace work and all.

They quietly formed a delegation and went off to talk, quite privately, to the ostensible enemy, the administration. They later confessed they had hoped to get the administration's assurance that if they could somehow break the strike, they'd get use of university facilities for peace work. Initially the secret negotiations were carried on with Ralph S. Halford, the university's vice president for special projects. Halford is a kind of trouble-shooter who denied in 1968 that the university had any connection with the Institute for Defense Analysis. Later the intimate but official tie was undeniably exposed. Halford, an open enemy of the radicals, liked the peace group's proposition very much.

It was never explained how the strike steering committee had the right to negotiate anything. The hectic mass meetings that called the strike stipulated that it was to last "indefinitely" until the three major demands were won: an end to political repression, the immediate withdrawal of troops from Southeast Asia, and an end to university complicity in the war. Technically, the strike should still be underway at Columbia and around the country. At any rate, the mass meetings had charged the steering committee with administering the strike, not with selling it out.

An amazing number of groups that moved into the strike

steering committee actually were never really in favor of a strike. As it happened, although they had never openly opposed the strike, they seemed to have almost no commitment to it once the committee began to function. So the group set about doing something besides striking. Since the radicals had dissociated themselves from the committee almost at the outset because they saw it as inherently tainted with loyalty to the university, those who remained were free to scrap the strike they were supposed to be running.

The negotiations with the administration were undertaken almost the same day the Moratorium ended and the full-fledged strike began. Halford figured the idea of opening up the university for anti-war activity was a harmless way to end the strike. Several people involved in the talks admit the vice president seemed quite delighted to be offered such an easy solution by the very body the administration had thought was causing it all the trouble.

There was an initial legal question of how much peace activity could be carried on without endangering the university's tax exempt status. Halford saw an easy way around that through the establishment of a "student activities center where students could play Ping-Pong or politics." Such operations were functioning even at state schools in New York and elsewhere without fear of the government. So while Halford wouldn't put the university publicly on the line to create such a center, he privately gave his assurances during an all-night negotiating session that the delegation would get what it was after.

After two days of uncompromisingly militant picketing of classroom buildings by SDS, the Third World people, D4Mers and a host of other students, the administration apparently had made its mind up to move, one way or another, to open the buildings up. But Cordier drew on his years of crisis-ridden diplomatic experience and moved to try to avoid a direct confrontation with the radicals. Monday afternoon, he discreetly called his friends, the strike steering committee negotiators, into his office and tested them as allies.

The president described in grave tones the way buildings were being blockaded, professors enraged and roughed up, and said it was his absolute responsibility to keep the university open. The contingent from the peculiar strike steering committee assured him that they had nothing to do with the picketing and also wished to see the school open. But that wasn't enough to convince Cordier. He pulled out the text of a statement he said he was about to release and to the astonishment of the group read a threat: either the picket lines come down or he would call in the police. It was unthinkable. Another bust, with all the broken heads and outraged students of 1968. Cordier's reputation had made it seem such mistakes would be avoided at all costs, then here the man was, ready to do it. Quentin Anderson, using his role as English professor, tactfully asked if he might edit the statement. When it was handed over he ran his pencil through the whole section with the threat of the police.

And then the delegation began imploring Cordier to understand such threats of force wouldn't be necessary. They were the leadership of the strike, they said, and if they could hold another mass convocation on Low plaza, declare "victory," and say the university had granted their demands, student support for the picket lines would evaporate. Cordier inquired how they would manage to hold such a gathering since the radicals were bound to attack the deal and might even storm the platform. The Student Mobilization Committee people assured the president they'd have at least 100 "marshals" out to defend the speaking platform while the declaration was read.

Cordier responded with gradually increased interest and enthusiasm for the plan. He acted, as one participant later put it, "as though the whole thing had never been discussed with Halford and it was all a new idea to him. He made it seem like a brand new option he hadn't ever heard of." Months later several of the negotiators were looking back on the whole encounter a lot more cynically—and some even decided they'd been had.

Even Professor Anderson, a staunch Cordier loyalist, later admitted: "With that old fox it's perfectly possible that he was using the threat of the police to inspire us to make as good a case as we could for our plan. With a man like that you don't consider the rhetoric important, it's what he does that counts."

The self-appointed negotiators never actually got Cordier's absolute assurances that their plan for making the university an anti-war center would be given full official support. The president avoided even mentioning Halford's approval of it. But their faith in the institution and the "good faith" of its administration left the negotiators quite confident that they had secured their goal.

Certainly Halford had led them to think so.

So the convocation was called for the next day. The radicals could smell the "Trojan horse" coming. They'd been warning about it all along. SDS had a leaflet ready the morning of the convocation declaring: "A strike is not a moratorium; it is not a picnic; it is not 'opening' Columbia to all sorts of political activity. It is shutting down all normal operations of the university, threatening the trustees and men like them by exercising material leverage over them. We must attempt to stop all university activity in order to pressure Columbia to meet our demands."

SDS had even learned through its own intelligence network what form of co-optation the university would use to halt the strike. The leaflet went on:

> The administration, however, is hardly stupid. It will attempt in countless different and subtle ways to blunt the attack. It will offer itself as the leadership of our movement; we must reject it. It will portray itself as a friend and potential ally; we must expose and defeat its lies. It will offer to "close down" the university and thus "open it up" as a center of anti-war activity. . . . WE MUST NOT BE FOOLED. . . . The administration will allow us to make telephone calls, use its business machines and exhaust its paper supplies; we are welcome to sit in its offices and classrooms day and night. Yet while we are organizing discussion groups, canvassing teams and "alternate universities," the essential functions of this institution—its administration, its business operations, its financial transactions, its relations with corporations, banks and foundations, its military research and "social scientific studies" will all proceed. The official termination of academic activity is a minor move for Low Library to pay. Under the cover of a "people's university," in the persuasive guise of an organizing center, Columbia will continue to fulfill its role as an instrument of oppression.
>
> We should not let this happen. We must uncover and defeat the intentions of the administration and the sell-out strategy of the Mobilization-led Strike Steering Committee to run the same exploitative university

under a "revolutionary guise." Most of all we must make primary in our minds and in our actions the political character of our movement as formulated in our six demands. To continue the strike and build militant picket lines and other actions may not be the most convenient course. But in the long run it is the only way we can win.

The convocation turned out to be the most tumultuous event of what had been far from an orderly week. President Cordier began with a keynote address which carefully skirted making any personal or official commitment to the resolution that was to follow:

"The students gathered here today have chosen to devote their full time to action programs aimed at the early cessation of the war. This meeting aims at crystallizing, focusing and increasing the effectiveness of those efforts." And at just about that point several dozen SDSers and blacks from the Third World Coalition charged through the crowd, heading for the platform. They were intent on stopping the "sell-out" and put the Mobe marshals to quite a test. Cordier rushed on with his preliminaries while the students pummeled one another just below. "I hope that all members of the university family will understand and respect these [anti-war] efforts while, in turn, those who are committed to this form of action will respect the position of those others who wish to pursue their academic work to the conclusion of the semester."

The marshals weren't holding the line very well and a contingent of university policemen had to come to their aid with clubs, holding the militants off for a while. They were screaming "Who killed Lumumba?" and "What about the workers?" when Cordier turned the convocation over to the strike steering committee, thereby evading all personal responsiblity for the proposal that was about to be read to the crowd.

Robert A. Bone, an English professor at Columbia Teachers College, came forward to deliver the coup de grace. "A new alliance must be forged," he said. "For the faculty the price will be a new level of commitment; for the students, a new restraint. Disruptive tactics must cease and those who cannot see this will be rendered politically impotent." And the prospective eunuchs, by this time fully surrounding the podium just outside its ring of police and marshals, bellowed "SELL-OUT."

The resolution: "Resolved: That the members of the university community here assembled [the 'here assembled' had been added by Professor Anderson to fuzz up whether the whole thing was really binding in any official way] pledge our efforts to bring about the immediate withdrawal of all U.S. troops from Indochina, to combat racism and political repression at home, and to oppose the involvement of universities in war research. In the months ahead we will focus our energies in organizing against the war. Our intention is to continue to utilize the university as a center for effective anti-war activity. We choose these priorities freely and will respect the right of others to disagree." The swarm of radicals around the platform immediately exercised that right vocally and vociferously.

And finally the resolution was submitted for approval to the crowd of about 1,200 people, only a fraction of the huge mass of students, faculty members and workers that had crammed into the plaza the week before. The resolution "passed" in a surprisingly apathetic fashion. Only a few of the people in the crowd bothered to vote "aye," and radicals yelled "bullshit," rather than vote at all.

Mathematics Professor Lipman Bers really bewildered everyone by calling on the crowd to raise their fists as a symbol of unity. A great many faculty members and even only moderately liberal students went along, shyly raising their fists, embarrassed at being called upon to exercise the gesture they had always so disdained when it was used by the radicals. And the radicals, for their part, resented what they considered the pirating of their devout symbol of militancy in the name of an effort to smash their strike. The radicals howled "fascist" and "pig" at Bers and he shouted back: "Don't try to impress me with your obscenities because I can curse in Russian, and that is much worse. I was expelled from kindergarten for using foul language." He told the crowd to go out and talk to the city's workers who don't understand that they too should be against the war.

And an SDSer called out:

"You've got a lot to learn from the workers, Bers."

"I certainly have, but you are not a worker, my son, you are an idiot," the mathematician vollied back.

And finally Roger Rudenstein of the Student Mobilization

Committee vowed to the crowd: "We want to open the university to transform it into an anti-war center *but we will not be tricked by any attempts to return to business as usual.*"

That turned out to be the most important declaration of the convocation. The radicals were completely convinced that Rudenstein and the other "sell-outs" had *already* been instrumental in allowing the university to go back to business as usual.

The summer was to bear the radicals out. Columbia quite abruptly informed all the peace groups that they would have to relocate off the campus. No apologies were given for the breach of the arrangement by which the strike had been ended. Dr. Bone, one of the men who had engineered the settlement and the one who actually presented it at the convocation, later told me the university "reneged shamelessly on its agreement. SDS and the others proved to be right not to trust the university on that business," he said.

Nothing can make people more righteously indignant than to warn that something dreadful is going to happen, be ignored, and then have it come about just as they'd predicted. That's how SDS felt after the convocation. All the tricks they'd predicted would be used to tantalize the students into giving up their fight had been brought into play. It was almost more than the SDSers could stand later that afternoon when they went underground again to meet in the basement of Carman Hall. They had cut knuckles and even deep bite wounds from the tangle with the marshals. And the strike was in deep peril.

At first the radicals seriously consider pretending they are taking the administration at its word, showing up at the dean's offices and saying: "O.K., we're here to work for peace. You guys better quit all that other work you're doing and leave because you're obstructing us." Perhaps even starting to hold meetings in President Cordier's office and send him off to the radicals' Carman lounge to do his work. Andy Kaslow can't quite believe that a strike could be ended on such a useless basis as access to the university's facilities. "Man, it's like selling out a revolution for some lousy bourgeois machinery: Xerox machines and telephones and electric typewriters. How the hell can they go on strike and call it a victory when that's all they're getting out of it?"

As far as the SDSers are concerned, it's what's to be expected from groups like the Student Mobilization Committee and the

Young Socialist Alliance. SDSers, being militant Marxist-Leninists, disdainfully call the broad-front peace groups "Trots" because they adhere to the theories Leon Trotsky applied to criticize Lenin and the Bolshevik revolution. In their attempt to build a mass movement, the militants say, the Trotskyist groups totally sell out the political potential of a radical alternative. They'll settle for anything that's popular—like "peace" instead of the destruction of the imperialist machine that made the war. So in the end they have to do it all over again with another war because they didn't do it well enough the first time.

"Stalin had the right idea about taking care of Trotskyists," Andy Kaslow says after a brief lecture in revolutionary history. "You give them an ice pick in their skulls."

SDS decides to make one last challenge to the university. The militant picket lines will be thrown up again the the next day. Platoons will be organized for all the main buildings and every bit of support for picketing will be raised by canvassing the nearly empty dormitories that night for extra manpower on the lines. And the platoons are nicknamed: The group assigned to blockade Fayerweather Hall becomes the Fayerweather Friends. The Dodge Hall contingent proudly dubs itself the Dodge Rebellion.

Only about twenty of the most committed make it to the sundial before nine o'clock the next morning, though. The fatigue of almost two weeks of continual meeting and marching and battling has taken its toll. And because the strike is already nearly diverted into nothingness, many don't have enough hope to get up early. The group splits up to cover three main buildings. Hamilton Hall, where the Columbia College deans work, is the most critical.

A dozen radicals walk over to the entrance to Hamilton and in half an hour or so their ranks have grown to two dozen. They form an oval picket line and begin marching in front of the doors. A small crowd slowly gathers on the walkway in front of the building to see how anyone who tries to get in fares. The radicals gibe at the onlookers for their lack of commitment:

"Spectatorism is a disease of the mind!"

"Apathy is the mother of persuasion!"

"Apathy is a mother."

And then Associate Dean Stuart, as usual taking comfort and assurance in his pipe, smokes his way up to the picket line and tries to involve the picketers in an academic discussion of their politics. "What I don't see," says the dean, "is how you can say you believe in Marx, when you don't know anything about Spinoza and Kant and Aristotle, from whom Marx is derived."

Neil Mullin shoves his face in front of the dean's before anyone can answer and bellows: "Don't answer this pig. He's total scum." That brings gaunt Carl Hovde, the lanky and literary dean of Columbia College to the scene. With a note of official and legal inquiry, he demands of the picket line:

"Are you blocking the entrance way into this building?"

"We're on strike," says the line. "This school is shut down, haven't you heard?" And the picket line begins to whistle "Old MacDonald had a Farm," giving particular emphasis to the part that goes: "With an oink, oink, here, and an oink, oink, there, here an oink, there an oink, everywhere an oink, oink."

The dean states what everyone knows: "I want to get into my office."

And Neil leans into him and shouts fiercely: "Just wait a minute. We're going to have to discuss that."

Still a third dean, Robert Laudicina, a grim looking man with deep-set eyes and a dark goatee, a face that would make a perfect villain's, saunters up and banters with Alan Egelman about the disciplinary tribunals he's got backed up for him. "How about starting them next week, Alan?"

"Well, gee, I don't know. I'll have to check with my lawyers," and he gestures to the rest of the picket line and then sweeps his hand out over the campus.

The dean, quoting the rigid regulations of the university's tribunal system, says Alan can have only one lawyer and an associate.

"Well, gee, I don't know," Alan replies. "My law firm is Livingston, Hartley, Jay, Carman and Furnald," ticking off the names of the men's dorms.

Then a short, middle-aged man in a stiffly pressed suit, unusually narrow necktie and perma-press shirt joins the doorstep gang. Dean Hovde announces, "Let him through. He's a rabbi." The students know Ismar Schorsch, an often indignant history instructor from the Bronx.

"As an individual, I have a right to enter this building," the rabbi declares.

"Individual rights are superseded by the rights of society," one of the radicals replies with equal confidence.

"You are condemned by your own actions and attitudes. You are condemned by your own principles."

"What the hell does that mean? How would you respond to repressive violence? Would you sit down and take it, or would you move against it, Rabbi?"

"It's none of your business how I would respond."

"How did Judah Maccabee respond, Rabbi?" asks one of the well-schooled Jewish radicals, plucking the greatest militant after Moses out of his heritage.

"Your minds are as closed as the door," the rabbi replies, shifting to a metaphorical approach.

"Right on!"

"Don't be so proud. For the last decade you have been condemning society for oppressing blacks. . . ."

"Does it? Does it?"

"Your system is no better. You oppress those who disagree with you."

"Aw, you're just upset because you can't get in and shuffle your papers."

"You are condemned by your own principles."

"You talk about us. Look at the way the U.S. is exterminating the Panthers. The way it's committing genocide in Southeast Asia. The tactics of a strike may not seem fair, but they're necessary. When you go on strike, you just don't conduct business as usual. Do you know how unions were formed in this country, Rabbi?"

"No. I don't know."

"You don't know, for Christ's sake, and you're supposed to be a teacher here? You ought to learn some of these things. Strikes can't allow scabs. That's all there is to it."

"Oh, stop with this strike business. A strike is when you withhold your labor from an employer who oppresses you."

"RIGHT ON, Rabbi! Now you're getting it."

The rabbi finally walks away toward the cluster of deans who are caucusing near the corner of the building. Three times he thinks of something to add, stops, starts back toward the picketers, and then gives it up and heads on.

About five minutes later a phalanx of sports-jacketed students, the organized conservative contingent on campus, which calls itself Students for Columbia University, bursts out from near where the deans are talking and charges toward the door. They smash down a blackboard barricade and burst into the building. And the deans slowly stroll up in the wake of the attack, all looking quite pleased. A D4Mer can't stand the sight and wails into Dean Hovde's face: "We're going to build and build, Hovde, and we're coming back to smash you."

With that, the last Columbia picket line of 1969-70 comes down so the radicals themselves can enter Hamilton Hall to meet and discuss where to go from there. It's a standard practice in SDS whenever a fight has been won or lost, a demonstration aborted or accomplished, or just when there isn't much else to do, to call a meeting. The radicals are bitterly disappointed in the apathy the bulk of Columbia's students have shown about fighting the university. There would have been broad support for the strike if people really cared as much as they professed to about fighting racism and the university's complicity in the war, the radicals say. Instead, nearly all of Columbia's students had either gone home, or gotten stoned for the ten days of the strike. A few had even conspired to break the strike through negotiations, and now, some had actually attacked its picket lines. While several of the radicals were confident that eventually, with a good "long-range" strategy, their fights would be won, the strike was over and there was a heavy sense of failure in Columbia SDS.

Columbia and many other colleges and universities around the country, which had taken surprisingly identical steps to end their strikes by "opening up" as anti-war centers, soon betrayed their alliances with the peace groups. Though no laws were changed at all, during the summer the government started making grumbling noises about all the peace work that was going to be done on the campuses. The Internal Revenue Service, which can be an effective political lever, suddenly raised the question of whether political work could be legally carried on at tax-exempt institutions. The universities panicked at the idea of paying taxes on endowment. The IRS had made similar noises earlier when ecology groups like the Sierra Club and others became effective forces in fighting or promoting legislation. (Though the "conservative" lobbying groups such as the American Medical Association or the National Rifle Association have rarely been similarly threatened.)

A great many legal experts and the more liberal academic officers are fully persuaded that the IRS could never have made its threats stick in a court fight—and probably never would have tried. But the American Council on Education, acting in the most timid way imaginable, meekly inquired of the IRS just what would be tolerated, and then quickly recommended a set of repressive guidelines on the basis of what the IRS wanted. It was a collective capitulation of academe without any fight at all, and left a great many peace people (and of course the radicals, too) quite convinced that the member colleges never were very serious about all that peace work in the first place. They welcomed the council's recommendations as an easy way out, confidently telling the astounded anti-war groups it was out of their hands—which it wasn't.

The boom fell on the peace people during the summer. At Columbia the shocked campaigners were simply told that they'd have to find quarters somewhere off campus. The university faintly mentioned it would help them in their search, but ignored the groups' pleas that it was essential to be right on campus in order to have access to the students, their whole reason for existence in the first place. Halford's confident assurances during the negotiations that the establishment of a student activities center would take care of any tax problems were immediately forgotten and the university laid down very stiff guidelines.

The blow shook the faith of many of the trusting anti-war people who had arranged the end of the strike. They had stood up to the rage of the radicals because they felt they would actually be accomplishing something to stop the war. In one head-on debate after another, they had dismissed the radicals' refusal to deal with the administration as naive paranoia. Their respect for the university had brought with it the conviction that the men who were running it would deal with them in good faith. The radicals had argued that, "No one gives away any power without a fight," and the liberals had answered, "Don't be silly. Intelligent people can work things out peacefully." Now they held a peaceful solution that had proven to be worthless.

"I was astounded," admits Dr. Bone, one of the faculty guiding forces in the arrangement. "I've been around a lot politi-

cally. Way back in 1947 I was the national secretary of the
Norman Thomas Socialist Youth Movement and ideologically I'm
still a socialist. I knew all the business about struggles for power in
theory, but I was still astounded. Under the pretense of those IRS
guidelines they were betraying the students who had negotiated in
good faith.

"Cordier was the guy who got all he wanted out of the deal.
He got everything and gave up nothing, and he came out absolutely clean because he wasn't the president anymore when the
deal was scrapped. [The political guidelines were issued as one of
the first acts under the newly installed president, William McGill.]
We reached into the fire for Cordier and pulled his chestnuts out
for him. We burned our hands; the radicals hate us. But that
doesn't hurt him. He proved that those sectarian radicals, who
were saying you can't negotiate with anyone, were right. But
believe me, that left a lot of bitterness with the people who helped
bring that strike to an end. In the end, what might have seemed
like a shrewd move then for the university will turn out to have
been very stupid. What they did will build more distrust than all
the polemics of the radicals ever could have. It's just going to drive
people into the SDS camp. And you can bet that I'm not going to
go pulling the chestnuts out of the fire for them again."

Several of the students who had taken the initiative in approaching the administration still haven't gotten over the shock of
the reversal. Chet Wollner, an education student and perhaps the
key figure in pushing the arrangement that ended the strike, calls
the whole thing "a smelly carcass that's best forgotten."

But Dr. Cordier, as might be expected, sees it as something of
a triumph. "I never use the word pride," he said the next fall, "but
I was certainly glad to see the way the strike ended, and I must
admit that I got quite a few favorable comments from other
university presidents on the thing. We do talk amongst ourselves as
college and university administrators and we shared our problems
to some extent during the strike. I think what we did at Columbia
set a pattern for the whole country. A lot of schools followed our
lead as it became known around the country that Columbia was
staying open."

I asked him how the administration could have been acting in
good faith when it gave the student negotiators the assurances on
an anti-war activities center only to back off when summer came

and the strike was over. "Well," he said, "the IRS ruling was only part of it. There were also New York State and New York City real estate laws which were a good deal more severe."

"Yes," I acknowledged. "But they've been on the books for years. Halford wasn't worried about them during the strike negotiations."

"Well, ah, yes, ah, they are old laws," he said. "But it wasn't until the summer that we were fully aware of their consequences." It was a hard claim to accept. Columbia had reportedly consulted its own distinguished legal experts on the anti-war center scheme before Halford had ever given the students his assurances. What Cordier really seemed to be saying was that in the spring he had the radicals on his hands and they were a direct threat that had to be contended with. Come summer, with the radicals gone and the strike broken, he could proceed unhampered in obliging the government.

CHAPTER SIX

AT WAR WITH ROTC

While many SDS chapters were in agonizing isolation during the spring of 1970, at Berkeley SDS broke out. It led the most militant uprising that's ever been seen on that campus—the place where American students first tested their strength. In many ways the Berkeley battle was the most fervent one American students have ever fought.

An SDS chapter without much backing on its campus is probably the hollowest threat on the Left. Cut off from the masses of students who are a prerequisite of radical effectiveness, the chapter becomes a pathetic cadre of impotent rhetoricians. Members rant on about smashing the American system while people either give them no notice at all or snicker and gibe at their blustering: "Ah, you guys couldn't liberate a pay toilet." It's an administrator's dream.

But there's nothing hollow in militant calls to action from an SDS chapter that has won itself a massive following. When the students trust SDS enough to consider themselves part of it, and believe in a struggle enough to mobilize for day after day of pitched battle, SDS is a fierce threat.

Students alone will probably never bring the government down, of course. SDS has acknowledged this and set out to ally with a far more numerous force, the workers. But that doesn't stop SDSers from slipping into the kind of ethereal calculating that follows:

There are over eight million college students in the U.S. *Playboy* magazine, which is hardly the sort of revolutionary journal that would exaggerate such things, surveyed campuses last year and reported that 15 per cent of the students are committed to making a violent revolution, which they feel is the only hope for instituting real change in the country. That would give you about 1.2 million students who are trying to smash the state. By way of comparison, the National Guard has only about half a million men. And the New York City Police Department, the biggest in the country, has only about 35,000 men.

While none of this is thought of as a line-up for the opposing sides in the greatest confrontation ever staged, it's the sort of figuring that can give a good deal of optimism to the student movement—and it's figuring that doesn't seem the least bit outlandish if you've ever seen an entire university, especially a huge university, up in arms.

The University of California at Berkeley is one of the most tremendous education mills ever created. There are 27,000 students at Berkeley and 10,000 more campus workers. The city itself, which is almost exclusively oriented toward the campus, is among the biggest in California. When the campus erupts, most of the city does. It's something to fear—if you're part of the power structure.

For most of the 1969-70 school year, Berkeley SDS had been sticking closely to the organization's new strategy of building an alliance with the workers on campus. There was fearsome potential in the concept. If the thousands of workers on the Berkeley campus could be combined in a fighting force with the students, who had many times shown their readiness to do battle, it would be hell to pay for the University Regents, Governor Reagan, the Berkeley Police Department and their lethal back-up force, the "Blue Meanies" of the Alameda County Sheriff's Office. Even President Nixon and his National Guard might not escape the power of a united Cal community in rebellion.

But while there had been some limited successes in the building of a Campus Worker-Student Alliance, at Berkeley, as almost everywhere in the country, the new SDS strategy had failed to organize huge ranks of students. So Berkeley SDS met when spring was coming on and began to look for other issues. No one wanted to scrap the idea of trying to ally Berkeley's "two oppressed groups"—the workers and the students—but several of the chapter's leaders pushed the approach that this could be accomplished through other struggles than just strike-support. Several members were assigned to investigate the weapons research going on at Berkeley. They came back to report that several Berkeley technocrats were involved in the Institute for Defense Analysis' high-powered "Jason Project" and were perfecting techniques for night bombings in Vietnam. Others in the chapter uncovered university programs to break down rebellions in American ghettos, and a whole curriculum of courses and research aimed at stopping the overthrow of pro-American governments in Asia, Africa and Latin America. Still another group from the chapter tried to assess how much interest there might be on campus for a fight against the university's increase in its tuition.

Anything seemed like it could lead to a big fight against the university, and each member had many arguments about why a particular struggle should be made primary. But in the end it was agreed that the response of the thousands of students at Berkeley would be what would mean victory or defeat for the prospective campaign, and leadership or isolation for SDS. So the members went out to canvass student opinion. Everywhere they went around the neo-fortress concrete buildings that make up the campus, they got the same message from the students: What about ROTC?

Reserve Officers' Training Corps is the oldest and most prominent form of co-operation between America's military and the academic spheres. Many schools have already eliminated the increasingly unpopular program and others are phasing it out. But ROTC is still going strong at state schools like Berkeley whose government-appointed administrations couldn't afford to take the "un-American" step of refusing to train any more officers for the armed forces.

In their search for the hidden shame of the university, the SDSers had overlooked the most obvious and offensive aspect of the university's militarism. But the students they sounded out had been watching the ROTC teams in their drills and thinking about the same men becoming officers to lead the war in Vietnam. Cutting off the supply of military managers seemed like a clear way to hurt the war.

The student Left has been fighting ROTC since the American

Student Union (an SDS ancestor) first attacked the Corps back in the Thirties. SDS chapters have led battles against ROTC all over the country. The 1969 Harvard strike and bust, which was sparked by SDS, grew from a campaign against ROTC. Berkeley SDS sent for the wealth of information on ROTC that had been compiled at the organization's national office in Boston. From that material and from their own research, several major arguments emerged for why Cal students should fight to kick ROTC off campus.

Most primary was the military's own assertions that it badly needed the ROTC program as a key source of officers. The *New York Times* had reported that ROTC was providing the army with half of its officers, and the navy and air force with a third of theirs. And a Colonel Pell, the director of ROTC at Harvard, had declared in defense of the program: "Today reliance upon colleges and universities for officers is greater than ever. For example, the 1968 graduating classes contained over 11,000 newly commissioned officers who will fill 85 per cent of the required annual input needed to provide the junior leaders for today's troop units. And more than 1,000 of these young men will become career officers to furnish the hardcore leadership for the future." And he added an almost irresistible enticement when he asserted that "beyond question there is at present no acceptable alternative source of junior officer leadership if ROTC is driven from the college campus."

SDS would like to ally with the fighting troops of the army, preposterous though that idea may seem. Revolutionaries have always cherished the knowledge that armies are built from the same class of people that make revolutions. There is the fervent hope that when the people finally do rise up against the government, the army will rise up with them, or will at least refuse to defend that government. It would certainly make revolution a lot easier. So there are two reasons for SDS to fight ROTC. When the people of Vietnam are fighting off attempts by the American government to rule over them through "puppets" like Thieu and Ky, SDS wants students on the side of the insurgents, not being trained in ROTC, to become the officers who will manage the war against those people. And when the blacks, Latins and working class whites who make up the troop ranks in the armed forces begin to fight their officers, SDS wants them to feel they have the support of students who are waging the same battle on their own front by attacking ROTC instead of joining it—and by hitting every other appendage of the military they can get to.

This isn't farfetched, either. A continual series of incidents have shown Leftists that the soldiers are already resisting and even fighting their officers. GIs coming home from Vietnam tell of repeated cases of soldiers "fragging" their officers—killing them with hand grenades or other explosives. So many latrines have been booby-trapped to get officers that many unit leaders reportedly insist on having a well-liked soldier come with them when they crap. Several SDSers who have gone into the army to organize resistance (rather than taking what many feel is the racist approach of evading the draft and having a less fortunate black go in their stead) have come home to report that often when an officer is shot in Vietnam the army medical men probe out the bullet that killed him to see if it was Vietnamese or American.

And there have been several inspirational television and newspaper accounts of the men in a Vietnam fighting unit flatly refusing to follow their commanders' orders into combat. "Search and destroy" missions search and *avoid* now. Radicals now have sustained hopes that the resistance to fighting that's growing within the army will put a severe crimp in the American effort to gain control over more and more peasant lands. On campus, the Left wants to do everything it can to help this along, and that means, among other things, trying to cut off the flow of officers from ROTC.

For most of the 1969-70 school year, thirty extremely dedicated people had been keeping SDS going on the huge Cal-Berkeley campus. They had held a long chain of demonstrations that were primarily in support of campus workers' grievances against the university, but they rarely succeeded in getting more than one hundred people to come out. All too frequently the turn-out had been more like fifty people or less. While that might not have been an especially miserable level of activity as such things can go (some SDS chapters in the country were getting only half as many people out) it was obvious that SDS had been failing to involve even a tiny fraction of the thousands of Berkeley students everyone knew were already committed to battling the system.

But the Berkeley chapter had barely begun laying out the arguments for fighting ROTC when interest in the group suddenly surged on campus and new people started coming around. It was exhilarating for the members who had been frustrated all year. "We saw we weren't going to just let the monster lie undisturbed," explains Anita Roger, a strikingly gutsy twenty-seven-year-old woman who was to help lead the fight and prove herself one of the most effective SDS organizers in the country. "With massive support for the fight against ROTC we knew we'd really be able to attack the university, the war, imperialism, racism—everything. It was all there."

So the planning moved ahead for the first anti-ROTC demonstration. Maria Fuentes of the Puerto Rican socialist group, the Liga Socialista, a fraternal organization to Progressive Labor here, would come to Cal to describe the tremendous fight against ROTC that had mobilized thousands of students the month before at the University of Puerto Rico. And fortuitously, a campaign against ROTC broke out at Stanford, Berkeley's neighbor and rival across the Bay. "If those rich kids at Stanford are fighting to kick ROTC off campus," people started to say, "we can certainly do it here at Berkeley."

The demonstration was announced for Tuesday, April 7. Thousands of leaflets were circulated around campus, demanding in huge letters "END ROTC" and showing a picture of the tens of thousands of Puerto Rican students marching against ROTC. The leaflet stated that half the American officers in Vietnam are ROTC grads, and five of the six commanding generals there. Berkeley, with 450 ROTC cadets, was one of the biggest sources of officers the military had on the West Coast. The leaflet was topped off with a clincher quote someone found in a *Wall Street Journal* article. A university president who was a member of Secretary of Defense Laird's ROTC advisory committee had declared: "Right now the [anti-ROTC] trouble is manageable, but if it spreads to such key campuses as Wisconsin, Michigan, and *California* then we're in serious difficulties." That's just where quite a hearty number of Cal students wanted the military.

"What this means is that by building a movement to abolish ROTC we will be concretely working to end the war and get the U.S. out of Vietnam and Southeast Asia NOW!" the leaflet declared.

SDS members worked like hell to get word out about the

demonstration and to convince students that it was vital. There was none of the trouble there had been earlier in the year getting people to do the tiring work of canvassing the campus with leaflets. The chapter had an enthusiastic sense that this struggle could be something big. And few people work harder than SDSers when they think they've got a powerful new campaign underway.

The usual contingency plans were made, according to how many students turned out. If there were about a hundred, the group would rally, hear the speakers from Stanford and then Maria Fuentes would describe their anti-ROTC campaigns. Then they'd march down to the army and air force ROTC headquarters in the gymnasium building for picketing. If there were more than 300, and the possibility was only a quiet hope, the crowd would be led to Callaghan Hall where the navy ROTC operation was located. SDSers would attempt to lead the crowd through the police lines that would inevitably be thrown up to protect the building, and once inside things would be "messed up." People were to bring sand for the guns, the glue—whatever might help to hurt ROTC a little.

The *Daily Californian*, whose student journalists were to be on the run for quite a while with the ROTC battle, helped things along with a front page story the day of the demonstration: "The presence of ROTC on this campus, always a smoldering issue, will surface once again at a noon rally today sponsored by Students for a Democratic Society." One of the SDSers told a reporter that how the demonstration developed would depend a lot "on the size and the mood of the crowd."

The crowd turned out to be surprisingly big—about 700 people at one point—and after Maria Fuentes finished speaking, it was amazingly militant too. Women had really started it all at the University of Puerto Rico, she said, giving great encouragement to the women's lib people. Three hundred women from the Women's Student Action Committee had marched to the ROTC building and were attacked by the cadets. One of the Liga Socialista leaders was shot in the incident and that made the students really rise up. Puerto Ricans hate the American military because of the imperialist milking and oppression of their country which those troops are instrumental in carrying out, she said, and it didn't take much to mobilize them against ROTC. The university dean called out police and even helicopters for back-up, but the fight kept swelling. Later, 3,000 students poured out and set fire to the ROTC building, as well as an air force office on campus. After about four hours of pitched fighting the police managed to clear the campus, but during the battle a woman was shot to death and thirteen other demonstrators were badly injured. And even after the police had gained control of the campus the battle raged on in the streets for another five hours.

It was an inspiring story, but the people in the crowd which heard Miss Fuentes tell it had no idea how much it was to foreshadow Berkeley's own militancy against ROTC. An SDS speaker tried to make the distinction clear between the mass violence that had destroyed the Puerto Rican ROTC building, and the Weatherman-style attacks by a few furtive bombers in the night. "They can always rebuild a building. But in Puerto Rico, the mass struggle that wiped ROTC out once will wipe it out again and again. It's the people they're afraid of. It's mass action by thousands of students that will really hurt the war and imperialism by kicking ROTC the hell out of Berkeley."

With that, the crowd moved out of Sproul Plaza, and headed for the naval ROTC building behind SDS' leadership. "U.S. OUT OF VIETNAM—ROTC MUST GO," was the chant. But the police weren't even going to let the crowd reach Callaghan Hall, let alone enter it. Two dozen of them totally blocked Cross Campus Road, decked out with riot helmets, stone-proof Plexiglas visors, flak jackets, clubs, gas masks and guns. No one had especially planned on such a confrontation, but the SDS leaders knew that if they got enough strength together to threaten the building, the police would be there to protect it. It had been agreed that if such a situation arose, the SDS leadership would not fail to display militancy. They would do their best to fight through the lines.

At the sight of the police, one of the SDSers suddenly tries to stop the crowd. "Back. Go back to Sproul" he starts yelling. But other SDSers fight him off and move toward the police lines. About twenty fight their way through, but the police capture Vic Coffield, Anita Roger's husband-to-be (for female dignity and identity, Anita would keep her "maiden name" after the two SDSers married). The police try to drag Vic off. SDSers grab his long legs and start pulling the other way. Finally the tug-of-war is won by the police. The next day the *Daily Cal* prints a big headline: "It's Springtime in Berkeley," and under it, stretching clear across the page, is a picture of two burly cops hauling Coffield away. One has his legs and another is up on the body, straining to hold on to Vic under his arms. Vic, militant to the end, is raising his right fist high to encourage his comrades.

The line of police moves in at the demonstrators with clubs swinging. The students fight back, throw rocks and only back off slowly. The SDSers who had broken through come back to help, then move through again. Finally, Anita climbs onto a truck and tries to get the demonstrators to help decide the next move. The adrenalin was pumping in Berkeley again. The same SDSer who had tried before to turn the crowd around climbs onto the truck and attempts to seize the bullhorn from Anita to curb the crowd again. Some people later suspected him of being a cop. Anita's warm smile must have misled the guy into thinking this was a gently meek girl. She gets him off the truck. Then she calls for the crowd to head for Harmon Gym to disrupt an ROTC class which was scheduled to begin in a few minutes. The people readily agree and move off again.

Several hundred make it into the gym, but the police are waiting inside for them. As the group pours down a long corridor echoing their "ROTC MUST GO!" chant through the building, the police block them off from the front. Prevented from reaching the ROTC classroom, about fifty of the demonstrators head downstairs to reach the ROTC armory. But the police are there too and box the smaller group in by moving in two pincer-contingents from either end of a corridor.

Forced out of the gym, the demonstrators finally rally still again and the call is made to gather at a mass Student Mobilization Committee meeting that night to make sure that anti-war activity at Berkeley and especially the fight to smash ROTC "remains militant."

About four hundred people showed up for the meeting that night, along with several policemen. Two of them deliberately identified themselves, saying they were "off duty" and in attendance simply because they wanted to be. The meeting voted overwhelmingly for the police to leave and when they still refused, half the assembly moved to throw them out bodily, and the police retreated. It was generally assumed, however, that a number of other more covert policemen remained—perhaps even participated—in the rest of the meeting.

The basic factions that vied with one another at Columbia were clearly in competition at the Berkeley meeting as well. In fact, it is remarkable how closely various groups' local chapters adhere to their national organization's lines, and how perfectly the groups replicate the political conflicts among each other on every campus. At Berkeley the Student Mobilization Committee wanted to build for massive, non-violent peace marches on April 15, a traditional day of peace protest, but the radicals of various shades were archly cynical of that strategy and proposed alternatives of their own. SDS wanted an on-campus demonstration against ROTC and speakers specified that such an action should be "militant" with the specific tactics to be left up to the SDS steering committee. The ROTC proposal was opposed by SDS' other rival organization, the Radical Student Union. Despite the enthusiasm shown that afternoon, the RSU claimed students wouldn't relate to an anti-ROTC struggle on a very massive scale. But the SDS proposal won the major vote.

The SDS-RSU rivalry at Berkeley was only one of dozens of similar conflicts that sprang up on campuses all over the country after national SDS broke apart at its 1969 convention. Those radicals remaining on campus who no longer liked the new, Progressive Labor-oriented leadership of SDS, broke away to form their own organizations. At Berkeley they called themselves the Radical Student Union, at Columbia they were the December 4th Movement. Underground, they were the Weathermen.

The following Wednesday night, SDS held its own meeting and drew easily three times its usual attendance. The group approved a proposal to march Thursday to Edwards Field behind the gym, as a leaflet put it, to "witness the actions of 200 of our fellow students—armed and in uniform—as they train to protect and perpetuate the interests of U.S. imperialists in Third World countries around the world." "REVIEW THE TROOPS," the leaflet trumpeted above a picture of a company of drilling ROTC cadets. Again hundreds of students turned out for a heckling session. An effigy of an ROTC officer was burned.

There were two major reasons why some college men were

still signing up for ROTC: many figured they'd be drafted when they got out of school anyway and decided that if they were going to have to go in, they'd rather do it as officers with authority, dignity, more power, and a lot less danger of dying in Vietnam. As cadets in their last years of school, they'd be paid $50 a month for giving the government relatively little time.

But, once in a very rare while, someone might actually join ROTC because he wants to serve the government. Berkeley naval ROTC Midshipman Alan Kirkpatrick told the *Daily Cal*: "I guess you could just call me a patriot. I want to spend some time in the military. I feel I've gotten a hell of a lot out of this country and I want to put something back into it." SDSers were aghast when they read Kirkpatrick's statement, but it made more sense when they noted that he was a business administration student. ROTC and big business work together, SDS had been saying. And the government agreed. ROTC recruiting literature even quoted endorsements from several big corporation executives saying they think a lot more of a man if he's a ROTC man.

The Berkeley ROTC struggle was following SDS' ideal pattern for building a successful political movement. A massive educational campaign was being carried on through the distribution of leaflets and even a ten page pamphlet detailing why ROTC should go. And the demonstrations were getting bigger each time, an obvious sign that the whole campaign was creating a "consciousness" in students who hadn't especially had it before, and was bringing those students into the action. One-shot attacks are no longer SDS' way to win a fight. Instead, a steady long-term struggle that keeps growing and remains militant is much more likely, SDS feels, to pose a real threat to the power structure. A hit-and-run demonstration with nothing to precede it and nothing in its wake really demands no action on the part of a government or college administration, SDS postulates. But day after day of highly committed demonstrating, with a constant display of ever increasing militancy, really shows power that has to be responded to.

In a sense, SDS views all its campaign campaigns as if they are mini-revolutions in the making. Although no one ever puts it that directly, no SDS campaign is taken on unless it will lead ideologically to a broader attack on the system. And because it is supposed to be thought of as part of such a long-term struggle, it's supposed to be built on a durable basis from the very beginning.

The SDS leaders at Berkeley did their best to build the ROTC fight with a two-pronged strategy. They would carry on as clear and direct a propaganda campaign as possible by carefully setting out their case and trying their best to anticipate the opposing arguments. They'd hold debates with ROTC cadets and officials (if they'd show up), hold forums if they couldn't involve the opposition, and get their literature out as well. All the while they'd provide a series of *actions* that would attract the people already won to their cause. And they vowed that those actions would be as militant as anything Berkeley had ever seen.

"It was kind of heavy," Vic Coffield admitted later on when he could look back on the whole struggle. "We wanted to show that if you are trying to succeed with anything in the movement, you've got to fight really pitched battles. But that meant asking people to face clubs and maybe even get shot at. They shoot demonstrators out here. That's pretty high aggression to expect from middle class kids."

But the Berkeley students showed they were up to it. October 15 started out deceivingly like many previous days of anti-war protests. SDS had called for a "militant march" on the ROTC building following a rally in Sproul Plaza. Word had spread that some radicals were ready to go all out in an action against the ROTC building. The Radical Student Union had recommended that people come prepared with rocks to hurl at the police from behind bushes. SDS call that "chicken shit." If the people wanted to throw rocks, fine; but the action wouldn't be militant just because guerrillas were lobbing stones from behind trees. The lines of police would have to be attacked frontally, SDS said.

At Sproul Plaza, a great many groups spoke out for fighting ROTC, linking it to the imperialist war in Vietnam. The Cambodian invasion was still two weeks off. The crowd, easily a thousand strong at the very beginning and growing rapidly as the action picked up, moved out of the concrete plaza towards the administration building. But the gathering only paused at University Hall. Speakers were jeered to silence by calls for "action."

They got action. Police were surrounding the ROTC building and the students massed in front of them — there was no cowering behind bushes — and began hurling rocks, sticks and even a few balloons filled with paint and water. A contingent of police moved in on the flank and the fight was really on.

Several times the crowd rushed the police. The sight of the riot squad contingents almost seemed to guarantee the prospect of violence rather than ensure peace. The police fired tear gas and drove several times into the mass of the crowd in an attempt to break it up into sections that could be more easily dealt with. But for the first time in the history of student combat at Berkeley, the crowd kept hanging together—convinced that was the only way to preserve its strength. Instead of just running away from the tear gas the students would actually scramble for the smoking canisters to hurl them back at the police. "I've never seen such vicious crowds," a cop declared. All the while people were chanting, "U.S. out of Southeast Asia. Cops out of Berkeley. U.S. out of Southeast Asia. ROTC must go."

Several SDSers from down the Bay in San Jose were driving into Berkeley that noon, unaware of the action that had been planned. Blocks from the campus they smelled the tear gas and began to lament the massacre of students which they assumed was once again being carried out by the police. But when they reached the area of the ROTC building, they happened on an astounding reversal of the usual sight: a crowd of several hundred students chasing a whole covey of police across the campus. The police ducked into a classroom building for refuge and the students followed them in and turned a fire hose on them.

It went on like that for hours. Old timers who had lived through all the Berkeley uprisings, from the Free Speech Movement through the People's Park fight (where one man was actually killed) said that the April 15 ROTC fight displayed militancy never seen before. Cars full of police would pour into the campus and be stoned before they could be unloaded. The police tried to form a protective barrier around the University Chancellor's building but that too was attacked and many of its windows were stoned.

At first the administration tried relying on its own police force, the city of Berkeley police, the Alameda County Sheriff's men and the California Highway Patrol, but when it was clear that was far too feeble a force to cope with the open rebellion, Chancellor Roger Heyns declared his campus in a "state of emergency." He summoned all the police reinforcements that could be raised on the basis of a "mutual assistance agreement" Berkeley has with surrounding cities.

At about that time 300 students charged into the usually placid north section of the campus behind the militant leadership of several SDSers. They scrambled over a fence to stone the chancellor's house. Up screeched a line of black limousines, and the students thought the Mafia had been called in as well. But more police poured out and the students scattered through the yards and even into the homes of Berkeley's well-to-do hillside suburbanites.

For a total of five hours groups of marauding students would meet up with groups of marauding police and exchange rocks for tear gas. All the tried and trusted police methods of crowd dispersion were failing. The police even began firing tear gas into classroom buildings. That would just empty them of whoever was actually in classes and strengthen the student forces. Police, desperate for some domination, would charge small pockets of students who weren't participating in the action (the "demonstrators" knew not to isolate themselves into too small a group). Police swarmed into the Student Union building where people who didn't want to be part of the action thought they could watch in relative safety. Many were clubbed, some were dragged out, and nearly all were terrorized.

The *Daily Cal* reporters described one scene where a group of police on Berkeley's main street suddenly piled on a black man standing in front of a bookstore. "They grabbed him on no visible provocation and while two held him down, the third came running over and beat him with a club," a witness reported. The Bank of America, perhaps the greatest target of anti-imperialist radicals on the West Coast, had bricked in most of the front of its campus branch well before the ROTC fight, but the few entryway windows that were left in the pillbox facade were smashed in. It was clear both the Berkeley police and the students had been bruising for just such a battle.

By nightfall the campus was cleared, though tear gas was still very heavy in the air. Trash can fires were still flickering. Twenty-two students had been arrested, most on felonies, and fifteen people had been seriously injured. Chancellor Heyns issued a statement to the press somehow blaming most of the day's violence on the Weathermen and saying the "pre-determined intent of today's violence was clear." A great many politicians and university officials told the news reporters that the campus had witnessed "astoundingly mindless violence." The radicals, who were never asked by the press why they had fought so incessantly, countered with leaflets trying to explain to those students who didn't already know, just why they had led such a militant fight.

"The students are angry about the expanding war and want to do something about it. Many people see the racist nature of a war against Asians where Third World GIs are the first to be killed. ROTC is essential to this systematic racism; it trains the officers who direct the murder of Vietnamese, puts down ghetto rebellions, and breaks strikes," SDS' leaflet declared.

As at Columbia, SDS tried to head off the probable co-optation efforts of the administration. "They will try all kinds of tricks to turn this fight around. They may offer negotiations, or hold out the bait of no credit for ROTC courses—but murder without credit is the same as murder with credit. We have to remember that we want to end ROTC completely and keep fighting until we have done it."

Not letting up a bit, SDS called for another rally the next day at "High Noon." Easily 1,500 students came to Sproul Plaza for the action, but the administration tried to stall things off. Willis Shotwell, co-ordinator of campus facilities and regulations, a stern man who'd taken disciplinary action against a student because he'd called him a "scrawny turkey," arrived on the scene with one of the "liberal" student senators. The youth was prepared to give a "cooling off" speech but never got a word out. The SDS contingent arrived equipped with a potent portable sound system and suddenly Anita Roger was on the air, urging the group to march to the chancellor's office.

Several policemen emerged from the crowd to make the first of many attempts to arrest Anita, but she stood her ground, announced what was happening, and the crowd swarmed around. It was obvious they weren't going to get out with Anita so the police let her go to save their own skins. Then the crowd moved out for the administration building. The planners had hoped that the chancellor would come out to attempt to quell the crowd himself. If he did they'd grill him about ROTC and war research and "generally expose him." But the chancellor didn't emerge so the building and the squad of police that was guarding it were bombarded with rocks and eggs, and the group headed out again for the ROTC building.

The crowd was packed with high school and junior high school students this time. Word had gotten around that the action would still be on at Berkeley and the younger kids came along for some big time experience. Activists start young in California. Earlier in the year a group of students had picketed the ROTC table at an activities fair and it was a *seven-year-old* who finally "took militant action" by lunging forward, grabbing the tablecloth and yanking the whole display over.

"ANTI-ROTC WAR RAGES ON," the headlines trumpeted. The second day of massive, head-on battling was beginning to seem like war. The police gassed the crowd from the ROTC building only to have it regroup again up on Sproul Plaza. So they were gassed there too, conveniently sending hundreds running right into a much smaller contingent of police who were clearing another area. The isolated police were pelted with clouds of rock. They lobbed off a few rounds of tear gas and high-tailed it into the basement of one of the buildings.

But SDS began to really lose control of the group which was constantly being egged on by the Radical Student Union people and others. When Vic Coffield, out on bail from the first day's action, climbed onto a car to remind the group of its supposed political target—ROTC—one of the rival faction's members shoved him out of the way and moved the easily directed crowd out toward Sproul Hall, where the campus police were headquartered. Things were beginning to edge too close to the absolutely needless destruction that SDS leaders feared would eventually hurt their hopes of winning ever broader support. Windows were being smashed. People were burning flags. A university truck was sent careening down a hillside and the crowd later tried to set it afire. The Men's Faculty Club was heavily "trashed," with furniture demolished and windows smashed. Some of the RSU people even stoned a group of campus workers, which to the SDSers was the ultimate atrocity.

Once again the storm didn't quiet until evening. Thirty-five more people had been arrested and lots of others injured. The next day SDS was banned as an organization from functioning in any way on the campus. The group was declared "a danger to the health and safety of persons on the campus and the property of the University."

But knowing full well that the leaders could continue to rally militant crowds whether or not they were doing it under the banner of SDS, the administration went further. A lengthy and repeatedly extended list of SDS leaders was drawn up. They were forbidden from setting foot, in any capacity, on the Berkeley campus. The first to go were Roger and Coffield. SDS immediately moved to fight back against the ban and the repression it represented. The organization immediately called for another rally the next day and vowed it would keep up the fight. But the ban would eventually badly hamper the functioning of SDS at Berkeley. And as word spread of how the U.C. administration had kicked SDS off its embattled campus, many other threatened college officials around the country readily took up the strategy to relieve themselves of the SDS threat.

The Cal campus had been placed under martial law. All political gatherings were illegal. Between 500 and a thousand policemen always guarded the campus. There were no longer any rights to free speech or assembly—even classes were unofficially canceled. SDS held a mass meeting Thursday night just off campus and the crowd overwhelmingly affirmed that the fight must be kept going, "legal or illegal." People started talking about a strike. "This university just makes cannon fodder for the system we are fighting. We've got to build for a strike and shut the motherfucker down."

And that renewed interest in allying with the campus workers. The university was threatening a whole series of layoffs and the unions were threatening to call a strike if the men were actually thrown out of their jobs. The prospect of a unified fight of students and workers suddenly came to life as the radicals began to anticipate how that could effectively close down the campus. Even the Radical Student Unioners, who had been baiting

SDSers all year for their "old fashioned" socialist approach, started talking about how the workers could help "our strike." It was hardly a two-way alliance the way SDS envisioned it, but at least people were beginning to remember the workers.

Police from more than twenty different cities in the Bay area were on campus by noon the next day. (The radicals might really have outsmarted them by demonstrating in the morning, but there's a limit. After several days of combat and several long nights of tense meetings, no mobilization stood a chance if it was called before noon.) SDS had generally decided to be much more directive in the demonstrating. Rampaging was out. Marches and rallies had to make a point.

SDS had its folding table set up in Sproul Plaza as usual before the rally. The new day's leaflet was distributed, urging the fight on, but with discipline. People kept gathering to rap about how the fight should be waged, what mistakes had been made, and where the struggle should be directed in the future. Dean Shotwell came to the table and announced quite officially to the group that SDS was banned from the campus. One of the bystanders told him to "fuck off." And an SDSer replied in official tones: "We will not leave voluntarily." The dean declared he'd have them arrested and left in the easy quest for a policeman.

As usual tactics were a problem. SDS was opposing any mass action that day because there were so many police on campus and action the previous day had gotten so far from the fight against ROTC that members felt a lull in the action would allow for more building on the educational level. But the RSU proposed that the crowd of about five hundred (without the prospect of another campus battle not as many people turned out) march to the Berkeley courthouse where people arrested in the previous day's demonstrations were being arraigned. All the while Anita Roger and RSU's Matt Ross were presenting possibilities for the day's activity, a loudspeaker blared out the warning that their assembly was illegal and anyone in the area might be arrested. Behind a flapping red flag, several hundred people quickly marched out of Sproul Plaza and headed off campus toward downtown Berkeley and the courthouse.

Police were blocking an intersection and the march poured through a parking lot to avoid them. But the police stayed them a block further on with tear gas, and then three police cruisers came barreling into the crowd and one man failed to dodge in time. A cruiser hit him and he sailed backward and smashed into the street. The police dragged him into the car and sped away behind a cloud of tear gas. The crowd broke into several smaller groups and eventually reclustered in front of the courthouse.

Again stones were traded with the police for tear gas canisters and the demonstrators eventually left the courthouse area and marched onto the Berkeley High School campus. Most conceded later that was a mistake. They were bringing down the wrath of the police on high schoolers who hadn't asked for it and were hardly expecting what came. The police charged several groups of students. A CBS camera crew filmed one Berkeley policeman trapping a young girl against a fence and then clubbing her to the ground. A police sergeant finally dragged the officer off his victim. The afternoon ended with another eighteen arrests and as many injuries requiring hospital treatment.

The weekend brought a respite in the series of violent demonstrations. SDS, which was having trouble finding rooms off campus that were big enough to hold the hundreds of students who were turning out for its meetings, held several discussions about the role of violence in the movement. Some people said all the rock throwing was just bringing down more repression on the campus. Some people said repression is inevitable anyway and violence is a necessary way of standing up to it. SDS said violence is fine as long as it makes a political point and it's done by a crowd and not a few individuals.

Monday the demonstrations began again. SDS held another illegal rally and marched the crowd over to California Hall where the chancellor was having lunch. The crowd swarmed in front of police at the entrance to the building but there was no stoning and this time, no violence. People chanted "U.S. out of Southeast Asia. ROTC must go now!" Finally the group headed for the plaza again. They chanted there throughout a peace group's singing of "We Shall Overcome," "Ain't Gonna Study War No More," "If I Had a Hammer," "Blowin' in the Wind," "Yellow Submarine," "Mickey Mouse," and "Marching to Pretoria." There were no arrests and no injuries. The anti-ROTC fight was still big, but it was cooling down.

Tuesday the university opened the second phase of its counteroffensive with the issuance of a special commission's study of ROTC. It was the third such official appraisal of ROTC at the university since students first questioned the propriety of a military program on the campus ten years before. The commission study had been underway for about ten months and no one seemed to know when it was really due to be issued, or for that matter much cared. The study group's credibility had been almost nil from its creation since people in the University of California community generally agreed that the Regents had hurriedly set the commission up to stall off a move by a faculty committee to cut off credit for ROTC.

No effort was made to explain the strangely opportune time the report was released from the university president's office. The fifty-six page document failed to recommend any major changes in the program and was generally interpreted as a somewhat hollow attempt on the part of the administration to make it look like ROTC's status was being given very careful consideration so that the students didn't have to worry about it.

Chancellor Heyns invited "student comments and criticism of [the report's] recommendations" when it was released. But the university had had very little interest in how students felt about ROTC when it created the commission. At first students were totally excluded from participation in the study. Later, apparently seeing that was not the wisest approach to an issue that periodically aroused student interest, the university named four students to the panel. But they were not given any real sway in the decisions and were actually prevented from voting or even from issuing a "minority opinion."

But several of the students made their dissent clear after the report came out. "The whole orientation of the commission seemed to be: 'For God's sake don't offend the Regents, don't offend the Department of Defense, and don't offend the Armed Serivces Committee and [its chairman] Mendel Rivers," John McKenzie, one of the student members, told reporters. He said the commission took it for granted from the start that without question ROTC should be maintained on the campus. Commission members were extremely afraid, he said, that if the ROTC program were eliminated, the Department of Defense would make good on its long-standing threat to cut off all the other funds it was pouring into the university.

That struck the radicals as pretty inspiring: kick ROTC out and have all the other Defense Department influence in the great educational conglomerate dry up at the same time. They didn't believe the government would be so co-operative. But before the struggle could heat up again, the university attacked on still another front. Using what might be called a "hostage," the administration tried to force the radicals to cool it.

A "Black and Blues Jazz Festival" had been scheduled for the following weekend. It was being organized as a fund raising effort for the Educational Opportunity Program which provided scholarship money to poor black students. The festival might bring in as much as $20,000 and the administration openly threatened to cancel it if there were any more disturbances on campus. It was an openly racist threat—as far as SDS was concerned. If the administration was as liberally concerned with the plight of poor blacks as its officers continually claimed, how could they imperil the educations of many blacks as a means of disciplining the entire campus? The gun was clearly being held to the black students' heads and SDS didn't see any way to avoid the intimidation. Other radicals argued that the black students would be able to see the need to keep the fight up and would consider that primary, but SDS thought it better to hold off.

"DON'T BE DUPED.... DON'T MARCH TODAY!" said SDS' leaflet. "Clearly any action today which would give the University the excuse to suspend the Festival is racist and plays into the hands of the Administration. They are willing to steal thousands of dollars from black students just to divide us and save ROTC.... SDS urges that after the rally today we COOL IT. Then we should organize another rally and march for Tuesday when we can give this racist University of California and its racist ROTC exactly what they deserve. SUPPORT THE JAZZ FESTIVAL! NO VIOLENCE TODAY!"

Anita Roger now thinks that was one of the biggest mistakes SDS made during the campaign. It allowed the university to get away with a racist challenge, she says, and encouraged them to do it again. Later when Chicano students had their own festival scheduled, the administration pulled the same strategy, but the radicals expressed their intention to go ahead with a demonstration and the Mexican-American students gave them full support. A thousand people turned out for a massive but decorous demonstration and the administration, with its bluff called, never tried to interfere with the festival.

When it moved into its third week, the anti-ROTC battle was still growing. The rampaging and somewhat aimless marauding by demonstrators toned down, but thousands of students poured out for teach-ins and debates about ROTC, and their sympathies were quite one-sided. *ROTC had to go.* Nearly a thousand students crammed a hall for a debate with ROTC supporters and even a few cadets.

The pro-ROTC people claimed it was an individual's right to sign up for the program if he wanted. They said it was a threat to freedom of speech and academic freedom to bar students from that choice. SDS said it's a "perversion" to use academic freedom as a "justification for teaching genocide." No individual has rights beyond their social consequences, SDS said. It's like yelling "fire" in a crowded theatre.

ROTC would help insure that the army was educated, humanitarian and liberal, supporters said. If officers come from purely military spheres instead of the more socially conscious environment of the universities, the armed forces will be led by uninhibited, blood-lusting fiends. SDS said the armed forces are already led by such people, and they're coming out of ROTC programs anyway. The troops in Vietnam are primarily led by ROTC trained officers and they're still carrying out genocide. Captain Ernest Medina, one of the key figures in the My Lai massacre scandal, was a ROTC grad, SDS pointed out. The real humanitarianism in the army is coming from the foot soldiers who are refusing to carry out the racist orders to kill Asians that their ROTC trained officers are giving, SDS maintained.

And finally there was the most basic argument of all: we need the strongest armed forces we can get to protect the country from aggression by the communists. The smarter our officers, the more capable our defense. Smart officers come from the universities. But SDSers quoted a vice president of the Chase Manhattan Bank on the war and its relationship to foreign investment: "In the past, foreign investors have been somewhat wary of the overall political prospect for the Southeast Asia region. I must say, though, that the U.S. actions in Vietnam this year [1965—the big Johnson escalation year]—which have demonstrated that the U.S. will continue to give effective protection to the free nations of the region—have considerably reassured both Asian and Western investors."

So ROTC trained officers are not defending America from totalitarian communism, at all, SDS concluded. They're not keeping the world safe for democracy. They're keeping it safe for the expansion of American capital.

Right while the debate was underway, two plainclothesmen attempted for the second time to arrest Anita Roger. The police were intent on getting her out of action. She slipped away from them again though, made for the front of the room, and announced to the crowd what was happening. "Those guys are the criminals. Not the students." The crowd chased the foiled detectives from the hall.

But the police and the university were intent on cracking down on the SDS leaders. A few days later Anita was setting the SDS table up in Sproul Plaza when the never-say-die plainclothesmen sprang out again and seized her. She screamed and the usual plaza mill-in quickly surrounded the trio. Students began kicking the police and trying to get Anita away. One of the police went for his gun and still the students tried to hold her—but this time the police made it. She was sped óff to the police station and booked on charges of inciting to riot and two counts of resisting arrest. The booking officer looked at the girl's pretty, always beaming face and shook his head: "What's a nice girl like you doing down here in all this trouble when you could be home having children?"

Anita was in jail the next day, SDS having run dry of money for bail, and so was unable to attend a hearing the university had scheduled for her and two other SDS women through its own judicial structure. Student radicals face a double jeopardy sequence of discipline nowadays. The university sends them to jail and makes them face up to the state for their crimes, then, whatever the court's findings, they haul them up on campus proceedings to determine whether they are entitled to continue to enjoy the status of studenthood since they quite obviously have no respect for the institution which is supposed to be educating them.

SDS' whole strategy is to bring as many students as possible to the campus courtrooms. They hear how the university ignores the larger moral questions, such as whether or not ROTC belongs on campus (or anywhere else), while administrators try to press lesser questions of infractions of their own rules. In the process, the display of mass interest in the issue and support for the "offenders" is supposed to intimidate the university out of railroading the leaders out of school.

It's an awkward situation for the disciplinarians. They can't very well perform their "justice" utterly behind closed doors without seeming ashamed of their mock courts. But experience has continually shown that the radicals' purposes are consistently achieved when the tribunals are opened up. The quasi-judicial proceedings simply become a new context for the political struggles that brought them on in the first place. So what usually happens is the administrators attempt to strike a compromise—or what they present as a compromise. A few witnesses are let into the tribunals, but only about a handful so that they can't "disrupt the proceedings." In turn, the radicals usually refuse to be tried without a fully "open" hearing. That leaves the university able to expel the students for refusing to submit to discipline.

At Berkeley the first ROTC hearing turned out to be more bitter than most. Roz Epstein, of SDS and Progressive Labor, was the first to be tried. She had been promised an "open" hearing but as usual definitions were a problem. Ron Yank, an instructor of a "Law and Social Institutions" course, brought his entire class to the hearing "to see 'democracy' work." Yank is quite sympathetic to SDS and has been known to give awfully good grades to students in his class who are "politically active."

The class members arrived about half an hour before the hearing was to begin but were informed that there was no room for them all in the tiny hearing room. The class remained however, and someone quickly found a "moot" courtroom in the building which was not in use and could hold the principals involved in the hearing and quite a goodly crowd of spectators too. But the university officials didn't especially welcome the discovery. The crowd began to chant "WE WANT AN OPEN HEARING" and "ROTC MUST GO." When an official finally poked his head out the door and peered around the group to inquire, "Is there a Miss Epstein here?" somebody howled, "Here we are." The crowd ripped the door clear off its hinges and poured in.

The hearing would have been open then, except that the Berkeley officials fled it. So the students decided to go ahead with it themselves. They found Roz Epstein innocent, and the university guilty of repression and maintaining a racist, imperialistic institution, ROTC. But then police invaded the small room and there being only a limited amount of space, the prosecuting attorney, the defense staff, the jury, and most of the witnesses fled through the window. Others not so fortunate were beaten. Two were arrested.

A couple of hours later Dean Shotwell arrived at the jail with a retinue of staffers. He called for Anita Roger and attempted to hold her hearing there at the jail. The dean was incensed about what had gone on that morning. "Miss Epstein was twenty minutes late for her hearing," he muttered. "Gee. That's not like Roz. She's usually very prompt," Anita responded. She refused a closed hearing.

That night brought word of the sudden invasion of Cambodia. For all practical purposes it killed the Berkeley ROTC fight. Governor Reagan shut University of California campuses down tight as soon as massive student reaction to the invasion developed. Not being able to take the liberal political approach of deploring the war, the Governor said the schools should be closed "in order to provide time for contemplation and rational reflection on the events of the past few days." Police sealed off the campuses. When they were re-opened the next week, the great bulk of Berkeley students thought SDS' urgings to "get back to fighting ROTC" were largely irrelevant.

The rest of the spring progressed almost exactly as the events after Cambodia had at Columbia. There were a few isolated attacks on the university itself. One crowd even tried to burn down the ROTC building by heaving a burning police barrier into it, but that only charred a wall. Finally the University was "reconstituted" by its strike steering committee into an anti-war center. Little more came of the move than had at Columbia. Students somehow forgot about fighting ROTC in their zeal to put an immediate stop to the war.

And while the university was involved in a mass meeting in

Berkeley's Greek Theater coliseum, the city's police department fanned out and rounded up most of the SDSers they'd been waiting for a chance to arrest without prompting still more student protests. Plainclothesmen swept them out of the area. Vic Coffield was busted still another time; Anita was beat up trying to seize the platform at a meeting. Even Professor Yank was led off the campus in handcuffs on the charge of "creating a disturbance" during the disciplinary hearings.

The ban on SDS was strictly enforced. Undercover police trailed known SDSers around the city and immediately arrested them if their feet set down on university property. SDS telephones were tapped as well. A group of SDSers from Denver came to town months later and arranged by telephone with the Berkeley leaders to post some SDS signs around the U.C. campus quickly and leave. They were unknown to the local police, but as soon as they reached the campus they too were arrested for violating the ban on SDS.

The organization was badly paralyzed by the ban for all of the next school year. The hearing which is supposedly required to uphold such an organizational ban wasn't held though the chapter demanded it for most of the 1970-71 school year. SDS urged students to "pass this leaflet on" at the top of all its flyers since whatever the group issued was in a sense contraband and hard to distribute without risking still more arrests. Across the usual SDS logo at the bottom of every leaflet had been added a diagonal strip declaring the organization "BANNED." From its sanctuaries just outside the fringe of the campus, SDS pointed out time and again that it wasn't being disciplined but "repressed."

It wasn't because it had been naughty that the university didn't want it around anymore, but because it had been such an effective threat to the university. The students SDS managed to reach with its forbidden leaflets and off-campus rallies seemed to agree that SDS should have the right to come back to the Cal campus, but nothing much was being accomplished to change the situation. For three memorable weeks SDS had led huge crowds in the fight against ROTC. Day after day the students had swept over the campus chanting "ROTC MUST GO!" But ROTC stayed, and SDS went.

Six months later, Anita Roger and Vic Coffield, who she married that summer, went on trial together to answer to the State of California for the numerous infractions of the law they were charged with committing during the ROTC fight. On their jury were a former secretary to the president of the university, a former ROTC cadet, and a real estate broker who'd been one of the many targets of a student housing battle. They made their trial a political one, defending themselves and attacking the political nature of the courts. They were convicted as everyone had predicted and sentenced to a year in prison. Anita was as happy as ever. She and Vic were already building a political fight around their appeal trial. Anita was elected to the SDS National Interim Committee in recognition of her leadership in the ROTC fight. SDS was planning a new offensive to try to fight its way back onto the Berkeley campus, and many people were beginning to talk about another push against ROTC in the spring.

We were sitting in one of the many tumultuous hamburger joints that fringe the Cal campus and Anita was reconstructing some of the incidents of the ROTC fight. One of Berkeley's many anti-war and anti-SDS professors sat down at the table with us and made it clear how distant the campus liberals still were from SDS. Anita began slowly, patiently, even sweetly, to cope with the kinds of accusations and misapprehensions she's been struggling against since she became an SDS leader.

"It was the biggest thing that's ever gone on at this school," the professor said of the ROTC battle. "But you must admit that tolerance for SDS was unusually low."

"Oh, no," Anita replied. "We had hundreds of new people pouring in to join us. Some people may have felt threatened, but we were never stronger."

"Well, of course you had a lot of *off-campus* people with you."

"Not really. They were all my friends. I know them well. They were students who cared about ROTC and wanted to fight it."

"But of course there's no way to fight something like that. It was never possible to succeed in getting rid of ROTC."

"But they've done it at New York University and a lot of other schools."

"ROTC is only a symbol anyway; it's just a symptom."

"Melvin Laird says without ROTC the war effort would really be hurting."

"Do you think for a minute you can abolish military officers? If you do, you're sadly mistaken. You may be able to cut the limbs away from the military. But they'll grow back. And you'll never cut the roots and kill the whole tree."

"We want to make it as expensive and as difficult as we possibly can for them to run that war. If we could kick ROTC off . . . "

"Yeah. Sure. 'If'."

"Well, we know it's not easy. But that doesn't mean we shouldn't try to do it."

Finished with his hamburger, the professor gets up to leave: "Well, let me know when they send you to prison. I'll say I knew you way back when. But remember, now, your effectiveness is going to be greatly reduced if you're in jail."

And Anita gave him still another smile and said she'd remember. But she was really planning to organize prisoners as soon as she began serving her term. I later asked Anita why she and Vic had been so indefatigable in keeping the fight going. The police had arrested the two of them, or tried to, five times. A total of about two hundred students were arrested in the campaign. And many others were thrown out of school. "We've worked a lot in struggles and we've seen time and again how much people in this society are being screwed," she answered. "We knew about their tricks and we wanted to defeat them. To do that we knew we had to be ready to move ourselves. Hell, if 300 million people can do it in China, we can do it here.

"And it was a fantastic time. We had enormous support. We even had grammar school kids with us. Grammar school kids! We could have won if we had prepared people more to see that fighting the war meant fighting ROTC, not circulating peace petitions. More groundwork might have done it. We got out 5,000 pamphlets about ROTC, but there are 27,000 students at Cal. It went so fast we couldn't keep building understanding. We were really sad after Cambodia when they tricked everyone into thinking ROTC had nothing to do with the war. But we learned some things, too. We'll use that knowledge the next time around, and maybe the next time, we'll win."

PART TWO

PEOPLE, POLITICS AND PROBLEMS

CHAPTER SEVEN

CHILDREN OF THE NIGHTMARE

If all the cliches you hear about SDSers were true, their parents, the government and big business would have nothing to worry about. Supposedly, student radicalism is just a passing fancy. The popular misconception is that SDSers are having a ball tearing up their campuses. They might spout some political theory but everyone knows it's really just a cover for going out to pillage the once sacred academic community. And while the students think they know everything, their understanding of real life is actually terribly naive.

The "truth," as people who have no way of knowing it will tell you, is that the radical students haven't got the foggiest idea what kind of viable political system would be better than the one we've got already. If they ever succeeded in tearing the system down, most people believe, they'd find themselves up against the hard realization that it wasn't so bad after all. The self-assuring public impression has it that if there's anything left of the establishment when the SDSers get out of college, they're likely to join it. Up against the inevitable hardships of life in unsheltered society, they're bound to try just as hard as everyone else does to get ahead. Then, people seem to think, all that talk about racism and capitalism and imperialism will suddenly be quite irrelevant and forgotten.

The real truth is that working with SDS demands such an absolute commitment of time and courage and conviction that it very often leads to a burning of the bridges back into "success" oriented middle class life. Many SDSers couldn't go back if they wanted to. A member who takes his share of a chapter's work is bound to spend virtually all of his time building SDS and its political struggles. SDSers tend to be strikingly intelligent and usually get by at even the most demanding schools without much studying, but eventually many of them find the minimal requirements of writing papers and cramming for tests too much of an encumbrance on their political work. It's a chronic crisis for SDSers and very often it's resolved with the student dropping out of the academic rat race altogether to commit himself totally to his political work.

For the radicals who once embraced great ambitions of material success and whose parents are virtually living to see them attain that success, it becomes a grueling ordeal to cut the cord finally, leave the college they've scrambled to get into, and head off in an utterly different direction in life. For others who have been deeply cynical about college and what it was supposed to lead to, it's a lot easier. In either case, it's a major step to extend the commitment to radical political principles beyond the student stage.

A great many SDSers never get a chance to quit school, however, since the most natural thing that can happen to a student radical who's doing his job well is to be *thrown* out. College administrations have no use for a cadre of organizers who spend all their time launching attacks against the institutions. In the past year or so, officials seem to have increasingly come to the conclusion that the only effective way to combat the radicals is to expel them. Total bans on SDS as an organization have been followed up with court injunctions barring individual leaders from the campus, as was done at Berkeley. Often now, to be sure they don't accept one another's troublemakers, schools ask transfer applicants to get certificates of "honorable withdrawal" from their previous college.

Prison records aren't the greatest assets to prosperity in mainstream America either. It should be clear by now that jail is often where SDSers continue their radical educations. A month after the ROTC fight at Berkeley finally died down, Anita Roger and Vic Coffield were married in a backyard ceremony that was publicized with SDS leaflets and resembled a demonstration a lot more than it did a wedding. Seven months later the newlyweds were sent off to Santa Rita prison; Vic to serve a six months sentence and Anita to serve a year. Though they were both in the same prison, they were never allowed to see or speak to one another. The only desperate exchange of words men and women get at the prison are by calling to one another in the dark from the balcony to the main floor during sexually segregated movie showings; or possibly by sewing notes into Vic's prison uniforms between their trips to and from the prison laundry where the women work.

The life of a convicted criminal is hardly like the life of a budding future businessman, and for many SDSers a jail sentence actually seems like an affirmation of personal accomplishment. When he was arrested after the Columbia strike last May, Steve Cohen had to face his father's wrath and bewilderment. "I understand your ideals and I can respect them," the man told his son, "but what the hell are you trying to do—ruin your future? What if you decide to be a doctor or a lawyer? Even teachers can't have prison records." And Steve answered him: "Maybe that's what I really want—something that'll prevent me from ever copping out."

Jail is a likelihood rather than a vague jeopardy for the fully committed SDSer. While no one much wants to go to jail, being a "political prisoner" is seen as just another way of organizing people for the revolution—just like being a soldier or a factory worker. Jim Sober, an SDS organizer in Connecticut, was convicted this winter of a string of charges stemming from a demonstration in which students broke into a University of Connecticut administration building. There had been no real combat with police and the only damage was the breaking of a glass door when the crowd moved into the building. But the university and the state wanted to make an example of Sober. So his "crimes" were given the most felonious interpretation possible and he was charged with breaking and entering, with violence, inciting damage to persons or property, and assault. Armed robbers face far shorter prison terms than the seventeen years in jail that the charges could have brought Sober. But the grave jail threat didn't shake Sober's fighting spirit at all. "You get hit hard when you fight those guys," he says. "But if you don't fight them, they screw your life a lot worse in a different way."

Sociologist Kenneth Keniston studied "young radicals" in 1967 and concluded that they have no clearly defined ideology or political goals. That certainly isn't the case with today's SDSers. In fact it's as specious to claim they aren't much interested in ideological questions as it is to say they're in the struggle for the fun of it. They are political scholars and avidly read Marx, Mao and Lenin, often in SDS-organized study groups. They can spout revolutionary history down to the remotest incidents. They devour the "bourgeois business press" more faithfully than most middle managers and can rattle off corporate profiles, with special emphasis on foreign investments, a lot better than many a stock-broker. A few years ago SDS gatherings were weird sessions of brow beatings and freaking out. Now they are droning collo-quiums of political discussion.

The outside world gets to see very little of the internal political theorizing beneath SDS' active assaults on the univer-sities. The radicals' primary task *is* to smash the existing system. Without accomplishing that, all the ruminating about what could come afterward is moot. But to conclude that the radicals them-selves don't know where they're going is silly. No one would fight as hard as they do for something they haven't bothered to figure out yet.

During the 1968 Columbia rebellion, then-University Presi-dent Grayson Kirk made the charge that the protesting students were out on a foolish anti-authority, hate everything jag with no real goal: "Our young people reject authority and take refuge in turbulent, inchoate nihilism," he claimed. Mark Rudd, though he later lost track of his vision and for himself validated Kirk's attack, answered for the SDSers:

"Your cry of nihilism represents your inability to understand our positive values. We do have a vision of the way things could be: how the tremendous resources of our economy could be used to eliminate want; how people in other countries could be free from your domination; how a university could produce knowledge for progress, and not waste consumption and destruction; how men could be free to keep what they produce, to enjoy peaceful lives, to create. These are positive values—but since they mean the destruction of your order, you call them nihilism. In the move-ment we are beginning to call this vision socialism. . . . We will have to destroy at times, even violently, in order to end your system, but that is a far cry from nihilism."

SDSers as a group have more hope and positive dedication than a whole government full of Hubert Humphreys. They fight the cynicism and defeatism of drug culture and often transfer away from ultra-permissive schools where politics has been replaced with pot. They despise the cynical liberals who actually admit that things are terribly wrong in America but figure it isn't worth the trouble to really change the system.

More than anything else, SDSers have an unrelenting sense of their own personal morality. They are driven by the concept that their efforts fight against the oppression of millions of people. Giving up the fight in favor of greater personal comfort and prosperity, they feel, would be at the cost of those millions of people's potentially free lives. Cast in that way, SDS becomes a purpose in life—a justification that resolves the great existential neurosis that plagues students. When their parents have obviously wasted their lives pursuing and accumulating material wealth; when nihilism merely leads to self-destruction on drugs; and when even hedonism grows stale in an anything-goes society, SDS, with its almost missionary commitment to change, holds out an inspiring purpose to all those who wish to free themselves of their guilt and go to work.

Student radicals, one after another, describe how they were nearly "out of struggle"—swamped by their own alienation—when somehow they got swept up in an SDS campaign and haven't doubted life or people or themselves since. These students want to inspire others with what they've found—and once they really can reach a person, they pour that inspiration out to him. It often works. Students—and everyone else in this society—are badly in need of that kind of purpose. The challenge to do something real and stop complaining is a welcome one. It takes a steadfastly selfish person to resist the practical idealism of a good SDSer who's trying to persuade him to join up.

Existentialism and drugs and psychiatry are part of a great pacification program as far as SDS is concerned. They're all aimed at convincing people there's something wrong with them, not the system. They seem to say to people: you'd better adjust to society or drop out of it. SDS' answer is to fight instead. One SDS woman I know actually intends to become a high school counselor and tell all her rebellious "patients" to keep fighting. "The rebels are the healthiest ones around really because they haven't been broken down yet by the system," she says. "But they have to be made to see their fight is just, and how to win. So I'll just keep showing them that it's the system that's immoral and where to hit it until the bosses who run the schools fire me."

To a great extent the radicals' mere existence proves the system's in trouble. If there were nothing wrong with the structure of American society, it wouldn't be creating thousands of young people from every economic level who are vowing to smash it.

THE FRESHMAN "FELON"

Steven Simon Cohen was a student rebel in nursery school. He became extra energetic just when his teacher announced it was nap time. He set out to play with the blocks when the teacher said everyone had to finger paint. Before he ever got to kindergarten, he'd been suspended from school.

They threw him out again in the fifth grade when he kicked his teacher during an argument about a book the class was reading. Steve doesn't remember what started the quarrel except that "it had something to do with farms." In the sixth grade he discovered socialism. "Communism was quite a forbidden fruit," he recalls, "so I figured I'd check it out." He started by reading the *Communist Manifesto,* but now admits he wasn't really ready for Marx. "I missed getting a real grasp of the class conflict concept, but I did pick up on the idea that things should be public property instead of private."

He went on to read several more Marx tomes, and then moved into Lenin voraciously: Lenin's own political theorizing, then biographies, and finally revolutionary histories. "I really dug Lenin and the Bolsheviks. Lenin was a great intellectual, and a great revolutionary. He made a tremendous impression on me." In the tenth grade Steve applied Lenin's theory that imperialism is the highest stage of capitalism in a paper analyzing how the First World War began. His teacher was shocked. Kids didn't write things like that in high school back in those days.

SDSers come from every level of society, but a great many of them are boosted along in their emergence as radicals by somehow not quite fitting into the mainstream's rush to materialism. A great many come from extremely wealthy suburbs but from families that were never as wealthy as the rest of the community. Their parents are always frantically trying to keep pace—often through sheer pretense—and the exhausting scramble really frightens and disgusts the kids. Both SDSers whose parents have never made it and SDSers whose parents have agree that, either way, it isn't worth the hassle.

Steve's parents haven't quite made it in the context of Pikesville, their very plush Baltimore suburb. Steve's father works for a brother at a commercial laundry in the slum of central Baltimore. Steve has always felt his family is very self-conscious about its standing amidst all of Pikesville's prospering businessmen and professionals. So he always felt set off from most of the local kids. And to compound the isolation. Steve is brilliant. His mind certainly wasn't much like his schoolmates'. "Everyone was obsessed with clothes style when the only style I cared about was literary style. I didn't know shit about what to wear. My mother would get me my clothes and I'd wear them. I'd go around in flannel shirts and baggy corduroy pants and white sox. But junior high school culture is incredibly vicious and they'd really knock me for what I was wearing because that way they built themselves up. I got the idea really early that I couldn't make it doing that capitalist-materialist thing. But I was really pretty fucked up. I kept vacillating between feeling superior and feeling inferior."

A school psychiatrist wasn't being especially creative when he cautiously diagnosed that Steve was "anti-authoritarian" after a series of interviews in which Steve made it inescapably clear that he hated hypocritical authority figures, and that he didn't know any authorities who didn't fit that description.

In high school, when some value begins to be placed on intellectual ability, Steve's classmates began seeking him out. They paid him $5 to write six-page papers for them. They elected him to the student council where he quickly decided the student government was made up of a bunch of administration "lackeys." He remembers having a lot of hate, but also being a devout "rationalist." "I thought if people would only get together in rational discourse, truth would prevail. I even began to see myself as part of an 'intellectual class.'"

His parents sent him to a Left-leaning Labor-Zionist camp, quite by mistake Steve thinks, since they've never cared much for the socialist politics such camps teach. "They saw it was Jewish and that it was cheap. That's all it took. They could never understand why when they brought me food I was required to 'pool it' with everyone else." The camp's annual Color War competition the first summer pitted "labor" against "management." (Political sophistication declined a bit the second year and the war matched the Jews against the Romans.) At the end of each summer the camp held a "Day of Revolution" when the campers rose up and overthrew their counselors by running them out with shaving bombs. But the camp held long discussion sessions and examined socialist theory quite deeply. The U. S. had invaded the Dominican Republic just before one of Steve's summers there and he came out quite fully convinced that American troops were terrorizing and oppressing people all over the world.

Instead of being crushed into humiliation in the fashion-show, dating-game atmosphere of the high school, Steve sought out his few working class schoolmates and they began hanging around together—mostly smoking pot. "We were the *'lumpen proletariat'* of the school. We didn't talk much, but we blew a lot of dope. I remember mothers wouldn't let their daughters come over to play with my sister because of the kids I was hanging around with." Steve, who'd always been an excellent musician, became the guitarist in a rock band and the group actually got a local recording contract. He was heading down the mainline to youth culture.

To complete his hodgepodge of lifestyles, he was also reading extensively about the plight of the Jews in Nazi Germany. He read every Leon Uris book he could find and began to groom himself to be a Jewish scholar who would "counter all the lies people tell about the Jews." His strong sense of justice and vengeance was pushing him to become a champion of the Jews. But the same impulses have since led him to forsake his Jewish background altogether and take a distinctly opposite stand. "After a while I began looking around and seeing that the ghetto merchants and landlords were all Jewish and were exploiting blacks like mad. And all those self-righteous Jewish liberals openly spout the most incredible racism. That finally clinched it for me." At Columbia last fall SDS debated a Zionist group about the situation in the Middle East. Steve sided with the Arabs while a different Steven

Cohen, not yet lost from the flock, argued for the Israelis.

There were a few semi-political incidents at the high school that gave Steve some inspiration. First, people sat-in on the principal over a strict dress code. Later, a marine corps band came to perform for a school assembly. The vice principal introduced the group and Steve and his cronies began to applaud vehemently. The rest of the kids picked it up and applause rained on for fully five minutes. The band leader finally got a chance to thank the students for their flabbergastingly warm reception. And they went into another endless ovation. With the concert quite totally blocked the vice principal screamed from the stage that the students were to be returned to their classes, and with the invincible marines corps totally beaten, the students roared again.

Steve remembers his old gang with a good deal of respect. "For the rest of the school, those working class kids were just cast-off refuse. But they were really sharp. They were the only ones who knew enough not to salute the flag."

Steve worked in several liberal political campaigns but he was cynical about all politicians pretty early. He read attacks on "Lily White Liberals" in SNCC literature and remembers anecdotes about blacks being forced to ride in the backs of the "Freedom" buses. He felt a lot of sympathy for ghetto rebellions. When the blacks in the ghetto at Cambridge, Maryland, rose up, he was thrilled. He remembers driving into the ghetto of Baltimore with his father, around Gay and Asquith Streets, amid incredible squalor. His father said it was contemptible that human beings chose to live like that, always "filthy and drunken." But Steve couldn't accept the idea that the blacks had chosen that life. "It was bullshit. I knew everyone had the American Dream of a good place to live and clean clothes. If they didn't have it, it was because they couldn't get it."

Things started crystallizing at the end of his junior year of high school. In May, 1968, the greatest month in the history of the world student movement, students in Paris began fighting the police in the Latin Quarter behind barricades. Then France's workers called a general strike and joined the students in the streets. And when DeGaulle tried to send in the troops, they too went out. It was almost a revolution. The same month, Columbia blew. He remembers the headline: "Student Rebels Seize University Buildings." Right then he decided he was going to go to

Columbia, "so I'd be able to fight in the streets too."

A month or so later, Steve and his father were sitting home watching the Democratic National Convention televised from Chicago—and Steve's radicalism was clinched. "We just sat there seeing Walter Cronkite freak out on the air because thousands of kids were demonstrating in the streets and getting the shit kicked out of them by the cops. No one could watch that and not be radicalized. I'd always hated cops, but that convention made you want to kill them."

The next fall Steve was in the streets marching in support of the Berrigan brothers and the Catonsville Nine, who were being tried for an assault on a draft board. Steve remembers the cops along the curbs in riot gear with mace and helmets and lead batons and thinking to himself that the streets were where he belonged.

Steve's parents had set their hearts on their son going to Harvard, but Steve was convinced that Columbia was where he'd learn about revolution. He didn't tell the admissions people that was why he was applying, of course. Instead he hit them with all the stuff that he figured they wanted to hear about Columbia's being a place where he could get a rich classical education in the intense urban atmosphere of New York City. But Steve insists that learning revolution was "absolutely" the reason he was heading for Columbia. It was a little bewildering that spring, after he'd been accepted at Columbia, to see that school remain totally quiet while Harvard blew instead.

The first thing Steve did when he got to Columbia was seek out SDS. The jumpy, wiry guy with intense wide-set eyes, whose high school yearbook had called him the "most intellectual" student in the class, went to his first SDS meeting ready to be awed. But he was cruelly disappointed. The Columbia chapter was still fighting out the split between the Progressive Labor-Worker-Student Alliance people and Mark Rudd's Revolutionary Youth Movement-Weathermen faction. The RYM guys were dominant at the first meeting, screaming, "RIGHT ON! RIGHT ON!" as one of their group read out PL for its reservations about the Panthers and the NLF. Then they started chanting, "HO, HO, HO CHI MINH. THE NLF'S GONNA WIN." They sickened Steve, with his unrelenting sense of rationality, but he didn't much like PL's approach to SDS either. He'd always thought the Panthers and the NLF were heroic fighters.

He could talk to the Worker-Student Alliance people, though.

For several hours after the meeting Steve listened while Andy Kaslow and Alan Egelman satisfied his sense of reason with explanations of their political positions. There was a lot of talk about nationalism and how no revolution has ever been built or sustained on the basis of the kind of in-groupism that characterizes the NLF and the Black Panthers. (Andy later began to see both groups a lot more favorably.) They told Steve the Panthers spend most of their energies fighting in the courts, which is a losing situation. They told him to go down to the civil court and watch the way landlords run roughshod over tenants. The courts are no place for revolutionaries, they said. The streets are. Steve liked the idea.

For several weeks he got into long ideological discussions with Andy Kaslow or one of the others, and, while he wasn't finding all the great battling he'd really been looking for, he was slowly becoming extremely impressed with the WSA's reasoned approach to revolution. He was "won" quite fully to SDS. Throughout that first year he kept wishing the chapter—which emerged totally Worker-Student Alliance—could get something really big going. He thought SDS was being too charitable in the way it was trying to support campus workers; instead of fighting and inspiring support, they were pleading for sympathy for the workers.

When the strike came in the spring, Steve thought things were finally ready to move. He was at the head of the battering ram, smashing down the doors to Low Library. He was ready to fight as he faced the campus police rapping their clubs into the palms of their hands. Then Steve heard the liberals down below pleading that the strike be "saved"; for the radicals to come down. It was a heavy blow, but it was what he had come to expect from middle class students.

Columbia was proving to be a cruel disappointment. He was arrested on felony charges at the end of his first year of college, in the Low Library bust, and then thrown out of school for a semester, but as far as Steve was concerned, the year had been a political failure. Despite all the talk about workers being politically backward, he was a lot more confident that they were ready to fight the rich rulers of the country than students were. "Hell, even the most successful and progressive student movement will only be a supporter of the working class' struggles." And he laughs with the recollection of a bit of history. "Do you know what the

Czar's last line of defense was when the people stormed the palace in the Russian Revolution? Students! Cadets! Fucking ROTC!"

Steve decided to give elitist, middle class Columbia one more chance to rise up again. "But if I'm not satisfied this year," he vowed in the fall, "I'm leaving. I'll go to some large state school or to a community college where the people really want to fight. I can't keep shitting around like this." And then he chuckled at chasing around after revolutionary lightning. "Watch. I'll probably switch and it will be just my luck to be gone right when they have the greatest battle this place has ever seen."

The best SDSers totally overcome their radical isolation by showing an almost religious respect for other people. Anita Roger and Vic Coffield are like that. They really seem to like everyone. Without giving an inch on their politics, they travel around Berkeley relating to everyone. They aren't the least bit pompous or moralistic about what they think people should be doing—but they make clear what they're doing and how much it inspires them. They're always reaching out to other people to join them in the struggle—but they do it so that it doesn't intimidate or turn people off. SDSers like that build a circle of people who are willing to fight with them. A successful chapter will always have one or two of them. You'll ask people in the chapter how they came to SDS and they'll say something like: "Well, I met Vic working in the cafeteria and we got to talking one day about the war . . . so he suggested I come to a meeting and . . ."

The good organizers have an excellent sensitivity for bringing new people in. They speak casually to them at meetings without swarming all over them and pressuring them into agreement. They're totally without suspicion of newcomers and quickly entrust them with responsibility. They pay extra close attention to the new recruits' opinions because they'll be getting a valuable new view of political conditions or strategy. They're ready to change direction pretty quickly if someone comes up with a new idea. And they've got encyclopedic minds packed with political tidbits that are always falling into just the right place to make convincing arguments. At meetings they know their leadership potential and hang back so the others will push their minds and the group will find its own direction. Then, when they see a really critical point, they come in. They speak quietly and confidently and quickly. People listen and often they agree and follow.

The worst of the SDSers can almost singlehandedly repel even the most sympathetic from joining the organization. They feel persecuted and oppressed. They've been isolated so long they're paranoid about newcomers. Anyone who disagrees with them must be a cop. They argue caustically and with incredible impatience. Often they fail to give anyone else much chance to explain his position, and tend to attribute to one person who disagrees with them the arguments they've gotten from someone else a long while before. To them, SDS really isn't supposed to be a vehicle for massive organizing but just a platform for their own dissertations. When really big campaigns develop, they usually shrink back in bewilderment. People don't listen to them anymore and they don't have much zest for battle themselves. They'll never build a movement, but they can really dismantle one. Fortunately for SDS, there aren't too many of that sort around.

SDS has a few glory seekers, but not nearly as many as most people think. There's still room in SDS for charismatic personalities and incendiary speakers who can handle a bullhorn and capture a crowd, but as in any organization, there's far more need for ultra-committed workers who are inspired even while doing drudgery—people who can keep handing out leaflets day after day, their hands black with mimeo ink, always putting out a meaningful call to others to join them. As style and politics have changed in SDS over the past two years, the organization has become almost totally composed of such hard workers. The glory hounds for the most part have gone off to find glamor elsewhere.

The traditional image of the SDSer as a weird and unpredictable individual is now almost totally unfounded. SDS members of late tend to be almost shockingly drab and astoundingly well disciplined. Newcomers have a hard time relating to the group because of it. Steve Cohen had to fight himself for a year to tone down his temptation to just leap into battle when everyone else was still trying to figure out how to win a following. "I just wanted to go out and trash buildings. I knew it was illogical if I had long-range political goals, but it's hard to resist my own personal adventurism. I have to keep telling myself it's a question of whether you want to have some fun, or you really want to be a revolutionary."

A great deal of SDS' internal functioning is directed at breaking down the individual interests of members and winning

them totally into a commitment to the group. Everyone is expected to think for himself and can certainly speak as an individual whenever he wishes (as opposed to members of Progressive
Labor and other "democratic centrist" parties where no differences are tolerated outside of the internal discussions of the
group). But if someone disagrees with an SDS position it's accepted practice that the disagreement be discussed openly and at
length—with the hope that either the dissenter will see he's wrong
or win over the rest of the group to what is right. I've been at
many meetings that started out with major splits of opinion but
lengthy discussion finally produced unanimity.

Members are expected to give up most of their personal
privileges too. If something has to be done, it isn't cricket to say
you don't feel like doing it—or that you've got a date, or that you
did it yesterday. A member supposedly believes in the political
goals of the organization and he's expected to do whatever is
necessary to accomplish them. When he drags his feet he's given an
intense political pep talk to get him moving again.

Impatience and immaturity are also integral parts of the
SDSers' traditional media image. While it's obvious that politeness
with your political enemies isn't considered much of a virtue,
patience is an absolute prerequisite to being an SDSer. Not many
"mature" adults would have an SDSer's self-control, sitting
through endless meetings, giving everyone the chance to express
without interruption his own analysis of the state of the world and
what has to be done. And only selflessly committed people could
keep working day and night for a far-off goal while most of the
people around them are settling into television and drugs and
booze and self-advancement.

The glamor of SDS' name still brings a lot of new glory
seekers around, of course, but they don't last long. Early last fall
a chubby boy named Barry came wandering onto the Columbia
campus after running away from home in North Carolina. He had
a tattered bag full of his clothes in one hand and a much-thumbed
copy of *The Strawberry Statement* clutched in the other. He
roamed around the campus for a while in awe—he was only about
fifteen—stopping people to find out the names of the buildings
and then flipping through his book to place them in the heroic
history of the '68 rebellion.

He found the SDS table set up on Low Plaza and declared he
had come to help fight. A few days later, he stole a map some-

where of the underground campus service tunnels because he thought that might come in handy. Later he went to the library and looked up explosives because he thought that's what SDS was into. And he spoke up at meeting after meeting to throw in irrelevant contributions. He hung around for several weeks, begging for pocket change. But eventually after breaking the mimeograph machine, he shuffled on. He'd come to the same conclusion a lot of students a good deal older than he often arrive at: working with SDS can be more boring than glorious.

The fight against individualism in SDS is carried on at the psychological level. The whole practice of chanting slogans in a march and raising fists in unison is initially abhorrent to many nonconformist students who have sought SDS out in large measure to be different. But the basic assumption of a group like SDS is getting people to fuse identities in a united fight. Chanting openly together to express a *mass will* is part of that process. It doesn't come easily. One active member from Ohio told me he was too self-conscious to stand up years ago when a civil rights rally began to rise spontaneously to sing "We Shall Overcome." Now he throws himself into chanting sessions almost triumphantly, as if to show the world he's with SDS and its politics completely.

With all those individuals uniting in struggle and sacrificing so much of their isolated identities, SDS begins to become a shared personality. Perhaps much more than is politically wise, SDSers hang around together on campus. A few will meet up, join a few other regulars, and soon the usual SDS coterie has gathered itself. SDS is like a big fraternity, with politics instead of prestige as the basis of unity. SDSers become one another's lovers; couples break up and new ones are reformed within the same circle. To some extent SDS provides a kind of prefabricated cluster of friends and every once in a while people seem to join it more to gain some kind of social context than because they're interested in anything political. But those kind never last either. To deserve the friendships, you've got to hold up your end of the work too.

While SDS chapters tend in concept to be only loosely federated with the national structure of the organization, political problems and goals are almost always the same around the country. SDSers can travel from state to state during vacations, staying with the local chapter members, talking about the same problems that the chapter at their own school was discussing.

In-groupism does a lot to hold SDS back, of course. SDSers

tend to develop a jargon that sounds pretty hollow to outsiders, and the highly critical stand SDS takes toward the establishment, commercialism and pop culture, leads to a general disdain for movies, rock music, hip clothes, drugs and lots of other things that most of the rest of the campus is into. Progressive Labor people, in their intense desire to relate to the working class, even tend to reflect some of the stereotypic worker prejudices against long hair, youth and all its trappings.

Almost any SDSer will admit how strange the group seemed to him at first, but the same person, once he's been around for a while, doesn't find his fellows that odd any more. Though few were conscious of it while it was going on, the newcomer was being assimilated into the whole SDS milieu. Probably he too begins to strike others outside SDS as kind of strange. Unless members are very careful to hold on to their old lives while they are becoming politically involved, they end up quite totally cut off from their former friends. The old buddies shake their heads and say: "You just can't talk to him at all since he's joined SDS." It's one of the worst problems the organization has and it's going to have to be solved before SDS will ever approach fulfilling its goal of organizing the great bulk of the nation's students.

The estrangement a new SDSer suffers from his other friends is minor compared to the sudden but furious conflict that usually comes when his parents learn he's working with the group. They cut off money, often haul the students home from school and sometimes even break contact with their children altogether. The father of one extremely dedicated SDSer from Long Island is constantly threatening to use his power as an attorney to go to court and block his daughter's participation in conferences and demonstrations. One of the SDSers arrested after the Low Library assault at Columbia broke word of plans to stay in New York with SDS friends over the summer. "Those aren't your friends," the father snapped back. "Those are your enemies. You're coming home."

The strain with parents can lead to some strangely awkward times. Many SDSers depend on their parents for money so they can spend their time in political work instead of in part-time jobs. Often the money won't keep coming if the parents suspect it's helping to sustain their son or daughter's radical politics—so some hide the whole SDS side of their lives. One daughter had been doing that quite successfully for several years until she was sentenced to several months in jail and had to break the whole story because there was no other way to explain her absence.

The problem seems twice as bad with Jewish parents. When New York Regional SDS scheduled a major conference on a Jewish high holiday, Yom Kippur, families all over the area were suddenly thrown into bitter conflicts. The parents insisted their kids shouldn't plan for revolution on a holy day. The kids didn't see what difference it made what day it was. It was a political question. Either you work for a revolution or you don't.

But some Jewish parents are more tolerant of SDS politics than they are of some of their kids' social customs. SDS tends to produce inter-religious couples with name combinations like Rotstein-Murphy. One Jewish SDSer's parents took their son's emergence as a communist fairly placidly, but when he told them he was dating a Catholic girl, his mother gravely informed him: "Son, you're killing us slowly."

While it's untrue that the great bulk of student radicals quickly sell out their politics when the time comes to leave academe and make a living, they all do have to work. The career crisis hits SDSers hard and there's no good resolution for it. In our capitalist economy there isn't much work a person can do without somehow being tainted because he's supporting the system. For several years the Progressive Labor Party was sending its young radicals into the factories to organize the workers. This was largely a failure. Volunteering for the oppression of a factory worker, who wants nothing more than to get out of his enslaved situation, is unrealistic. Even if a former student adapts himself to factory life, he's not likely to do very well as an organizer when his fellow workers think he's "slumming."

(PL now tries to make contacts with sympathetic workers inside the plants and have *them* bring the Party's communist politics into the working situation. On the outside, the Party works very hard to sell its newspaper, *Challenge*, to get out word of militant rank and file worker struggles around the country and to build support for the Party's revolutionary strategy.)

For SDSers there aren't many careers they can justify politically. They abjure the professions for the most part. Being a lawyer is just strengthening the racist and oppressive court system. Being a doctor is a bit better, but consigns the person to a life that leaves little time or spirit for political work. Being a businessman is obviously out. Teaching seems to be one of the only viable alternatives and at this point probably 80 per cent of the SDSers in the country intend to be high school or college teachers. They hope to bring their radical politics to the students and they fully expect to be harassed and even fired for doing it. Many figure on teaching social studies with a heavy emphasis on economics and socialism, or history—lingering for months in the retracing of various revolutions.

Those SDSers who've already actually taken teaching jobs seem to find the situation only partially satisfactory, however. The students, particularly at the high school level, are almost always incredibly hostile to the whole school situation. It's brutally hard to reach them. And the school administrations are vigilant about keeping radicals out of their midst.

Most of the radicals who have seriously examined the whole career problem seem to have resigned themselves to a lifetime of unsatisfactory work of one sort or another. What's vital, they say, is that wherever you work, you declare your politics clearly. And your life, after making enough money to live on, has to be dedicated to working toward revolution. As long as you don't become a "boss," and you don't give up politics to become prosperous, you're O.K. There are really two levels to paving the way for revolution, it's felt. The primary one is actually winning enough people to the idea of getting revolution going; the secondary, but still vital level, is convincing others not to fight against it when the revolution comes. A sincere SDSer after college approaches most of his contacts with people in these contexts.

Whatever their "class backgrounds," SDSers generally consider themselves Children of the Nightmare—American capitalism. Comparing backgrounds is a favorite SDS pastime. Members love to describe the experience that helped them realize that the status-oriented nature of American society was a lot more ruthless than their schooling ever let on about America, the "Land of Opportunity." Being an underprivileged suburbanite like Steve Cohen seems to have been a sure route to radicalization. Instead of cavorting at the local country clubs, the money-pinched kids worked in them. It was enough to turn envy into hatred in many cases. Suddenly they were seeing the luxury their parents were scrambling so frantically to attain from the perspective of workers instead of that of would-be possessors. They waited on their school friends' parents at dinner dances, brought them towels in the locker rooms, carried their clubs on the golf course, and served their friends lunch at the pool. On the basis of what they saw, they decided that the well-to-do were often arrogant, foul, insensitive people. For the future SDSers, such work was enough to convince them that they didn't want to reach that level someday, as their families hoped they would.

There are a goodly number of quite wealthy students who come to SDS, too, and they also have scintillating stories to tell. The chapter will be talking about monopoly capital and one of them will pipe in with an anecdote about how his father took over an aluminum company. Or the discussion will be about imperialism and they'll chip in a first-hand account of how the family's company has "expanded" its manufacturing operations to Latin America for the cheap labor. They too have seen the scramble for money. Even the rich in America don't seem to stand pat with what they've got, and because the money hasn't brought their families much happiness or security either, rich radicals-in-the-making empirically reject the system as inadequate for even those on top of the heap.

And of course there are working class SDSers. A precious few, admittedly, because working class kids don't as often go to four year colleges. But how the chapter members envy the lucky SDSer who can say, on the basis of his own family, what workers think and want. And what lethal weapons the working class members are against the ubiquitous SDS baiters. "Aw, what the hell do you kids know about workers, anyway?" some guy will call out during a demonstration. And the workers' child can step out and really give it to him: "I know plenty, mister. My old man's a mailman and my mother works at Woolworth's. They make about $9,000 a year combined. So don't tell me how well off the workers are!"

One of SDS' sorest points is its lack of black members. The group constantly indicts American society for its racism, but SDS itself is virtually all white — and always has been. To a great extent that's an indication of how absolutely divided the races in American society have become.

SDS isn't happy with its own de facto segregated status and never has been. Periodically during its history SDS allied itself closely with black groups in order to work more directly to fight racism. In the early civil rights days, SDS was the white radical arm of the Student Non-violent Co-ordinating Committee. But as black nationalism intensified and SNCC made increasingly frequent attacks on all whites in the movement, the relationship became strained to the point of schism. And in the days just before the split in SDS, the RYM faction was tying itself directly to the Black Panther Party. But that relationship also proved short-lived and never really functioned except on the symbolic level.

Black students in the country today are probably the most militant group on the campuses. Their militancy thus far has been directed chiefly at restoring pride and privilege to their race and not really at attacking the system. Some major college struggles have been fought by blacks (Cornell University, where blacks brought guns with them for self-defense when they occupied a building, is the chief example.) But the demands have usually been for black studies, black student centers, greater black enrollment, and occasionally the firing of a professor or dean accused of being racist.

As far as SDS is concerned, these goals are all diversions away from making a really concerted attack on American capitalism. SDS sees the system prospering by exploiting people and dividing them with racism so they can't fight it. When black students have come out to fight the system, SDS has allied with them enthusiastically, as the Columbia chapter tried to do with the Third World Coalition. That alliance brought Warren Tull into SDS. And while he is one of only a few dozen blacks in the entire organization, his presence is a faint indication that black and white radicals are beginning to get together under the same banner.

"The problem is that if you're into nationalism you see everything from that perspective. And if you're into socialism, you see everything from that perspective. It takes a while before you can see the two at once," he explains.

The long-range goals of SDS seem too remote to black students for the most part, he says. "SDS comes off looking like an elitist white group that's just trying to agitate without really winning immediate goals on the campus that blacks can identify with." Blacks would like to "restructure" the universities to relate more directly to their needs. But SDS says such restructuring means reforming, and reforming means keeping things essentially the same but giving them a prettier appearance.

"I want to really fight the system, but only if the fight is going to win some changes. I'm skeptical enough to not want to waste all my efforts just bringing down more repression. I know we've got to fight for a non-capitalist system. Hell, I can see how cruelly impersonal this system is. Only circumstances decide what rung you're on. We need a system that will bring the most good to the most people. When you go through what I'm experienceing now — being refused work for six months — you have to start thinking: 'This system isn't working for me, and it's probably a lot worse for a lot of other people.' Once you're that far, it's a simple thing to decide to start fighting." When Columbia SDS reembraced the Panthers as allies, several more highly committed black radicals joined the chapter.

"I'm going to keep working with SDS for a while and see what happens," says Warren. "If we do something concrete, I'll stay. If we don't, I don't know. You can't fight alone, but there aren't any other groups that seem to offer much of an alternative."

A surprising number of SDSers are the children of fallen capitalists. Their fathers ran stores or restaurants and were embezzled or trusted their money to con men and were broken by them. One's father kept speculating in oil lands and the family gyrated from bankruptcy to wealth and back to bankruptcy several times. The experience certainly created a lot of cynicism about the system. One, whose father's business was wiped out, describes his own reaction. "First you blame him for the family's sudden poverty. But then you begin to realize everyone's going through that sort of thing and you begin to see it's all part of how the system works."

And finally there's the group of SDSers whose parents have deliberately groomed them for radical politics—though they may not feel that great about their young rebel's affiliation with SDS. The sociologists call them "Red Diaper babies" and the student radicals apply the term to themselves with a good deal of pride. Their parents were in Left politics in the Thirties and Forties. Many were in the Communist Party and many more were extremely close to it. They bred cynicism for capitalism into the kids quite deliberately. They put them into the W.E.B. DuBois Club and into civil rights activity. But most of them seem to worry now that their radical offspring will get into too much trouble and ruin their lives.

These parents are still haunted by the terror of McCarthyism. They were witch-hunted out of their jobs and red-baited into paranoia. A great many of them finally gave up fighting the system altogether, though many still silently hate it. Nearly all of the old-

timers, if they remain at all political, have very carefully camouflaged their communist politics in a cover of liberalism. So it
horrifies them to see their kids working openly for revolution and
they warn them time and again not to put their names on leaflets—
or speak at public rallies. When times get tight again, they say,
you'll pay for that bravado. The young radicals find their parents'
submission to such intimidation enraging. They lacerate them for
their cowardice and hypocrisy. They attack the old Communist
Party as "revisionist." And sometimes the parents whose politics
were very close to SDS' end up having some of the worst conflicts
of all with their children.

SDS has largely resisted accepting the "generation gap" analysis of the conflict in this country. There are progressive people in
every generation, the SDS thesis goes, and they just have to be
united in struggle. Playing up "youth culture" just divides people
and it certainly turns off the vital working class. But the age
rivalry is certainly there. "I don't go in for generational chauvinism," says Steve Cohen, "but if there was ever a generation that
really sucked, it was my parents'. How could they just sit there
through Joe McCarthy and all that anti-communist crap? None of
them said a word against the Korean War. They just swallowed
that without question, while our whole damned generation op-
poses Vietnam."

SDS women have done a startling job breaking out of the
shy, retiring feminine roles into which they were bred. A newcomer to SDS is usually amazed to see all the women speaking
out, and speaking vehemently. But the women of SDS don't feel
they are always treated as equals in the organization, and they
make their grievances known. "There's still a hell of a lot of male
chauvinism around this organization that we have to fight," says
Kathy Murphy, a dedicated SDSer who quietly labored in the
background of Columbia SDS for months before really putting her
own leadership forward. "The men have us chair meetings and
speak at rallies, sure, but a lot of that is tokenism. When there's a
critical moment on a march and it has to be decided pretty
quickly whether we go through the cops or around them, no one
bothers to ask the women what they think."

For most college girls, militant radicalism is something that's
developed very slowly. They've been taught to be demure. They're
attractive when they're in need of manly protection, they're told,
and threatening when they're hollering and fighting.

One SDS girl says her mother keeps warning her that she'll never get married if she remains political. "I get these real motherly warnings: 'Remember you're only young once, dear. And this is the age when you can be your most attractive and feminine. Don't destroy your whole personality trying to act tough.' When she's done I tell her to go fuck herself."

Women in the U.S. clearly have been conditioned out of being political. SDSers constantly notice that when they're holding out a leaflet for a couple, it's the guy who takes it. An argumentative man is often considered forceful and a leader. An argumentative woman is more likely called a bitch.

Women have long had grievances with the way they've been treated on the Left. One of the most quoted things Mark Rudd ever said in SDS before he left to build bombs was: "Get me a chick to do some typing." And Black Panther leaders went through a period when their line was that the most appropriate position for a woman in the movement is "prone." Anita Roger dated men involved in Left politics for years but they rarely asked what she thought about various political questions. She has ended up asserting as much force and influence on SDS as any man has. She is a great encourager now for other women to come forward. "You just have to force yourself to speak out and take leadership," she urges others. "When you do, they listen. And you learn through struggle to rely on yourself more and more."

CHAPTER EIGHT

FOUR FOR THE REVOLUTION

AN INTELLECTUAL DISCOVERS COMMUNISM

"Most of us go to college because we want to help people and we think we'll be taught how. But it's hard to square the reality of the universities with your ideals. You want to fight racism, but you find that these sanctimonious institutions you'd hoped would show you the way are actually incredibly racist themselves. You want to fight poverty and you find the school where you've gone to learn how is itself keeping people poor, especially the ones who work for it. You want to fight the war and it turns out the schools are pushing it instead with their war research and their counter-insurgency institutes. If SDS weren't there on campus to try to make your ideals real, you'd never stay."

For a while at Queens College in New York, Robbie Nuremberg managed to blot out a lot of the idealism he describes. A gangling guy whose nature is to hang back and check things out cautiously, he spent most of his early years absorbed in athletics and culture. He admits he wasn't very conscious of the problems of society. But they caught up with him.

He graduated from Queens and was accepted into a doctorate program at Princeton with a sizable fellowship. "I was going to become a professor and write the Great American Novel on the side. I was totally apolitical. But I started coming around the summer before I went to graduate school. My job opened my eyes." He was working as a gravedigger in a New York cemetery. It was Robbie's first direct and close exposure to the working class. He was young and strong, securely middle class, and full of anticipation because he saw his life opening up before him. His co-workers were desolate, poor, older men, many broken by the difficult work and all of them without hope.

"I was deeply shaken by the contradiction between my life and theirs. It was a *class* thing. There's no other way to describe it. Here I was, accidentally working alongside these men, but I was just passing through — on my way to Princeton and the easy life. They were staying; there was none of that upward mobility bullshit with them. Their lives were bad and they were at a dead end. There was no way I could have ended up in their shoes. I didn't do anything to deserve my easy life and it wasn't because they were lazy that they were doomed to digging graves. Hell, *I was the lazy one.* But I was born higher. Somehow you're not supposed to think about those things when you've got it made. You're supposed to think everyone's got as much chance as you and the whole world's really comfortable. It hits you pretty hard when you realize what a lie that is."

When he got to Princeton in September, he joined SDS. The chapter then was strong; it was 1967–68, the year of the Columbia Rebellion and SDS' undeniable emergence as a threat to the whole academic establishment. Princeton, like Columbia, was one of the ten members of the multi-campus Institute for Defense Analysis, and SDS was going after IDA everywhere. For every IDA branch there was an SDS chapter to try to shut it down. In October, Princeton SDS staged a sit-in and blockade of the institute and much of the chapter was arrested. In the spring at the same time Columbia was under siege, SDS led a strike that shut down most of Princeton. Robbie was an active part of the fight which demanded not only the abolishment of IDA but of ROTC and of university investment in corporations and banks with links to the South African government.

SDS had good support on the campus for a while, but in one sense the campaigns were frustrating for Robbie. "Our goals were too liberal. We were trying to reform the university. We were saying, 'These things aren't nice and they don't belong in a nice place like Princeton.' The assumption was that you could purify the place by getting the war stuff out of it. It just didn't seem like enough to me."

He was starting to arrive at an understanding of capitalism as an economic system, and the lessons were coming primarily out of his own life. His father suddenly experienced business setbacks. It was as jarring an experience as it had been to discover he was from a privileged class. Somehow the same brutal and arbitrary forces had come down on his folks, through no apparent fault of their own, and thrown them into hardship. Robbie started talking about it with a friend in one of his English classes. The fellow was a Progressive Labor member who had studied the socialist analysis of capitalism. "It's not just a few mean guys fucking over some other good guys. It's the way the whole system functions," he told him. And he started pulling out some communist literature for Robbie to read.

"I considered myself a radical by then, but it amazed me to find a communist right there in my Anglo-Saxon Literature class. I remember saying, 'Shit, man. Here you are a perfectly normal guy with a wife and family, reading this stuff and talking openly about communism.' And he laughed and said, 'Sure, you've got to read those ideas to really understand what's going on. They try to build up all this fear and hatred of communism so you'll never get close enough to find out its right.'" Robbie started to read more and more political stuff and less and less English literature.

That summer he joined the SDS Work-in, a program Progressive Labor had put forward to bring students and workers into much closer contact. As many SDSers as could find them took jobs in factories, warehouses and the like. They worked alongside the people they were beginning to feel had the real power to stop the war and threaten the system. Wherever possible, SDS tried to mobilize support for workers who were already fighting.

The black and Latin workers in a sweatshop bra factory in Manhattan's garment center started wildcatting because they were earning only $65 a week. Every time they tried to organize, their leaders were fired by the company called "Figure Flattery" (the strikers said the only figures the company was really flattering were the ones on its profit sheets). Robbie and about fifty other SDSers from around New York started going down to the factory early in the morning, picketing to help the wildcatters keep the factory shut down, and leafleting at streetcorners in the teeming district to raise support. It was the first time SDS had linked up directly with a worker struggle, and was the clincher in Robbie's political transformation.

One of the leaders of the wildcat was constantly being baited by the company and the union for being a communist. The company eventually granted the workers a 4 per cent wage increase, but pressured them to abandon their organizers. The SDSers, who'd really come to respect the leaders for their militancy and their organizing ability, were afraid the workers wouldn't stick with them. One of the leaders got up at a tense meeting of the wildcatters and stood proudly on his politics. He was fighting for the workers *because* he was a communist, he said. That was why the executives and the union officials who were trying to break the strike were red-baiting him. As a communist, he was their enemy, and he was the workers' friend. The strikers agreed emphatically and the wildcat went on.

Several times the union brought in teams of "goons" who attacked the picket lines. Once a squad of them found a group of the SDSers isolated and swept in, flailing pipes and chains. Robbie remembers battling furiously — for the first time in his life. The garment strikers poured in to defend the students.

The Figure Flattery workers eventually won their demands and Robbie returned to Princeton the next year, convinced that the student movement had to be linked in a massive way to the interests of the working class. He joined Progressive Labor and began struggling inside SDS to redirect the organization's program out of student power and toward a worker-student alliance.

Princeton ended up throwing Robbie out of the PhD program after three years. His organizing on campus was obviously a thorn in the university's side. It struck many of Robbie's colleagues as a surprisingly vindictive move by the school, which even refused to give him the customary "terminal" Masters degree.

But by then he'd come to expect that sort of retaliation and didn't especially care. He started taking some graduate courses back at Queens College and intensified his political work. His whole orientation had changed. He wasn't thinking about writing any novels — let alone the Great American one. He'd decided to make revolution his life's work.

MR. LICHTY GOES TO PRINCETON

Dan Lichty went to Princeton for the prestige. He knew that wasn't the sort of thing he ought to do, so he joined SDS as soon as he got there. He'd very much like to lead the students now in tearing the place down brick by brick. But pastoral Princeton, though its students are now of more varied origins, is still an ultra-elite institution as it was in the days of F. Scott Fitzgerald and his kind. Dan and his fellow radical Princetonians have been terribly frustrated by the place.

Dan was perfect Princeton material when he applied, but was poison for the place by the time he'd arrived. He was a model establishmentarian for most of his school days in Johnson County, Kansas, one of the richest counties in the country. He was president of the student body. He even joined Junior ROTC at the beginning of his senior year. His grades were tops and he was on the debating team. Then alienation hit him.

His father had been going through a long series of business reversals and Dan was beginning to get pretty cynical about the idea of material success. He decided Johnson County was incredibly decadent, that its school system was farcical, and that the whole country and its ridiculous war in Vietnam was deplorable. He started getting drunk twice a week. They threw him off the debating team for cussing out the coach. Then he fell into LSD and any other drugs he could get hold of.

The summer before he came to college, he started thinking it would be better to work for change than to drop out. He really took a liking to the poor blacks he worked with in the kitchen of the local country club. "By the time I got to Princeton I'd done a lot more thinking," he says. "I was really pissed off and I was ready to fight."

Like Steve Cohen at Columbia, Dan checked out the Revolutionary Youth Movement (RYM) faction of SDS first and decided it was anarchistic and ridiculous. Then he met some of the Worker-Student Alliance leaders and was impressed intellectually with their strategy. "It made a lot of sense. Students had been trying for years to change things in the country and it was pretty clear that they simply didn't have the power. They could shut down a few schools and wreck some buildings, but they couldn't stop the war, and they certainly couldn't bring about a revolution. But if the workers joined up with the students, the country wouldn't be able to function."

General Electric Company was hit with a nationwide strike in the fall of Dan's freshman year, 1969. Under it's new Worker-Student Alliance leadership, SDS made supporting the strike a major campaign. Princeton SDS organized car pools to drive down to Trenton, N. J., very early every morning. The SDSers helped picket with the workers and lent what other support they could. The basic idea was to show the workers that students care about their plight, and to show as many students as possible that workers can be great fighters who are sharply against the system. General Electric is a major defense contractor, SDS pointed out. As long as those workers were on strike, the war machine was being slowed down.

It was a politically inspiring experience for Dan. The G. E. strikers at the Trenton plant were among the most militant in the country. They welcomed the students' support and talked at length with them about how power in the country rests in the hands of the few men who run corporations like General Electric. The students said the same guys who direct the corporations are trustees of the universities. There was a lot of agreement that they ought to all fight together. When General Electric made the mistake of sending a recruiter to Princeton during the strike, SDS completely sealed him off from anyone who might have been thinking about going to work for the company. "No Scabs" was the chant. Princeton SDS even raised money to buy several dozen turkeys for the strikers' families at Christmas.

But while Dan's commitment to a pro-working class student movement was deepening, the Princeton community itself was finding the idea quite peculiar. "Princeton is just that kind of place," Dan laments. "It's all shade trees and lawns and rich people's kids. They don't think about workers here. The students all know that they've got it made. A friend of mine was talking like a revolutionary for a few months and now he says he's going to be a corporate lawyer. That's what kind of a place this is." One of Dan's roommates adds: "The line on the working class here is 'Let them eat cake.' "

Not coincidentally, Princeton students seem to have a lot more faith in electoral politics than most other collegians. Dan calls it "rampant liberalism." The Movement for a New Congress and the whole idea of letting the students out two weeks before the Congressional elections in the fall of 1970 was centered at Princeton. In fact, the electoral recess, which failed to encourage much real student politicking, came to be known as the "Princeton Plan." SDS at the school was forced to struggle with students on a much lower level. While at Columbia the SDSers were struggling to rid themselves of pacifism, at Princeton several were openly espousing it. A few members would unabashedly refuse to take part in any demonstration that might lead to violence. While thousands of students were trying to smash the ROTC building at Berkeley, Princeton students were saying such matters are a question of civil liberties and academic freedom — bar the program and you're injuring the rights of the students who want it. When SDS raised the question of the Vietnamese right to be free of the war, it went unheard.

By the spring of Dan's first year at Princeton, most of the SDS chapter's leadership had either graduated or dropped away from the organization. It was like a college football team that had lost its whole first string backfield and half its defensive line the previous year and was trying to still seem tough. Dan was left trying to keep the chapter going with only five or six other members. Every once in a while a military recruiter would come to campus and Dan and his small chapter would plan an action. But almost no one would come to it other than the university's peacekeeping proctors. Dan worked on through the year hoping somehow to get something going. He had a vision of really attacking one of the recruiters, getting hauled up on university charges, and building a struggle around the 'trial.' But the opportunity didn't come. Every time he passed Nassau Hall, the ivied administration building, he itched to storm it — but he had no one to do it with.

A DISCIPLE OF LENIN

SDS was just another stage in Neil Mullin's development as a revolutionary. "I plan to get myself into as many different kinds of fights as I can," he says. "I'll go way out of my way to get experience organizing different groups of people. I've already been somewhat successful in relating to workers' and students' struggles. And I'm really going to keep studying Mao, Marx and Lenin. After years more experience, I hope I'll have become what Lenin called a 'professional revolutionary.' "

In SDS and elsewhere throughout his life, Neil says, people have "assumed" his leadership. Some of his political rivals accuse him of working the other way—of doing the assuming himself. Either way, his following is clearly there. He is a classically charismatic figure. He looks hauntingly like Mario Savio, leader of the ice-breaking Berkeley Free Speech Movement. His dark eyes glare. His black curly hair is unkempt. And he's a brilliant orator.

Neil is the son of two school teachers from the Bronx. His parents were somewhat sympathetic to the Left. The family moved out to a posh suburb on the Hudson River, north of the city, and Neil says he immediately began to despise the "ruling class kids" he was suddenly thrown in with. He remembers first taking part in a demonstration when he was nine (he's twenty three now). It was a march organized by CORE to integrate the town fire department.

When he was sixteen he helped organize a local march against the war in Vietnam. (It's startling to hear SDSers say they've been protesting the war, which is now the longest in our history, "since we were kids.") It was an extremely pacifistic parade, with people singing peace songs, but it was attacked quite brutally by a gang of right wing youths and no one fought back. That was the beginning of the end of Neil's own personal pacifism. Demonstrating seemed sensible but so did self-defense.

He wasn't ever especially committed to making a career for himself and kicked around from college to college and job to job. He wrote a pornographic novel for four hundred dollars, worked at the "underground" paper *Guardian* published by a former SDS leader, Carl Davidson, and ran Addressograph machines for Mobil Oil and several other big corporations.

He was at the Democratic Convention in 1968 and the Chicago violence, he says, "totally turned my mind around. My friends and I were maced and beat up. I can still see the blood spraying from the cops' clubs. We were gassed all the time. They shot at us in Lincoln Park. When I got back I was numb from seeing so many people beat up. And I was furious. I said to myself, 'We've got to smash those guys. The next time I'm going to have a gun.' "

He remembers an old man he worked with at Mobil who was retiring after being with the company for thirty-five years. The executives held a ceremony for him and presented him with a diamond tie clasp. "Here he was, making $135 a week and there they were on about $100,000 a year, not counting their stock options. The old man wouldn't take their diamond."

Neil had been writing a lot of poetry and it impressed one of the prominent professors in Columbia's English Department. The man got him accepted into the college. For about a semester Neil worked hard, full of ambition about the career opportunities he could have. He says he "was tired of piddling around in little jobs."

He got almost straight A's the first semester, and then decided the course work was utterly irrelevant and wasn't worth wasting his time on. He stayed up late nights reading Marx. A neighbor who was in Progressive Labor talked him into going to an SDS national council meeting in New Haven — it was there that he was "won" to the organization.

The New Haven conference was the first major SDS meeting following the split in Chicago in June of 1969. It was an exuberant gathering. PL - Worker-Student Alliance people for the first time were free from being baited and harassed by the Revolutionary Youth Movement faction which had bailed out of SDS in the split. The "campus worker-student alliance" strategy was put forward and warmly received by the crowd. Students would get jobs on campus, get to know the workers in the cafeterias, libraries and maintenance crews, and support them in their struggles with the administration at every opportunity.

Neil had already been captivated with classical Marxist politics and here they were being put forward as a program for college radicals. He began to take an increasingly prominent role in the Columbia chapter. He was one of the leaders of the successful boycott of campus cafeterias that got the militant shop steward rehired. And he was a heroic antagonist at confrontations. The following fall, the university called up Neil and five other SDS leaders for a "tribunal" because of the boycott, and when they refused to go in unless the proceeding was opened to anyone who wished to attend, Columbia quite happily expelled the whole group. While some of them took the sudden cessation of their college educations hard, Neil seemed distinctly pleased that his brief relationship with the university had ended.

He shared an apartment with Bill Lyons, the campus worker who had declared he was "proud" to associate with "those student radicals." For a while Neil was heading toward becoming a member of the Progressive Labor Party. He was going to "candidate classes" and doing a great deal of work for the Party. But the Party's politics were already quite rigidly formed, and Neil had major differences with them.

A crisis hit the Columbia chapter in the late fall when the tribunals against Neil and the other SDSers were scheduled. Dozens of workers came out in strong support of the threatened students. They even bought an advertisement declaring their alliance with SDS in the school newspaper. Several hundred students and workers marched to the controversial School of International Affairs where the university had tauntingly decided to hold the tribunals. They demanded everyone be let in to the proceeding. It was the most prominent display of united worker-student strength in the experience of the new SDS strategy, but it failed terribly in its goal of frightening the university.

Very soon after, the "SDS Six" were expelled. Neil began moving away from PL and the chapter followed him. The chapter members decided SDS had been distinctly racist in its failure to give sharp support to the Black Panthers in the past, and it issued a public self-criticism admitting the past error. A chapter meeting was called and a Black Panther leader came to speak. The Progressive Labor members who had suddenly lost the leadership of the chapter sat quietly in the background while the rest of the membership gloated.

At the SDS national convention in Chicago in December, 1970, the Columbia chapter put forward a proposal that sharply opposed Progressive Labor's political line against the Panthers and other "nationalist" groups, such as the Puerto Rican Young Lords Party, the National Liberation Front of South Vietnam and the Palestinian "resistance" movement. The Columbia chapter's proposal was voted down three-to-one by the convention, but Neil and other Columbia leaders considered it a preliminary victory. They began organizing nationally so the next time around they'd have a majority.

It may seem a minor question whether or not a somewhat isolated group of American student radicals supports some far off war of national liberation, but the fine ideological question was tied very directly into what SDS would actually be doing in the future. And it had been one of the irrepressible political conflicts underlying the 1968 split. The Columbia proposal was meant to be the basis of a broadening of SDS' program so that it would once again organize for fighting directly against the war and American imperialism. The failure of the Worker-Student Alliance at Columbia to lead any massive struggles had been enough proof to the chapter that a redefinition was needed. And if SDS could return to its old practice of driving war research and counter-insurgency institutes off the campuses, Neil and others argued, it would be doing its fullest to help the workers of America and workers and peasants around the world. Fighting to get campus workers their jobs back was good—they'd all done it, and would continue to do it. But concretely hurting the imperialist nexus accomplishes a lot more.

As part of his preparation for revolutionary leadership, Neil was out to set SDS back on the road to massive attacks against the system. In the process, he and a few friends even began talking about the possibility of forming a new revolutionary party. He was obviously taking a lot of inspiration from his reading of Lenin.

THE SDSER WHO FACED ROCKEFELLER

They confront deans all the time, and once in a while a college president or a visiting politician. But SDSers almost never gain access to the real enemy chieftains—the President of the U.S., say, or a Rockefeller. They joke a lot about what they'd do or say if somehow they could get close enough to one of the real "Mr. Bigs" of the power structure. But they never really expect to be able to carry out the fantasies: it's inherent in the nature of class conflict that the revolutionaries not meet the capitalist "rulers" until they've actually defeated them.

But once back in 1969 an SDSer faced a Rockefeller head-on. It must have been a jarring experience for David Rockefeller, chairman of the Chase Manhattan Bank, to find himself and his family suddenly being indicted for exploiting and murdering people all over the world. And to have the attack come, not from some incensed Latin American mob while he was on tour, but from a handsome young divinity student who was sitting in the sanctity of Rockefeller's own office.

A controversy had been smoldering at the ordinarily apolitical Harvard Divinity School during most of the 1968-69 year over $1.5 million the Rockefeller family had promised to donate for the construction of a new divinity building. The Rockefellers were steadfastly insisting the building be named "The John D. Rockefeller Jr. Memorial Hall," after the father of David and five other Rockefellers.

A tall young Protestant minister named Jim Fisher was at the Divinity School working on a PhD in religion that year—when he wasn't spending his hours on SDS projects. Jim saw himself joining the ranks of history's revolutionaries who happened to be involved secondarily in religious work. The cliché contradiction between communism and religion exists only when the communism or the religion have been distorted out of their proper form, he always explains when people ask how someone with his ideas can be a minister. "The only problem I have in reconciling my politics with my work as a minister stems not from my beliefs but from the very bad role organized religion has played and continues to play in working against the interests of the masses," he says.

Jim was leading the insurgent forces who were campaigning for rejection of the Rockefeller gift. He and several other SDSers at the school maintained that the money was dirty and the proposed building was a waste. The Divinity School shouldn't lend its dignity to cover the Rockefellers' shame, they argued. And the money would do a lot more good if it was used to build badly needed working class housing in Cambridge instead of a new academic building. "The gift was a clear-cut attempt on the part of the Rockefellers to undercut any criticism of capitalist society by academic theology," Jim says. "Here was the supposedly critical prophetic stance of the Divinity School running right into the money interests—and the administration was calmly ignoring the collision."

This was all bewildering criticism as far as the advocates of accepting the gift were concerned. They said it didn't matter how dirty the money might have been, since it would be purified through its assistance to such a righteous cause anyway. As Rabbi Martin E. Katzenstein, who was in on the tense meeting with David Rockefeller, stated the position: "If we are correct in seeing ourselves in the discipleship of Amos, Isaiah and Jesus, the Rockefeller family, symbol to many of the evils of capitalism, might have another side. Gifts so thoughtfully conceived and so generously given place the burden of proof on the recipient rather than on the donor. In accepting this gift, the Harvard Divinity School is saying to the world that the system of which we are a part is not wholly tragic, that it has elements of power within it that can be used for its own purification."

The whole question probably would never have gone beyond

the theoretical stage if SDS and Progressive Labor that spring hadn't seized University Hall, the Harvard administration building. They demanded that ROTC be abolished and that the university halt its bulldozing of working class neighborhoods. A police "bust" was called in, heads were broken, the liberals were finally mobilized, and Harvard, the one place they said it could never happen, was shut down by a militant student strike.

As is wont to happen in such times of political crisis, the university-wide strike kindled many satellite controversies at individual segments of the university over particular questions. At the Divinity School, the previously low-level ideological debate over the gift suddenly blared into a full-scale struggle. Many students who'd been aroused by the strike into opposing the university's complicity with imperialism through ROTC and its "anti-working class" expansion began to listen to what Jim and the others were saying about how the Rockefeller gift and the new building were part of all that. Opposition to acceptance grew abruptly. The radicals' fight against religion's role as a "charitable cover for capitalism" no longer seemed peculiar to many students who had earlier agreed with the administration that such questions are beyond the purview of clergymen and theologians.

Eventually the administration tried to resolve things by holding a referendum on the question. It was a risky proposition. Perhaps they didn't foresee how close the vote would be, or, very likely, they saw some way around the possible blow of a majority voting to reject the Rockefeller money. It's certainly hard to conceive of the school quietly abiding by a decision to turn down the money it had celebrated being offered. In the end, a "compromise" proposal squeaked through. It stipulated that the money would be accepted but that a delegation would explain to David Rockefeller the doubts the school had suffered in coming to its decision.

Jim Fisher and Harvey Cox, the bearded philosopher-theologian who has written somewhat sympathetically about the student Left, represented the opposition. Richard Niebuhr, an eminent theologian along with Rabbi Katzenstein, a nun, and another student made up the acceptance faction. Rockefeller declined an invitation to come up to Cambridge to meet with them—apparently sensing the possiblity of an embarrassing confrontation with the radicals—so the group went to New York to see the billionaire.

David Rockefeller himself, a somewhat paunchy and friendly looking man in his mid-fifties, who didn't seem quite at ease despite his wealth, sat them down and the awkward session started. Professor Niebuhr, the senior member of the delegation, began. But instead of reconstructing the conflict as it had developed at the Divinity School, he slipped into a lengthy description of how much American theological education owes to the Rockefeller family. Given the supposedly critical nature of the mission, Dr. Niebuhr was heaping surprisingly heavy praise on Rockefeller. Down the table, Jim sensed that the banker himself might be a bit uncomfortable with the enumeration of his family's acts of goodness. "It just wasn't as subtle as these things are supposed to be," he later said.

Then it was Harvey Cox's turn. Rockefeller seemed to brace himself for criticism from the Left-leaning academician. But Cox himself was far from comfortable. He had, by his own accounting, been "the only member of the Divinity School faculty who had opposed accepting the gift." That opposition had brought him under what he felt was a great weight of criticism from his colleagues. "It got so severe that at one point I very nearly left the faculty," he now admits. Cox came closer than Dr. Niebuhr had to mentioning the actual controversy at the Divinity School, but not much. Most of his remarks were in the form of a somewhat rambling description of "the critical problems facing society." He never clearly stated why he himself had opposed accepting Rockefeller's money.

Rockefeller seemed relieved, but Jim Fisher was really angered. He felt it was all a lot of "mumbo-jumbo" that was totally failing to present the grave fears he and others at the school, including Cox, had expressed about the detrimental effects Rockefeller's gift would have. His was the remaining opposition voice. "I was so mad I just let it all drop. Everything I'd thought about the Rockefellers and their interests came out. And everything I've come to believe about the class conflict in the world." It caught Rockefeller by surprise when the handsome young minister, who was dressed so conservatively and whose manner seemed so mild, launched into his indictment.

He began slowly in a dispassionate, almost cataloguing manner, reciting where the various Rockefeller interests were concentrated in the world and what effect they were having on the people of those areas. Jim had researched the "empire" during the debate at the Divinity School. Before the meeting with Rockefeller he'd carefully studied a report on the Rockefeller "nexus" that had been prepared by the North American Committee on Latin America (NACLA)—an old SDS off-shoot which has become sort of the research think-tank of the New Left.

First there was Venezuela, almost a "colony" for the Rockefeller family for the past century. The Rockefeller-controlled oil operations dominate the country's economy. In 1966 alone, Standard Oil of New Jersey, which is controlled by Rockefeller interests, siphoned a quarter of a billion dollars in profits from Venezuela. And because the oil industry had been so fully automated and most of the refining of Venezuelan oil was being done outside of the country, very few workers from the country were actually part of the industry, as the great myth of development of "backward nations" promises will happen. In fact, the Standard Oil subsidiary, Creole Petroleum Company, had in the past ten years actually cut nearly in half, from 9,000 workers to 5,000, the number of people it was employing in Venezuela. It was, Jim said, a clear and simple case of the exploitation of an entire nation by greedy capitalism.

The itemization of business interests was hardly strange to the board room situation, but the stinging explanations of what was happening to the people while the money was being made was something new indeed. Neither Rockefeller nor anyone else tried to cut the indictment short, but they were hardly cool about the situation either. Jim recalls seeing David Rockefeller pressing himself deeper and deeper into the high-backed seat while he endured the blitz.

Philanthropy and social concern can often be just a cover for more money-making, he said. Nelson Rockefeller had organized an international "development" organization called the International Basic Economy Corporation (IBEC) in 1947, as part of a series of groups that supposedly would help put Latin America on its feet economically. But the IBEC venture had turned into quite a gold mine for the family (as if it needed another one) which retained, as of 1968, 70 per cent of the IBEC stock. Nelson's original investment of $3 million had grown into a huge international complex with assets of about $160 million. IBEC had become the largest supermarket distributor of food in South America, had cornered Brazil's hybrid cornseed market, and had gained control of several other vital Latin American markets.

Rather than aiding in the growth of "indigenous" economic interests and production capacities, IBEC and other American investments had been killing the local businesses off, the radicals claim. It is "a business enterprise quite similar to the classic Standard Oil model in which weaker competitors are squeezed out and then prices are raised," according to NACLA. An example is the way IBEC's dairy company in Venezuela undercut the local competition by putting imported powdered milk into the watered fresh milk it was producing. Once the competition had lost out to IBEC's low price, IBEC jacked its own price up to the point where milk cost nearly half again as much in Venezuela as it did in the U.S.

Such business interests are hardly politically impartial, Jim pointed out. Any threat of a socialist revolution that would turn such wealth back to the people would quite clearly be attacked by the family's allies in the government and the military, and it has plenty.

Then Jim got to David Rockefeller's own Chase Manhattan Bank and its leadership in lending many millions of dollars which had supported the government and economy of South Africa and in the process propped up apartheid—"the most flagrantly racist and exploitative social and economic system in the world." Without that money, he said, the corrupt and evil government might have collapsed. "Whatever rationales about impartial investment capitalists give," Jim told Rockefeller, "it is clear that your support of the racist treatment and exploitation of the people of South Africa is an example of the racism and exploitation that is built into the American capitalist system."

He'd been going on for about fifteen minutes, repeatedly making the point that the main purpose of the Rockefeller empire was to exploit the rest of the world. Rockefeller's gift was an attempt to "buy off" the Divinity School and theological education in general, he said. It wasn't something the family had to do, of course, but it would certainly help sweeten its image, just as decades of philanthropy had already helped take some of the sting out of the old "monopoly boss" image of the Rockefellers.

Such gifts "tend to offset uneasiness about the system that produces the surplus in the first place," he noted later in a written explanation of his arguments. And "this pattern is not incidental to maintenance of the status quo and those who benefit by it. Such praise for the Rockefellers is important to their images and a typically essential part of the capitalist perception of social good and evil. Philanthropy is the ticket to our justification of 'inevitable' suffering."

"The only good I can see coming out of your Rockefeller Hall," he told the banker, "would be if the place was turned into an insurgency center. People from South Africa and Latin America could be trained there. And then they'd go back to their homelands to throw your family the hell out."

Rockefeller was shaken. He slumped in his chair and said he had no idea people felt that way about the gift. "If I had, I wouldn't have given one dollar to the school, and if I hadn't already promised the money, I wouldn't give it now."

The theologians were "vibrating" so hard Jim thought "the table was going to levitate."

"My father was the most Christian man I've ever known," David Rockefeller continued. "I don't feel I have to defend either myself or him." And then the man became deeply emotional. It shocked the SDSer who had expected such a paramount capitalist figure to be cool and untouchable. But instead, according to the radical minister, "Rockefeller came apart in a broken-record dissertation on the American Dream."

American society is an open opportunity for everyone, Rockefeller insisted. Perhaps wealth was distributed more equitably in a communist society, but power was certainly concentrated in a few hands. In America, everyone has the right to vote, and the right to make money. Money might be the source of power, but money is available to anyone who has the initiative and the energy to go out and make it. Many do make money and they are inspirations for others to go out and do the same. America is a country where the opportunities are wide open, and no one, certainly not the Rockefellers, are "buying off" any institutions.

Jim recalls it as an "incredible performance. I didn't think even the most reactionary people in the country were still pushing the line about opportunity for everyone without limitations."

Sister Augusta, the nun, tried to sooth things by commenting how good it was that people could communicate back and forth in such a healthy way. Rabbi Katzenstein said something about lifting up the gift from the Rockefellers "as an offering before the altar." And with that the six member delegation from the Harvard Divinity School took its leave of David Rockefeller.

They were all quite surprised when Rockefeller turned up back in Cambridge the next day to receive an honorary doctoral degree from Harvard University.

CHAPTER NINE

GETTING IT TOGETHER

A radical student he'd met during an organizing trip through southern Ohio made an urgent call to Education Secretary Alan Spector at SDS national headquarters during the Cambodia Days last spring. "Hey, we've got 150 students occupying a campus building," the triumphant voice declared. "You guys have all the experience. What are we supposed to do now?"

They talked politics for a few minutes just to get the goals straight. To win any permanent gains, Alan explained, SDS feels the student movement has to ally with the interests of the working class by fighting racism and imperialism. The caller agreed. Then Alan gave him two pieces of advice: First, stay in the building and try to organize hundreds more students to support you around a series of concrete demands. Then start a campus SDS chapter.

Students would be fighting the American system even if there had never been an SDS, but their battles would probably be so completely isolated from one another that the national effect would be nil. SDS exists as a national organization to devise a program that can be fought on a broad co-ordinated front. Student radicals from all over the country are brought together in meetings and through the newspaper, *New Left Notes,* to analyze what students are thinking and what the system is doing, and to figure out the best way to fight.

If only one school at a time rose up against ROTC, the military could simply pack up and leave the embattled campus to set up shop at another school where the students wouldn't give them trouble; but if SDS as a national organization succeeds in launching a program on every campus to insist that ROTC must go, it won't have any place to go to, and will be eliminated altogether. The same applies to war research and the fights against the corporations. The power structure of the country is well united, the radicals realize. The heads of corporations serve on one another's boards of directors, run the universities and control the government. They have the same goals and are very much together in accomplishing them. To fight that kind of a united front, SDS says, the radicals have got to unite themselves. As an SDS organizing poster asks: "They're together. Why aren't we?"

While SDS has hardly forged a union of forces that can match the power of those who are now in charge, the benefits of students working within a national organization are constantly visible. SDS' national interim committee (NIC), which is made up of about twenty elected representatives from around the country, meets every month or so to reassess the national situation and plan. Most of the meetings begin with discussions of specific chapter activities at different campuses and what can be learned from them in terms of victories and mistakes.

Someone from the Midwest may describe the beginnings of a fight against ROTC and a delegate from Berkeley, who's lived through a heated anti-ROTC battle, will caution him about the various means the administration might use to co-opt the fight: "Don't let them try to hold a referendum on whether the credit should be taken away from ROTC courses. We used the slogan, "ROTC Kills, With or Without Credit." And someone from Columbia will report the tremendous interest SDS discovered on campus in the Middle East question: "They really see that this might develop into another Vietnam, but Zionism is a really strong emotional force that is a lot harder to cope with than the old patriotic American line we used to get with Vietnam. You've got to really bone up on what Zionism has meant historically." Copies of leaflets and pamphlets and press clippings are brought and passed around.

NIC meetings are held in various regions around the country so that rank and file SDSers from different areas will have direct

access occasionally to the deliberations of their leadership. There is
a severe problem in SDS and other radical groups over how much
power the national leaders take in establishing policy and making
major organizational decisions. As is only natural, radicals have a
deep distrust for concentrations of power. While most people who
have worked in the movement for any length of time readily admit
that there has to be a cadre of officers who will keep things
rolling, the same members are likely to be suspicious of every
move their leaders make. At times when the organization is having
problems, this becomes severe paranoia. Inevitable grumblings
begin about the national leadership trying to "manipulate" the
organization for its own political interests.

At least once a year SDS tries to get the membership together
in a huge convention which will analyze the progress and problems
of the previous year. The meetings have become the battleground
for the factions that naturally crop up within the organization.
And since the NIC, three national secretaries, and proposals for
future SDS programs and policy are voted on at the national
conventions, to a great extent they determine the leadership and
politics of the organization for the coming year. There is always a
good deal of semi-tumultuous bickering among the factions, and a
lot of time is lost from devising a proper united policy for SDS
while the factions try to out-maneuver and out-organize one
another in winning the favor of a much-wooed but rare species—
the independents. There is usually some compromising among
opposing groups in order to get some balanced representation on
the NIC. Political proposals that don't exactly conflict with any
group's policies may gather broad support, or may fail miserably
simply because the factionalized members vote only for something
they have originated.

In the end, political factions that are absolutely in opposition
to the ideology and strategy of the majority may end up splitting
off. But usually the conventions serve to bring some new unity
and determination to the membership, and to move the thinking
of the organization forward. Certainly the whole change in character of the student movement, from relatively insignificant battling for student privileges to very weighty struggles to change the
nature of the world, has been reflected in the sifting of ideas and
feuding of factions at SDS conventions. To a great extent, much
of that change is directly attributable to what went on at SDS

conventions themselves, as we'll see.

SDS really lives at the chapter level. While a nationally co-ordinated strategy and structure is vital to its long-term goals, the organization does its proselytizing and fighting on campuses. Before the 1969 convention, when the political disputes in the organization became so sharp they broke SDS apart, it was estimated that there were about 300 chapters around the country. Now the number is closer to 150. "Regional travelers" for SDS are sent out every once in a while to schools where there are no chapters. They put up posters announcing an SDS meeting, talk to as many students as they can reach and sometimes go to meetings that other groups are holding. A good organizer can almost always come up with a nucleus of three or four radicals on a campus who want to go a lot further than any existing groups are doing and who have some general agreement with SDS politics. They're left with a pile of literature and best wishes. If they're effective themselves in bringing people together, before long they can build a chapter of dozens—and battles of thousands. "It's the ideas that really count," says Berkeley's Vic Coffield. "You can put a tremendous struggle together from just a couple of people if you're open to others and really want to build."

Like any organization, the chapters are kept going by a fairly small core of people. They do most of the calling to get meetings together and write the leaflets. Sometimes they are formally elected as a "steering committee" and sometimes they are left in the roles by default. But the central group's size has very little relationship to the potential strength of SDS on the campus. If only twenty-five people are coming to SDS meetings, there are probably another hundred who can be counted on to turn out for major demonstrations, and literally thousands who will be with SDS if a major battle gets underway.

It's become almost a cliché in the press that "the great majority of American college students are not radicals." Of course that's true; by definition a radical has to be in the minority. But it's also true, and SDSers never forget it, that the great majority of American college students can be rallied behind radical causes if SDS handles things right and the administrations don't.

"Less Talk, More Action" is one of SDS' major slogans, but one the organization doesn't especially practice any more. Meetings are what hold SDS together. They are the means by which the membership participates in the planning, policy making and administration of the group. They go on almost every night, for hours each time. They are tightly disciplined. There is always a chairman, and because experience has shown that a meeting can't be held together if it is allowed to get informal, no one is supposed to speak unless he's been called on. You can't read a newspaper during an SDS meeting, and you can't sleep. It's a lot more demanding than just going to college.

A lot of radicals can't bring themselves to tolerate SDS meetings. To arrive at a collective policy, a great many individuals usually have to participate in its formulation. That means everyone at the meeting has to say what he thinks, and almost every assumption the meeting is based on has to be questioned. So when a meeting is called to plan a leaflet for a demonstration, inevitably there will have to be a lot of discussion not only on what the leaflet should say, but why there ought to be a leaflet in the first place, and beyond that, why there even needs to be the demonstration. It drives sheerly action-oriented people crazy.

Several times I've seen people at SDS meetings freak out. They rise after the first hour or so and scream out something like "Political power grows from the barrel of a gun!" or "Fucking bureaucrats!" and stomp out. A radical from a rival group was sitting in on an SDS meeting being held in a Columbia classroom last year. He kept talking to the people sitting around him at the back of the room and the chairman kept asking him to be quiet. Finally, after about the fourth scolding, the visitor shouted back, "What the hell's the matter with talking in the back of a classroom, anyway? That's what the backs of classrooms are for."

Another problem that builds a great deal of impatience at SDS meetings is the bickering that goes on between established factions. Compounding that, there are a number of amazingly persistent little political sects that prey off of the big SDS beast. They constantly turn out for major meetings and conferences, droning the same speeches about their programs. But they do it in an argumentative way, attacking the political suppositions of the group at large. So then the others attack the small sects back and much of the business that was to be accomplished gets lost. Newcomers to SDS who happen to be unfortunate enough to get trapped in the midst of that kind of meeting get totally lost in the arguing. Since both sides know very well what the other is going to say before they say it, basics are rarely even brought out. Even if the novice is sharp enough to catch any sense of what's being debated, he still can't see why in the world it's important enough to be getting so much attention. And he's probably right. A great many people on every campus will say they were once interested in SDS and went to a meeting or two, but couldn't understand or relate to a thing and so gave up on SDS. A standing joke is that the biggest political group on campus is made up of ex-SDSers. Most SDSers know it's happening and they'd very much like to cut it out, but somehow it keeps going on. It could get so bad eventually that the parasites kill their host.

Knowing that the discussion is bound to be drawn out, and hoping to miss out on the useless preliminaries, many SDSers try to show up at meetings about an hour late. The result is that the meetings don't begin at all until about an hour after they were called for, and everybody ends up sitting through the whole thing anyway. Time and again when one meeting decides to call another, someone will make a speech saying, "Next time we've just got to get here on time and get done on time." Everyone will agree—and everyone will come late.

The fluctuations between almost euphoric optimism and paranoid discouragement that accompany building a revolution are reflected in the way an SDS chapter puts together a plan of action, and then slowly dismantles it in the face of real conditions.

The Columbia chapter last fall actually scheduled a forum on the Middle East for Monday night, a rally to protest the appearance on campus of an Israeli defense minister on Wednesday, a confrontation with the university president for Thursday afternoon, a mass meeting for Thursday night, and then a big area-wide conference for both days of the weekend. The forum and rally were held and were quite successful, but members were so exhausted from the organizing for those two events that the confrontation with the president and the mass meeting had to be scratched. The area conference would have been put off too except that other chapters had already been organizing for it and there was no way to get out of it.

SDS meetings are completely open to the public, with the exception of the press—"pig journalists." Contrary to the impression that has grown up as a result of the secretiveness of underground groups like the Weathermen, SDS is a totally open organization. It has to be in order to organize millions of students. While terrorists can function with only a few people no one knows, organizations that still believe it takes masses of people to get something accomplished try to make themselves as accessible as possible.

The result is that a lot of police are quite able, provided they bother to change into civilian clothes, to attend SDS meetings. And they apparently do. An SDSer from California who was on trial for charges stemming from a demonstration flew east to Chicago one weekend for a NIC meeting. He was amazed in court the day after he got back when a policeman repeated to him everything he'd told the NIC. Berkeley police know SDS leaders so well they tauntingly call to them by name in the street.

The universities themselves employ an elaborate intelligence network to keep track of the radicals. George E. Kotcher, a student at the University of Chicago, made an amazing confession last fall in the school newspaper about the cushy set-up he'd had going for him as a spy on SDS.

The university's office of public information hired him to attend SDS meetings, and in addition, to occasionally change the displays in a case in the administration building. He had to write up reports on each meeting and give a total of nineteen different copies of each account to the administration the day after each meeting. Later, the vice president of public affairs for the university quizzed him orally on the meetings to find out specifically which students made which statements. Once in a while the campus police would ask him to identify various students in pictures they had secretly taken at demonstrations.

He always sat near the door and never said anything. Eventually one of the SDSers got suspicious and, using her own intelligence sources, found out what Kotcher was up to. When she confronted him with being a spy, he denied it. But he later had a change of heart and admitted it. He then told the office of public information that he wasn't going to attend any more meetings. At first, perhaps to try to change his mind, the office upped his pay from $500 a month to $600, but he remained firm in his resolve and after a month of getting no more meeting reports, they fired him. When he publically confessed the set-up, the university public relations men were understandably embarrassed. At first they tried to explain George away as just part of the healthy interest the university takes in its students. "We wish we had the manpower to send our people to all the meetings that go on at the university," a spokesman stated. But in the end they made no real attempt to deny that George had been their spy.

No one especially worries about such visitors at SDS meetings. No hot information is going to come the way of a police or
university agent who "infiltrates" SDS meetings, though they will
get quite an education in radical political theory if they pay
attention. When SDSers plan a demonstration there's no way to
keep it a secret and bring out enough people to have it be a
success. So the assumption is you might as well be open all the
way.

There is a great danger, however, in falling prey to the police
provocateur. The oldest and most reliable police tactic for attacking groups, be they of students or striking workers, is to plant an
undercover cop in their midst. At a crucial moment the make-
believe student dips into his knapsack and starts heaving rocks or
bottles. His colleagues in uniform retaliate by swarming down on
the group, breaking heads and making arrests. SDS demonstrations
now are tightly controlled affairs in which the marchers stay with
others from their regions so that marshals will be able to isolate
any strangers who might need to be watched. Everyone links arms
so that no one is especially free to heave anything (though that
does put a crimp on militant fist raising). And everyone is made
well aware of the possibility that a provocateur might invade their
midst and that they should just leave him to the SDS marshals if
one turns up.

For most of the 1969-70 school year, a thin, jumpy guy who
said his name was Tommy toured upstate New York campuses
claiming he was an SDS regional traveler. SDSers, who know their
organization pretty well, had never heard of the guy and immediately assumed he was a cop. But a few non-SDSers weren't so wise
to the old trick. At tiny Hobart College in Geneva, he apparently
trained two freshmen in the use of army rifles and the making of
firebombs, then had them arrested after the ROTC office, which
was located in a dormitory, was firebombed at night. His boss,
Ontario County Sheriff Ray Morrow, said it was perfectly proper
for a police agent to teach people such things. When the story hit
the newspapers, students at other schools began to report that
they too knew Tommy: he'd slugged a dean earlier at Hobart,
tried to push bombings at Cornell and Syracuse, and led a few
march contingents in Washington. The sheriff would never reveal
where he found "Tommy the Traveler" other than to say, "He
came to us highly recommended."

Within SDS, the political objections to terrorism and indi-

vidual acts of violence are very clearly set out. You don't horrify
people you are trying to win to your politics. You educate them.
When someone comes along with the other approach, he is immediately presumed to be a cop without any other evidence. SDS
threw a long-haired insurgent member out of its most recent
convention after members from Boston reported he had been
preaching bombings. As one girl told the assembly: "We're 95 per
cent certain he's a cop, but even if he isn't one, he's doing the
work of cops by pushing that shit. Either way, we don't want him
around." The convention agreed wholeheartedly.

    SDS sells national memberships chiefly as one means of
raising money, but hardly anyone other than police infiltrators
bothers to buy them (though many do lay their money down in
order to have voting privileges at conventions). It's almost impossible to estimate the real size of the organization other than in
terms of the number of chapters since such a great bulk of the
people who make up SDS' numerical strength exist more or less on
the periphery of the central chapter groups. Before SDS split,
estimates were that about 35,000 students were working with SDS
chapters. National conventions in the past few years have usually
brought out about 1,000 people, with the bulk of most chapter
followings not showing up.
    Raising enough money to pay the phone bills and keep
printing literature is a chronic problem in SDS. Unfortunately for
the radicals, they do not get the subsidies from insidious foreign
powers that right-wingers always claim they do. For the most part
they are dependent on scraping up money themselves—and from
their parents. It's a common joke in the organization that members, especially those from well-to-do homes, pass their parents'
generosity along to SDS, though that's hardly where the folks at
home would like the money to be going. "I used to feel really
guilty about taking bread from my family," says an SDSer who's
the daughter of a New York millionaire. "Then I started giving it
to SDS and now it feels great." And another SDSer roars about
her father's suspicion that SDS gets its money from Moscow.
"Little does he know we get it from him."
    The SDSers give almost all of their own money to the
organization as well. It comes down to the old question of
whether or not you believe in the political goals of the group. If

you do, you've got to do everything you can to accomplish them. Very often that means cleaning out your pockets of the small amount of money you've got left from part-time jobs or parental stipends. Hats are constantly being passed at meetings. Al Furst, an SDSer at Boston University, even wrote a song about it:

"You can't run a car without gasoline/ You can't clean a brush without kerosene./ You can't hit a ball without swinging a bat/ And you can't beat the bosses without passing the hat.

"Have you heard the news?/ We aren't fighting to lose./ Sometimes it's bail; sometimes it's lit./ But you can't get either without cash for it."

When the real money crises hit because the phone company has cut off service to the national headquarters or because the politically sympathetic printer of *New Left Notes* in New York has finally frozen SDS' credit, the young revolutionaries are forced into momentary binges of capitalism. SDSers hold cake sales, peddling homemade baked goods inscribed with political slogans; "Smash Racism" cupcakes usually go well. Members sell blood for $15 or so a pint. They hold used book sales, and rent old movies to show on campus. (John Wayne's *The Green Berets* really packs them in. The college audiences love to root for the North Vietnamese.)

There are fund raising picnics and parties. Someone drives out to the country and negotiates with a poultry farmer for a cut-rate load of chicken parts (they're often the wrong parts) and then everyone turns out for food and political games, and they pay a dollar or two for admission. A great game of socialist football was underway at a Boston-area fund raising picnic last summer. The "Workers" were leading the "Bosses" 12-0, but the game broke up when someone ran into one of the huddles to announce that some people from the Student Mobilization Committee had attacked an SDS officer at a meeting. The huddle turned from pass patterns to "smashing the Trots."

Left optimism often gets in the way of the radicals' efforts at capitalism, though. There is a distinct tendency to overestimate the size of the market and bake far too many cakes or buy a few too many cases of chicken. Many a fund raising affair has had to be bailed out by another fund raising affair. Such failures aren't really terrible embarrassments. As one of the SDSers pointed out to a disappointed "lunch committee" that was trying to auction off about thirty pounds of leftover baloney and cheese: "Don't be ashamed at what you have to go through to get money for the movement. One of the Bolsheviks actually married some wealthy old dowager to get her money for the Party. And Stalin robbed banks."

Rich liberals used to give a lot of money to SDS but none do any more. A steelworker who'd been reading SDS literature available at a bookstore in Baltimore died last year and made SDS his beneficiary in a will. He'd been telling his friends about the great idea SDS had to get students and workers together in an alliance against the politicians and the corporations. There was only about a thousand dollars involved, but the family contested the will and SDS never got the money.

SDS' famous name is kind of a mixed blessing. It is still the only student organization that has ever done much to really organize big radical campaigns. Students still arrive at college and seek SDS out. But the politics of the organization have changed so completely in the past few years, and the group so totally disagrees with the Weathermen, who are still called "an SDS faction" in the press, that there is a feeling among members everywhere that when they say they're from SDS they have to add: "But we're not what you think we are."

And although the name may mean the rebellious students of a new order to many adults, on campus it has begun to seem a bit dowdy. After more than ten years of existence, not even SDS has been sacrosanct from the demand for newness. No other organization even threatens to replace SDS in organizing students, but its age, combined with its rediscovery of classical Marxist doctrine, have already given the organization an old-hat image.

SDS's difficulties vary from campus to campus and from area to area—as do the kinds of projects SDS takes on. In the South, particularly around New Orleans, SDS has virtually no freedom to function at all. The organization is banned from selling literature, having demonstrations or even calling meetings under its own name. None of the prohibitions are constitutional, but as far as SDS is concerned, neither is most of the rest of what the government is up to in this country. And SDS is reluctant to make a big fight in the courts around the violation of its civil liberties because it's a basic radical assumption (which some accuse the Panthers of forgetting) that radicals should not allow themselves to be diverted into fighting in the government's courts instead of "the people's streets."

SDS in New Orleans, however, took on a campaign in Bourbon Street that most chapters in the organization would never have approached. In a big "clean-up" campaign in the French Quarter, the New Orleans police began harassing and rounding up anyone with long hair or jeans and a great many homosexuals for whom the Quarter was once a mecca. SDSers called it "repression" and helped organize a coalition of groups to picket the street. They hoped to dry business up until the hard hit bar owners told the cops to call off the round-up. The campaign was partially successful, but most SDSers elsewhere in the country ridiculed it as a "degenerate" struggle that wouldn't do a thing to build revolution, fight racism, capitalism, imperialism, or help the working class. What was significant about the French Quarter effort was that the local SDSers disagreed and followed their own politics.

While some cities, and a lot of schools, are cracking down heavily on SDS, the organization is actually being given nominal official support on other campuses. A great many SDS chapters, along with other student groups, have university space and local phone service provided for them by the universities. Most schools freely grant the organization space to hold meetings though they all shun SDS conventions, and a few even give free duplicating services for SDS literature. It can be an awkward situation for both parties. When things heat up, the administrations often end up kicking SDS off campus anyway. And it's a little embarrassing for the radicals to be taking any kind of dole so "charitably" extended by the enemy.

It's easier on the radicals' consciences when the schools put up a little interference and SDS can resort to connivance to get by. At Berkeley, when the organization was banned from campus, a new organization called the Campus Arts Troupe, otherwise known as CAT, suddenly sprang up and served as an inadequate but helpful SDS front for a while. And at Columbia, when SDS learned that free auditorium use was given to campus religious groups, several members quickly organized the League of Militant Atheists. The League's organizers told the people in charge that they were "close to SDS." They didn't tell them that a group with the same name had been founded in Russia many years ago by a man named Lenin.

CHAPTER TEN

"JOIN US!"

It must have made chilling reading for the parents of Columbia College's 1970 freshman class. Along with the deluge of enthusiastic mail their sons were getting about their new college careers came a welcoming communique from SDS.

First there were the official letters notifying the new collegians of registration procedures, dorm assignments and some pep talking about the enriching experience ahead of them. Then there was the recruiting literature: not quite defunct fraternities trying to present a confident front, advising the youths to drop by for some beer and talk when they got to campus. A few student activities describing how much fun they are to work on. The various religious denominations sounding youthful in select mailings to their own brood about worship services and social activities.

And right at the tail end of the flood, just before the freshmen set out for school, came the letter to the in-coming class from the Columbia-Barnard Chapter of Students for a Democratic Society. It didn't say so, but the mailing had been made possible through the efforts of a friend of SDS who worked in the dean's office and was good enough to steal a roll of pre-addressed labels ready for mailing to all the freshmen.

Fellow student,
Welcome to Columbia. This letter is to tell you about SDS and to clarify some of the misconceptions

you might have about us . . .

We reject the notion that Columbia is a "value-free institution," an ivory tower dedicated to the pursuit of pure knowledge. Columbia is not isolated from the system; it is, in every way, a pillar of this society. The trustees of Columbia, who have ultimate say in all of its affairs, have an average yearly income of between $75,000 and $100,000. Most sit on the boards of directors of some of the largest corporations in the country and the world (IBM, Lockheed Aircraft, Consolidated Edison, Irving Trust Company, etc.). They include luminaries like:

William Burden—head of the famed Institute for Defense Analysis

Percy Uris—one of the largest real estate magnates in New York

Lawrence Walsh—second to Henry Cabot Lodge at the Paris "peace" talks

Frank Hogan—District Attorney for the county of New York and the man . . . who framed up the New York Panther 21.

Columbia serves its patriotic duty (and coincidentally the interests of its trustees) in:

1. Training diplomats and CIA operatives in the School of International Affairs.

2. Teaching counterinsurgency courses in the Southern Asian Institute (especially handy for use in Vietnam).

3. The Business School (future corporate executives of America).

4. Millions of dollars worth of defense contracts (in particular, through its ties to the Riverside Research Institute).

There is an added dimension to all this. Columbia is the second largest real estate holder in New York (the Catholic Church is the largest). Over the last few years Columbia has evicted thousands of families from their homes to make room for its expansion. This expansion has taken place mostly in black and Latin working class communities where Columbia, the slumlord, owns most of the buildings. This is racism in practice.

Now the question arises: how does SDS feel that the situation can be changed? First of all, we do not believe in isolated acts of terror or bombings as perpetrated by so-called "radical" groups like the Weathermen. Such acts are apolitical. We do believe in MASS action, organized with a clear political direction, around concrete issues and demands, involving large numbers of students in struggle. Adventurism does not build a movement. Mass political struggle with a long-range, serious perspective can and will succeed.

When you come to Columbia, you will sense a kind of assembly-line atmosphere. You will find that large numbers of students have feelings of frustration and alienation. You will note that the vast majority of Columbia students are into drugs as a hoped-for means of dealing with this alienation. You may discover that Columbia doesn't give a damn if every student sits and rots in his dorm for the whole year, disillusioned and alienated.

We are trying to broaden the base of our organization by offering people an alternative; a concrete political means for dealing with alienation by uniting students around a common goal of fighting the war and racism. We see all oppression and alienation, be it in Vietnam, the ghettos or the college campuses, tied in some way to the same source. We hope you will join with us and we are looking forward to rapping with you during Freshman Week.

Sincerely and in solidarity,

Columbia-Barnard
Students for a Democratic Society

The chapter was indeed looking forward to Freshman Week. For several weeks members who'd been around during the summer or who came back early to make sure things got started right had been planning a "counter-orientation" to introduce the university to the new arrivals giving a radical perspective. As soon as the university published its schedule of Freshman Week activities, SDS made up its own version. Columbia was running "tours of the university." So SDS made up its own itinerary for a "counter-tour." The same was done to match the official "community" tours. SDS would leaflet the "Kings Crown Activities Night" condemning the traditionally rampant vulgarity and male chauvinism of the men's assembly—then hold a discussion afterward.

All the while members would be leafleting and canvassing the dorm rooms to get everyone out for the first chapter meeting of the new year—which would be held the next week when the upper classmen would have arrived as well. But the freshmen were the key. A good number of them would have to be recruited into the organization if SDS was going to present a real threat that year to Columbia. The press had been full of speculative articles on how the students, inspired with the previous spring's nationwide strike, were heading back to school ready to tear the campuses apart. SDSers hoped to make good on those fears.

It's remarkable how many freshman come to colleges nowadays ready to shut them down. While SDS is no longer very active in the high schools, students are often veterans of radical politics by the eleventh grade and itch to get to college where their organizing won't be on quite so make-believe a basis. Many come looking for SDS. Others have to be reached out to and drawn in. SDS' campus tour made contact with more than two dozen of them.

Almost every freshman got one of the brilliant gold leaflets with SDS' version of a map of the campus. "See the university exposed in all its naked shame," members joked as they handed out their maps of the "REAL" Columbia. Highlighted were Barnard, "Where they teach you how to marry a rich doctor"; Low Library, with a dollar-sign dome and majestic steps, "scene of '68 bust, vicious and bloody"; the School of International Affairs, "where they teach you how to put down peoples' liberation struggles"; and Riverside Research Institute, "your friendly neighborhood bomb maker."

The group left the sundial right on time at 11 A.M. The freshmen arrived early, and the tour guides, Neil Mullin and Ed Connelly, found the group waiting at the sundial. Rather than risk losing them, they moved right out. A number of other SDSers, who felt like coming along, and a few more freshmen, who were already radicals in terms of their punctuality, were left behind.

They mounted the steps of Low, pausing momentarily to view the patched-up side of the Alma Mater statue which had been bombed by a "symbolism freak" near the end of the spring strike. "That's the sum total of what terrorism will get you," Neil lectured. "The press tells you we're the Weathermen, but we aren't. We want to get people together to do a lot more than that kind of shit." Inside Low, standing in front of the gold-inscribed Trustees' room, Ed began a long ironic rap on the lessons of the 1968 rebellion:

"It was a telling experience for us that stripped away the facades that exist around here. All the liberalism and atmosphere of open intellectual inquiry were gone when the community rose up with the students and the racist university called in the pigs. We stayed up there in the president's office for a few days. We sampled his sherry and his cigars and we found them to be second-rate. And we went to browse throught all those impressive foreign books he had on his walls, but their pages weren't even cut.

"Since then we've learned to see beyond the facades these guys put up. We've learned that they are the founders of the fine art of obfuscation. They have their public relations firms and their ad firms. And we have to really get our heads together to know that they're trying to give us a life of controlled psychology with all these 'positive and negative reinforcements.' We've got to shut all that shit out and go for what we know is right. We have to realize that what they keep sending down is just trying to fuck up our minds.

"The guys who run this place have one major concern and that's profits. You're part of their long-term investment program. This place is supposed to supply them with the manpower they need to keep running their corporations and their government and their army. If you graduate you'll find that they'll be pushing you into one of those places. But of course you could do something more relevant, like not graduating and spending your time in political work. But you have to realize that they channel people the way they want and if you aren't going to be a boss, they're going to make you pay the price. They'll screw you like they screw all their other workers."

After Ed finished, the group headed back down the steps of Low to take a look at the Graduate School of Business Administration. As they rounded the corner of Low, the image of Columbia's new president appeared behind the rippled surface of his

Plexiglas, rock-proof office window. "That's our new boss, fighting Bill McGill," Neil pointed out. President McGill gave the group a little wave. And one of the freshman responded by shooting up a clenched fist. As far as SDS was concerned, the new class looked like a pretty good young crop.

Freshman Week is an intensive period of recruiting for SDS, but unlike the fraternities that go hunting for new blood only during rush season, SDS is always trying to expand its membership. In fact, virtually everything the organization does is supposed to be aimed at bringing its politics to more people, thereby winning them into the common struggle. The radicals call it "base building." And they use a great many techniques. What distinguishes the people who are left in SDS from the Weathermen who broke away is that SDS tries to get as many people as possible to participate in its demonstrations while the Weathermen, while they welcome support, are necessarily furtive and alone in their terrorism.

The Weathermen don't leaflet. You can't from the "underground." But SDS around the country must give out several hundred thousand leaflets every month. At Columbia alone, where the chapter was actually trying to go a little light on leafleting last year, about one hundred reams of paper were stashed in the SDS office at the beginning of the first semester. That's half a million sheets of paper. In a month the supply had nearly been depleted. SDSers gathered in Chicago for a national convention and distributed a quarter of a million leaflets around the city building for a demonstration to fight unemployment which was hitting the highest level in a decade.

The incessant leafleting apparently wears down the patience of the enemy while it gets SDS' politics out and brings new people in. Retiring Harvard President Nathan Pusey, who battled one of the strongest SDS chapters in the country, actually complained in his 1970 commencement address about the "scores of SDS leaflets to which we—all of us at Harvard—have been continuously subjected." The radicals laughed and said "no one told him he had to read them." But it was appropriate of Pusey to institutionalize the SDS leaflet; it has become one of the eternal verities of life at the universities.

Almost nothing better illustrates the radicals' indefatigable campaign to break out of isolation than their constant leafleting. The SDSer stands for hours on campus or downtown or out in front of a big factory. He's trying to hand out pieces of literature that somehow express the driving force in his life. He wants desperately to reach the thousands of people pouring past him because he knows he needs them to achieve his goals. Not many of them have any regard for his fervor, though, and all too few are curious about what he wants them to know. But a few do go out of their way to take the leaflets and read them. It's fascinating to compare the varying attitudes toward political proselytizers that are shown by students as opposed to industrial workers and ghetto residents. Almost invariably SDSers find that workers, even if they are bustling into their plants, are a lot more interested in the radical literature than the radicals' fellow students. And when a group of SDSers went to Philadelphia last summer for a Black Panther gathering, they found ghetto blacks actually stopping them in the streets and asking for literature.

If an SDSer has to give out a thousand leaflets to bring one person very tentatively into contact with the organization or to a demonstration, that isn't considered too bad a percentage. It can always be said that the ones who don't come around might still have been interested enough in that leaflet to read a little further and even stop and talk for a while the next time. Some people do read the leaflets, and a few actually agree enough to join in whatever action the leaflets recommend. And that small accomplishment, as far as the committed radicals are concerned, more than justifies the hours of effort involved.

There are some techniques that help make leafleting more effective. One is to have a small rally going on in a conspicuous place and hand out literature to the people passing by. They usually won't stop to see what's happening, but their curiosity will often be aroused enough to read the literature to see what it is they're missing. Extremely aggressive leafleters get their ideas out by walking along beside a person while they are handing him the leaflet—giving a quick but hopefully arousing explanation of what it is the radicals are organizing for and why it's important for the recipient to come along.

For big conferences or demonstrations, SDS usually prints up thousands of posters along with the usual cases of leaflets. Walk around the business areas that surround almost any campus and you'll see tattered peelings of bygone posters which will make up something of a history of recent political activity. A problem is that postering on the brick walls of stores and granite university buildings and the sides of mailboxes and bus stop shelters is considered illegal defacing of public or private property. Such laws are rarely enforced against workers for campaigning politicians, but the police come down quite hard on the radicals for postering.

So the radicals have perfected a pretty effective clandestine technique for getting their broadsides up. Small cadres of three or four SDSers fan out into assigned regions very late at night, each group equipped with a bucket full of paste and dozens of the posters. They'll either stroll along the sidewalk casually or drive slowly in a car. They decide on a spot that's going to be seen by a lot of people in succeeding days but probably is not under police scrutiny right at that moment, and the group hauls up. One or two look out while the others smear paste with their hands onto the surface, slap the poster onto it, and then cover the front with paste to solidify the bond. A good group can get a poster up in only a few seconds—hardly breaking stride really. Still there are the excruciating times when the police swoop up suddenly (in Boston in particular the police are coy enough lately to hang back until they've got the posterers caught sticky-handed and then come down on them) and a getaway is impossible.

Many times the police have ordered radicals to bring the poster over to the cruiser so they can try to decide if its politics are threatening enough to warrant arresting the SDSers. In a great many cases the initials "SDS" alone are enough to bring on the dreaded order: "Get in!"

The most disheartening thing about postering is the fleeting life an SDS poster usually has on a wall. They stand up to the weather fine, but somehow by the middle of the next day, a great many of the posters are already torn down. Sometimes the store owners send workers out to peel them off until they can't be read, and sometimes it's done by "reactionaries" passing by. Distressingly often, members of rival groups tear them down or cover them over with their own posters. (Special "posting areas" in Berkeley often get five new layers overnight.) But optimism usually accompanies such opposition too. When SDS was organizing for a big national demonstration in Detroit last election day to support the General Motors workers who were out on strike, members plastered the whole city with stickers and posters. An amazing number of the posters immediately disappeared. "We can't keep a poster up around here for five minutes," one of the organizers told a group proudly. "The ruling class is scared to death of us."

Virtually every radical organization that is trying to build a movement publishes its own newspaper and pours a tremendous amount of manpower into selling it. The idea is not to raise money since most of the organizations barely break even on the cost of their paper. The purpose is to get the group's politics out and, by reporting the events which seem especially significant of the organization's program, to show people how immediate the radical strategy really is to their everyday lives. For the Black Panthers that means putting a great deal of emphasis on the brutal activities of the police in the ghettos. For Progressive Labor it has meant a constant report of rank and file militancy in both wildcats and union sanctioned strikes. And for SDS, through its *New Left Notes,* it means tying student campaigns in with the fights being waged by workers and blacks against the corporations, racism and imperialism.

In trying to sell the papers, the radicals get a chance to talk at some length to the people they are approaching, and that often means facing head-on the aspects of "bourgeois" life they have come to abhor.

Like drug crazed hippies. Really committed leftists condemn lives centered around drugs even more vehemently than the staunchest advocates of getting ahead in the system. The chemical euphoria of marijuana or LSD or heroin saps the political bitterness that's produced by the evils of the system. And you need that bitterness, the radicals know, in order to fight. A great many excellent organizers have been lost to the Left in recent years because of drugs. They seem to tire of the fight once they fall heavily into the "better living through chemistry" approach.

There are, to be sure, a goodly number of SDSers who smoke pot and perhaps even tinker with hallucinogens. It would be impossible to build a movement of college students these days without having some participants who use drugs. But the "dope blowers" worry the rest of the members. They can be busted for their drugs and have the political cause discredited (though many radicals who deplore drugs have been framed by the police on possession or use charges anyway). And there is a strong feeling among many radicals that using drugs is really playing into the hands of the enemy. Castro and Mao banned their revolutionaries from using them. Militant blacks and Puerto Ricans have been maintaining for years that if "the Man" didn't really want people pacified on heroin in the ghettos, the police would actually clean out the pushers instead of ignoring them. White radicals are convinced that whatever rhetoric might come from President Nixon and the rest about the dangers of drugs, the guys in charge would much rather have the students stoned than stoning. "Cultural" revolutions of the sort described by Charles Reich in *The Greening of America* are a cheap excuse for the real thing, the radicals say.

With the possible exception of rock festivals, there isn't another place in the U.S. where a greater percentage of the people are likely to be high on drugs than at the Bethesda Fountain in New York's Central Park on a sunny summer weekend. Bracing themselves for certain attack, several SDSers trudged into that frenetic scene last summer with piles of *New Left Notes* slung over their arms. For one of the SDSers it was like going home. He'd been, by his own description, "totally freaked out on drugs" until he gave them up after coming to SDS.

He walked over to two high school age girls who were lying on their backs under a tree staring up at the light show of the sky as it blinked through the leaves.

"Want to buy the latest issue of *New Left Notes*, the SDS newspaper?"

One of the girls didn't even seem to hear. The other just said, "Nah."

"Why not?"

"I just don't."

"Have you ever seen it?"

"Yeah."

"What'd you think of it?"

"I dunno. I'm not interested in politics."

"What are you interested in?"

The other girl giggled.

"Getting stoned and getting laid."

"Listen. Don't you care about what happens to other people? There are millions of workers and women and blacks and Latins who are totally miserable because of the way the system is grinding them up. Don't you care about them?"

"Nah."

One of the other SDSers was hitting the crowd sitting around the rim of the fountain. He walked up to a guy who was sitting with a woman wearing a see-through pants suit and no underwear.

"*New Left Notes*, the SDS newspaper. Seen it?"

The guy smiles and declares, "I'm against everything that's in that newspaper."

"Are you against fighting the oppression of women? There's an article in here about that."

"Women aren't oppressed," he says. He puts his arm behind the woman's back and reaches around to fondle her breast. "You're not oppressed, are you, baby?"

She smiles at him and says, "No, honey."

SDS and other groups have to go through all this leafleting and postering and newspaper peddling to counter what the population reads in the regular press. The radicals say all those newspapers are owned by and printed for the establishment. They have absolutely no trust in such publications because they are the mouthpieces of the enemy. And while SDS will, on occasion, issue a press release or hold a press conference, the organization makes a policy of throwing the press out of its meetings. It exults in doing so too. It is a rare opportunity to directly rebuff a representative of "the bosses."

There is good reason to throw out the supposedly impartial newsmen. Over the protests of a number of rank and file reporters, the heads of the various major news media organizations in the past few years have co-operated with the government when it was investigating or prosecuting radicals. The *New York Times*, which has grumbled about being thrown out of SDS meetings, brought on much of the radical resistance in the late Sixties when it had one of its reporters testifying before a House subcommittee about what he saw and heard at an SDS meeting he was allowed into.

The "reluctant" witness, Anthony Ripley, acknowledged to the committee that his testimony was going to make it more difficult for him "to cover the radical community." He was right. No *Times* man has been allowed into an SDS meeting since.

For the most part the news media has complained bitterly, both orally and in print, about being shunned by the radicals. After growing used to being wooed by publicity seekers, it hurts to find a group that doesn't want to have anything to do with you. But Eric Wentworth, a writer for the *Washington Post*, wrote an unusual column when SDS made its first official move against the "capitalist press" by barring reporters from the convention in 1969. Such ostracism, he said, struck most of the newsmen who were forced to hang around outside the hall as smacking of "silly naivete, acute paranoia or incipient facism." But he said journalists who gave the radicals' position some thought while they cooled their heels outside the convention hall "had to concede the radicals had a point or two."

The Public's-Right-To-Know argument, which newsmen usually employ to coerce balky sources, is ignored when Congressional committees and "august finance" powers often meet behind closed doors. And Wentworth admitted there was "serious question" whether supposedly objective reporters should play active roles in the political process by appearing before Congressional committees—even under subpoena. He said he observed a number of his colleagues proving the radicals' claims that the press would distort or misconstrue everything. "It was disheartening," he admitted in print, "to overhear a television newsman outside the Coliseum summarizing before camera and microphone what had been transpiring inside with an air of authority but, alas, with astonishing lapses in accuracy."

SDSers avidly read the press they refuse to co-operate with, of course. Most of the news revealing the latest scandal on judicial corruption or the internecine political maneuverings of the two major parties strike the radicals as being tediously irrelevant to what's really important in the country. But if they ignore what the power structure is pushing, they won't be able to deal with the information that's being devoured by others who believe things in the press.

SDS at Berkeley became so incensed with the right-wing slant that radical news was getting from ex-Senator William Knowland's *Oakland Tribune* that the chapter decided to plan a campaign of demonstrations against the paper. The *Tribune* sent a reporter to the meeting who actually spoke up and told the radicals they were right: the editors of the paper did consistently rewrite the reporters' accounts of radical activities to paint them in an unfavorable light. He gave them a casebook of clippings which showed that. SDS later found out that an undercover policeman who had been at the meeting reported the newsman to his editor and the guy was fired.

My own personal experiences working for the establishment press coincide with the radical appraisal, I should add. Proud declarations about objectivity that publishers make are very often forgotten when the reporters' facts seem to threaten the politics of the publication. A great many newsmen, including those with quite conservative views, complain that there's almost nowhere they can work and be certain that all the truths they report will be printed without interference from their editors or from higher up.

SDS does find a lot of truth in the media, however—mostly in advertisements. Every once in a while something hits print that so baldly seems to reveal what the radicals think is going on in the American system that they can hardly believe it's being so pompously displayed.

Everything SDS had been saying about American business gaining control of the rest of the world seemed summed up in an advertisement one SDSer spotted in *Fortune* magazine:

WHEN YOU NEED SOMETHING MORE DIPLOMATIC THAN A GUNBOAT

Times have changed. Empire builders can't shoot their way to success as they did in the bad old days. But there's nothing to regret about the passing of gunboat diplomacy: it was costly, it was risky—and in the long run it was ineffective. Today's way, the diplomatic way, is infinitely more efficient—but it depends on *inside* knowledge. That's why you'll do well to choose Chemical Bank as your international business partner.

We know the people who count in the places that

matter in more than 145 countries; their first hand advice together with our experience of international finance will help you establish yourself—diplomatically and decisively—in any of the world's markets.

And an SDSer who was flying youth-fare home from a planning meeting couldn't get over the ad he found in a flight magazine. It was far franker about admitting that America has a "ruling class" than any literature SDS had dared put out:

THE NEW ARISTOCRACY
There is a new aristocracy in America.

Its peers are plainly titled, like the barons, viscounts, earls, marquesses and dukes of old.

If you are a vice president, you are an earl. You are halfway to the top of the greasy pole. And if you are the president, you are there. You are a duke.

Your castle is the corporation. Your code is hard work. Your plague is ulcers.

You are the most powerful aristocracy in history. You decide what two hundred million people will eat, ride in, wear, laugh at, live for.

But you have never learned how to live. You treat yourselves like a corps of messenger boys. You wake yourselves, shave yourselves, shine your own shoes, lug your own luggage, then rent strange cars in strange cities and become your own chauffeurs. You indulge only one of life's joys: a vodka martini on the rocks, and that bolted down on the run.

We hereby suggest that you shed your hair shirts.

Who are we? The Carey Corporation. We operate chauffeur-driven cars in 12 cities.

Almost nothing aggravates the radicals more than to have the establishment media co-opt their very language. The media is rife with debasement of revolution. The Left no sooner coins a phrase than Madison Avenue rips it off for its own use. They have the nerve to declare, "It's revolutionary!" and then go on to talk about the latest washday miracle (perhaps the miracle people

resent that one too). President Nixon commited the most out-
rageous appropriation of radical rhetoric in his 1971 State of the
Union Address when he appropriated the Panthers' call for "Power
to the People."

Demonstrations themselves, while still aimed at displaying
enough power and militancy to win demands, have increasingly
become another means of reaching out with a political line.
SDSers chant "JOIN US! JOIN US!" to the people on the side-
lines. They approach demonstrations much more, lately, as "consciousness raising" efforts. As the peace movement has proven,
people tire of repeated demonstrations that don't bring them
awareness of more advanced politics and don't bring results.
SDS organizers hope that by keeping the politics of their demonstrations advanced and the spirit high, they will be able to sustain
the momentum it takes to keep going with that form of protest.
Everyone knows it's going to be difficult, but no one has any idea
what could ever replace the demonstration as a means of mobilizing people.

SDS and other groups have come up with a welcome method
of preaching their politics without bearing down too heavily on
the assembled group with the usual speeches. It's called guerrilla
theater.

Abbie Hoffman and Jerry Rubin's Yippies really developed
the idea, but their approach is a lot more guerrilla and a lot less
theater than the way SDS does it. There are SDS Radical Arts
Troupes, or RATS, in most of the major cities. They put on skits
featuring characters like: General Wastemoreland; General Motors;
I. Will Twistit, the famous journalist; Trusty Trustee, the university board member; Roadblock Woodcock, the union "mis-
leader"; Henry Kissass, the international affairs expert; Rocky
Tycoon, the billionaire; Nixon; Mitchell; George McGovernment,
otherwise known as Super Senator; the workers; the students; and
the people.

The plots usually have all the government guys, tycoons and
their confederates trembling because the workers and students
have gotten together and are spoiling all the great things the boys
in power had going for them. Everyone sings songs. Rocky, Nixon

and the rest of the power structure sing the Southeast Asia Theme Song, to the tune of the Beatles' "I Want To Hold Your Hand":

    Southeast Asia's got that something big business understands.
Cheap labor, and resources on which to lay our hands,
    Invest in Vietnam, invest in Vietnam.
Invest your energy, your money and your sons
    And you'll protect all our investments
With our guns, with our guns, with our guns.

    The people answer with their own song, "U.S. Out Now," which is to the tune of the Beach Boys' "I Get Around":

    U.S. out now, don't say you don't know how.
The Paris talks are a sham. Get out of Vietnam.
    Tin and rubber and the New York banks;
You protect your investments with your rifles and tanks.
    If you really wanted Asian people to be free
Then you'd cut out all your counter-insurgency.

    Although SDS is hardly forced to concentrate on court fights as much as the Black Panthers are, the organization does occasionally find trials another good organizing device—especially when the case is such that the role of the police and the courts as protectors of the wealthy and their institutions can be made plain. Then SDSers will often decide to make a "political defense," acting as their own lawyers, mobilizing as many people as possible to come watch the trial, and getting as much ideology as possible into the testimony. It's a strategy aimed at "putting the courts on trial" and it works awfully well when the facts of the case clearly support the radicals.

    Through a weird stroke of luck, SDS had a perfect opportunity for such a trial in Cambridge in 1970, where there had been almost continual feuding between the police and the thousands of Harvard and MIT students in the city. It was a political trial stemming from a political trial. The city had been prosecuting some of the Harvard students arrested during the SDS-led strike at the school in 1969, and at one point during the trial the courtroom exploded. One of the defendants was insisting that he was being put away for political reasons. The judge kept ordering him to be quiet and the youth kept insisting that he was being persecuted. Apparently working from a prearranged strategy, the bailiffs and deputies who were spread throughout the crowded courtroom suddenly moved in on all the defendants in a melee followed. The judge ordered the courtroom cleared and the students poured out into the street chanting, "THE COURTS ARE AFRAID OF THE PEOPLE. THE COURTS ARE AFRAID OF THE TRUTH. HARVARD OWNS THE COURTS." Four more radicals were arrested outside the courtroom.

The district attorney then charged them with the usual "cover" offenses: disorderly conduct and distrubing the peace and also tacked on the very serious felony of assault and battery on a police officer. He was apparently hoping that the usual pattern would develop: the students, fearing convictions on the weighty charges, would agree to plead guilty to the misdemeanors if the felony charges were dropped. But the radicals had an ace in the hole and told the D.A. to skip the deals.

They went on trial a short while later at the same courthouse where they supposedly committed their criminal acts. The prosecution put a string of ruddy-faced police officers on the stand and they all told the same story: The students came pouring out of the courtroom, swearing and yelling, and attacked the officers who finally managed to subdue them and put them under arrest. The "defense" sat quietly through it all and then sprang its surprise. An amateur photographer who lives right across the street from the courthouse heard the chanting and went to the window with his camera. He testified he had no affiliation with any political group and never knew the defendants before—and then he gave a slide show.

One photograph after another was beamed onto a screen, showing the students not attacking the policemen but slowly walking down the street with their backs to the police, either unaware of them or unconcerned. And the police were bent forward, charging up from behind the students, and clubbing them over the heads. One series had several police gathered around one of the downed defendants, pummeling him and stomping him. It was a graphic presentation of police brutality; proof that's rarely presented in a courtroom and documentation of the commonly heard accusation that the police were "framing up" radicals.

The SDSers in the courtroom were elated with the photographic proof of the cops' lies. They cheered for the pictures and laughed at the prosecution's befuddled attempt to cope with them. The defense managed to show the slides through several times until finally, when one of the defendant-attorneys said: "We'd like to run through the slides again to point out . . ." the judge interrupted and muttered, "I think I've had enough of the slides," and the students readily supposed that he had.

With their defense sewn up, the radicals moved on to try to make a few political points. Fellow SDSers or some of the unaffiliated students who'd come down to see the first trial were put on the stand.

Defense: What was being chanted at the time of the incident?

Witness: HARVARD OWNS THE COURTS. (The audience chuckles to hear the accusation being made right there in the solemn courtroom.)

Defense: Did that slogan disturb you?

Witness: No. I think it's true.

Judge: O.K., now don't try to slip that stuff in. (The witness peers over at the judge and blinks naively.)

Defense: Tell us what happened.

Witness: Well, we're all well aware of the court's complicity in the police attacks on the people of Cambridge and Harvard and MIT students. It's well known that . . .

Judge: Enough of that.

Defense: We're just trying to establish the motive behind . . .

Judge: I know what you're trying to do.

Defense (turning back to witness): Did you see anything obscene?

Judge (heading it off): Oh, that one's obvious. The only thing obscene was the police and their brutality. (The audience roars agreement.)

Defense: Are you aware of jailings of any other members . . .

Judge: Strike that from the record.

Defense: Were these part of a systematic attack on . . .

Judge: That's excluded too.

A new witness is called. This time it's one of the other defendants.

Defense: Tell us what happened.

Witness: The students were attacked by the courts.

Judge: No philosophy! Just tell us what happened. You are bound to irritate the court, aren't you? You are not here to make speeches. The right to defend yourselves does not give you the right to come in here and give speeches.

Defense: What did the police say when they arrested you?

Witness: One of them, the one that deliberately stomped on my eyeglasses, told the others: "It's those fucking Jewish commies again. What did I tell you? It's those fucking Jewish commies again. I wish to hell Hitler were still around." Then he said he'd like to do to me what they did to the students at Kent State.

The next day the judge found them all not guilty of assaulting the police officers. The pictures had clearly disproven that. But he said he was accepting the officers' testimony about how disorderly the students had been and fined each of them $200. The defense eagerly and publicly announced it was going to appeal.

CHAPTER ELEVEN

THE POLITICS OF RADICALISM

The system that SDS has set out to smash is a weirdly complex contraption. It has many mechanisms that seem absolutely vital to its functioning but that turn out to be just decoys once they are attacked. Time after time, SDS has charged in and managed to deal one of the many parts a potent blow. But just as the radicals were exulting in the damage they had done to the mechanical colossus, it became clear the damned thing was still functioning absolutely unhampered. Sometimes it seemed to be going even stronger than before. It had never really needed that part anyway, it turned out.

In its old age SDS is learning not to just throw itself into battle every time the machine comes within range. The Left, it is now clear to SDS, has badly needed its theoreticians, for it takes someone who is almost an economic and political genius to figure out where the system is really vulnerable and how to attack it effectively. So after trying it on its own for ten years of do-your-own-thing rebellion, SDS has turned to the master dismantlers of capitalism: Marx, Lenin and Mao. The young radicals have finally embraced the demanding concept of a "long-range strategy." Each well-chosen attack now is seen not only as an attempt to slow down the machine; it must also be a "building action" towards the next assault.

More and more people should become involved with each new encounter, and the group's radical convictions should be deepened by the struggles that have come before. If the fighting mass keeps growing and becoming smarter, it will finally make a revolution as its "ultimate demonstration." And that, if successful, will smash the entire system and replace it with one that will belong to all the people, serving them instead of exploiting them.

SDS is not *officially* a revolutionary organization. It wants to be broad enough to attract people who believe in its immediate fights without necessarily accepting the final goal of replacing the entire system. But I know of only a few people who have been around the organization for any length of time who don't consider themselves revolutionaries. So while SDS has to build the forces for an attack on the system, as well as lead that attack, it now also spends a great deal of its time devising the nature of the campaign itself. The primary question is always whether a proposed struggle will lead on toward the eventual revolution or will be co-opted into the sort of change that the system touts as a "reform," and that the radicals disparage by using the same word.

"Student Power" campaigns, it's now generally conceded, are dead ends. Not much substantial redistribution of power results from uprisings against rules that keep men out of women's dorm rooms, or vice versa. The chief problem is that student power demands are easily granted with hollow concessions that convince students they have won when they haven't. After massive fights like those at Columbia in 1968 and at Harvard in 1969, the student governments are reconstituted under the pretense of "involving students in the decision-making process."

But SDS has found all that to be a hoax. The new bodies remain in the control of the administration, and the issues the radicals consider crucial—university complicity with the government and the military, the university's ruthless expansion into poor neighborhoods, the survival of programs like ROTC, the treatment of campus workers—are almost all ruled out of the newly bolstered student government's purview. On the rare occasions that such groups actually go against the desires of the trustees who really still run the universities, they are quickly and often openly overruled.

The administrations make no secret of their efforts to co-opt. To do so would be self-defeating. Instead, they loudly broadcast their supposed acts of concession in hopes that the students will revel in victory and leave the administration alone. It often works.

"Columbia U. Reform Cools Student Revolt," the *Christian Science Monitor* headlined on its front page a year after the Columbia rebellion. "Reform, the nemesis of revolution, has instituted itself at Columbia University. With the first meeting of the new 101-member university-wide senate, Columbia has progressed in one troubled year from the image of a powderkeg to a firecracker." And Marquis Childs had a column in the *Washington Post* and other papers after Harvard blew, entitled: "Harvard Hopes Restructuring Will Neutralize Radical Left. . . . Restructuring, that favorite word of the reformers, may bring a stronger institution able to hold the line against the radical Left. That is the devout hope of the loyal sons of Harvard."

The loyal sons of the revolution, for their part, are now out to attack Harvard and every other university so directly that gestures of reform will seem comical. All the while, the tug-of-war continues between the radicals and the system over the people in between. A massive campaign is being carried on by the government and industry to "reinvolve" young people. And radical groups have to keep scrambling further and further to the Left to continue providing a full-fledged *radical alternative*. As Congress was moving to give eighteen-year-olds the vote, SDS was campaigning in its literature that "elections are a hoax."

John D. Rockefeller 3rd (David's oldest brother) wrote an article in the *Reader's Digest* not long ago actually titled: "We Need Our Young Activists." It was a call for tolerating youthful idealism and channeling it into peaceful and legal efforts such as Gene McCarthy's campaign. "The nature of our response is crucial," Rockefeller warned, "for it has everything to do with whether there will continue to be violence and whether violence will pay." Clearly he would rather arrange things so that it won't. By the classical Marxist dialectical approach, what Rockefeller wanted was exactly opposite what SDS had in mind. As far as SDS was concerned, the article showed that liberal politicians like McCarthy are on the side of the millionaires.

And a month before, the *Digest* ran an excerpt from a book written by Rockefeller's colleague at the top, Henry Ford 2nd. Ford posed the choices of "starting with what we have and working from within to build something better" or "to condemn society in all its works and to seek, like today's new revolutionaries, to tear down everything in preparation for a fresh start."

Obviously Ford chose the first option, of "working from within."
But a lot of radicals were quite astounded to read his explanation
of why he didn't choose revolution: "It is not really possible." The
more revolutionary violence there is, he said, "the more vigorously
it will be repressed." If the repression was all that was holding him
back from turning his factories over to the workers, SDSers
laughed, all he had to do was tell the President to hold back the
troops.

SDS often determines its own program by reading the
"bosses' press" to find out what the power structure is up to and
then moving further the other way. The power structure watches
the radicals closely, along with the response they're getting from
their potential followers, to determine its own strategy. It ends up
quite like a cat and mouse chase, though sometimes the mouse is
too tiny to be noticed and the cat is too fat to move.

Radicals, if they are to remain radical, have got to keep their
political lead on mass opinion. Periodically, when a onetime Left
cause begins to become the fad of the rest of the population, it
scares the radicals away from it. For much of 1970, SDS gave up
on the anti-war movement because it had grown so huge and
innocuous, it didn't seem worth bothering with.

When the Great Ecology Craze hit in 1970, the contradiction
between the radical and liberal perspectives was glaring. Nixon said
the enironment was going to be a major focus of his administration. All of the big publications, many of which own polluting
paper mills, ran great spreads on the crisis in the environment.
Everyone started talking about how the ecology movement was
going to become the new fascination of student activists—and the
university administrations eagerly echoed this hope.

SDS said *"pollution means profit."* It is the capitalist system
that pollutes the environment, and it is naive to expect a government that rests on the corporations to police them and cut their
profits by cleaning pollution up. SDS wondered how someone like
Ralph Nader, who seemed to be on the people's side, could keep
revealing the atrocities of the corporations and how they were
being covered up by the government, and still keep his faith in the
system. Capitalism hates people, SDS says. When medical pressure
against the sale of cyclamate foods got so great the government
finally had to force the products off the shelves, the manufac-
turers just turned around and sold their unhealthy stocks to

Europe. And companies that are terrible polluters, Dow, Monsanto, Allied Chemical, etc., are also arrogantly making millions selling pollution control equipment.

The whole ecology craze greatly irked the radicals. The people themselves were being blamed for reproducing and technology was being cited as another villain. In San Jose, students bought a brand new car and buried it to demonstrate where the evil lies in society. SDS agreed a lot more with the blacks who held a counter-demonstration nearby, saying, "Bury the system, don't bury the car."

Progressive Labor members in SDS maintained that the whole population control idea was a "genocidal plot" to hold down the numbers of workers who could help man the revolution. The Rockefeller brothers haven't limited their own offspring: Nelson had seven, David had six, Laurence and John 3rd had four each. And John is the founder of the Population Council! Only Winthrop stopped with the prescribed two.

The environment is not the "primary issue facing Americans today," SDS says, though the press and most politicians claim it is. The primary issue is capitalism, which not only pollutes, it oppresses, exploits and murders. "Fight pollution with revolution," a group of West Coast radicals urged recently. Ecology is a perfectly good way to demonstrate what capitalism does, SDS says, but to talk about it without mentioning capitalism is bizarre. Some people try to argue back that "communist" countries like Russia have pollution problems too, but SDS has no loyalty to Russia at all—in fact, it is quite hostile to the USSR's brand of socialism and considers it virtually the same thing as capitalism. No true socialist state, SDSers answer, would kill its people with pollution to cut production costs.

At the University of Utah, the SDS chapter launched a series of demonstrations against the Kennecott Copper Corporation, the biggest corporation in the Salt Lake City area and the biggest polluter. Kennecott's smelters spew hundreds of tons of sulphur dioxide into the air daily. The company's chimneys also give off lethal doses of arsenic. The plant managers and corporate executives live high in the hills outside the city, or back in wooded areas, where the pollution doesn't reach. The workers who run the furnaces live in the valley ghettos which are often choking in the pollution. The managers wear gas masks on their visits to the copper works, but some of the men who run the smelters weren't issued them.

The University of Utah SDS campaign against Kennecott Copper may not have done much to cut pollution, but it was a clear way for the radicals to help mobilize people in the area, especially the working people who were being most victimized, against the corporate giant. And that would just be a beginning. When the copper workers went out on strike, SDS would hit Kennecott again, hopefully with more people. And if Kennecott was attacked in South America by its copper miners there, SDS could try to turn people out against the company. Pollution, workers' wages, and corporate expansion into foreign countries clearly would all eventually become part of the same fight against the same enemy, SDS hoped. In time, the group hopes, Kennecott and all the corporations will be taken over by the masses of people who want to make sure the system of production doesn't go against their own interests.

1970 was a year for new movements. Along with ecology came women's liberation, another cause SDS found worthy, though not the way it was being trumpeted in the press or by the movement's "liberal leadership." SDS was one of the first radical groups to confront the whole question of the oppression of women. In fact, a women's caucus that formed at the SDS national convention in 1967 issued a "women's manifesto" which demanded an equal role within SDS and an effort by the organization to fight what caucus members called "male chauvinism." (The phrase was apparently coined by the SDS group and has since become the standard identity for the force that oppresses women.)

A heroic, crusader atmosphere exaggerates masculine warrior pride on the Left. Women used to be allowed to exist only on the fringes of the movement. They were tolerated only as concubines and typists (roles for which they were even recruited at times). And up until the 1967 SDS convention, women were almost invisible in the leadership of SDS or any other radical organization. Certainly none of the major officers of SDS, SNCC, the Black Panthers or any other radical group had been women. The idea that women were all right as movement sex objects and suitable for the "shit work" that accumulates in an organization was prevalent even at the 1969 SDS convention, when the group that was to become the Weathermen split off.

Since then a concerted effort has been made within the new SDS to correct the situation. While SDS women still complain about internal inequities and about the organization's failure to really concentrate much attention on fighting "sexism," most SDS women who have been around Left groups say SDS has come a long way toward recognizing female leadership ability. In fact, when SDS held its most recent convention in December, 1970, a woman, Marty Riefe from Troy, New York, was elected to the top office—national secretary. And no one considered it tokenism.

The problem of fighting male chauvinism outside the organization is a lot more difficult. SDS doesn't much care about the fact that women are shut out of executive posts in business the way the National Organization of Women and other such groups do. It wouldn't be very honest for SDS to demand corporate jobs for women when SDS doesn't believe the corporations themselves should exist. And the campaign against the sexual degradation of women, especially on campus, often comes off as prudish. Some chapters have tried to get *Playboy* taken off the magazine stand in the school bookstores. At San Francisco State recently, the chapter waged a hard battle which resulted in a number of arrests when members decided to occupy the office of the school newspaper because of a series of articles it had run which were degrading to women. Some other chapters have joined in the fights for free abortions and twenty-four hour day care centers. But an ideal anti-chauvinist campaign that would link up to the long-range battle against the capitalist system hasn't come along.

SDS sees male chauvinism with the same working class perspective it views racism. Both are considered devices that "bosses" use to get away with paying their workers less. Blacks are often given only half of what whites make for doing the same work. And women are wedged into specially designed job classifications and receive lower pay than men doing similar work. Very often now, when SDSers talk about the "special oppression of women" they cite sexist pay differentials as the primary atrocities, but to some women within the organization and many radical feminists outside, that kind of "economist" approach isn't enough to explain the dehumanization of women's lives. SDS' anti-male chauvinism literature will need a lot more than bar graphs and employment statistics, they say, to prepare Americans for a socialist system in which women will be treated equal in *every* way.

With its politics sharpened, SDS now has the nagging problem of being isolated from the masses of students the organization so desperately wants to lead. But being quite convinced that any way but its own way is the wrong way, SDS can hardly ignore what it considers the truth, in order to bring more people in. The organization is now riddled with sectarianism, the reclusive tendency that plagues nearly all the Left groups, causing them to shun anyone who doesn't see things entirely their way. But the problem is being corrected. SDS leaders openly admit now that in backing off from the issue of Vietnam during 1970, they were cutting off the group from millions of students who already had the desire to oppose the American presence in Southeast Asia. But because the anti-war movement was only "dissenting" from a part of American foreign policy while SDS rejects the whole thing, SDS considered struggle against Vietnam impotent.

SDS is now tooling up to lead the fight against the U.S. presence in the Middle East just as it led the anti-Vietnam movement in the mid-Sixties. Many SDSers are quite convinced that the unspoken U.S. alliance with Israel is going to lead to "another Vietnam." SDS teach-ins on the Arab-Israeli question have already gotten underway. While there is still dissension within SDS on the whole question and not much has been said "officially" about the Middle East conflict, SDS quite clearly sides with the Arabs. Israel is considered a bridgehead of capitalism in the area, and while some of the semi-feudal Arab monarchs such as Faisal and Hussein are no better, SDS strongly supports the "Arab liberation movement" which is fighting both Israel and the Arab rulers.

It is a very volatile issue, especially at heavily Jewish campuses such as Columbia, but the SDSers have researched their arguments very carefully. Israel was founded, they say, because of the racism and anti-Semitism that was rampant throughout Europe after the Second World War. Rather than absorb the Jews into their own lands, the western countries packed them off to "colonize" Israel. The Palestinian refugees never left on the "voluntary" basis Israel claims they did, according to the SDS position. Israeli officers, like Americans in Vietnam, were sent through Arab villages with loudspeakers warning the people to leave or face a massacre, and sometimes, Israeli troops actually raided towns and drove the Arabs out.

The Israelis refuse now to let the Palestinian refugees come back into the country because they say it would imperil "Israel's national character." That is as flatly racist a position, SDS feels, as was the refusal of European countries to accept the Jews during and after Hitler's reign of terror. Israel maintains its heritage as a racist state by consigning black Jews from North Africa to lower paying jobs and decrepit housing. And the plight of Israel's working class is desperate, SDS points out, as is demonstrated by the string of strikes that have been going on in the country for several years now.

On many campuses, Israel's supporters point to the *Kibbutzim*, the communal farms of Israel, and say the country is actually more socialistic than any other state in the world. But SDS doesn't buy that claim, either. A few farms that occupy a tiny fraction of the working population can hardly characterize the entire economy, the organization says, any more than the existence of the Boston Common during Colonial times meant that Massachusetts Bay Colony was on the road to socialism. Finally, the SDSers say, Zionism is just another form of hypernationalism that will prevent the workers of the world from rising up together.

It is awfully hard for American Zionists to hear Jewish SDSers indicting Israel, and there are many Jewish SDSers who do. At a debate between the heavily Jewish SDS chapter and a student Zionist group at Columbia over the Middle East question, a man near the back of the hall stood bolt erect when SDS' Steve Cohen charged that Zionists had actually negotiated an agreement with Adolf Eichmann stipulating that 6,000 Jews would be allowed to emigrate to Palestine in return for the deportation of a million Jews to Auschwitz. "Shame! Shame!" the man cried. "You make me ashamed to be a Jew." Later during the question period, another man rose in the audience and declared to the other SDS debater: "I have only one question. What the hell kind of a Jew are you anyway, Mr. Barry Sautman?"

"I don't consider myself a Jew," the SDSer answered. "I'm an internationalist. I believe the only way to overthrow the bosses of this world is for all the working people everywhere to rise up together."

At Columbia, SDS had several violent clashes with the paramilitary Jewish Defense League. Several times the young radicals tried to demonstrate against the appearance on campus of Israeli officials and the JDL decided to "kick the shit out of the dirty Reds." At one point last fall, a contingent of Jewish Defense Leaguers stood on one street corner just off the Columbia campus holding "Ivan Go Home" banners (which the "Maoist" SDSers agreed with) and sang a bungled rendition of "The Star-Spangled Banner." On the opposite corner, the SDSers stood and chanted for victory to the Palestinians.

SDSers have tried hard to avoid being anti-Semitic in their political condemnation of Israel. But for the young radicals, being Jewish is itself an irony that's hard to bear. No matter what stands they take, everyone still sees them not as SDSers but as Jews. Police and others keep telling them "Hitler should have killed off the bunch of you." Black militants often pay little attention to SDSers' opposition to capitalism and associate them with "blood-sucking landlords" and "quick credit" ghetto merchants. And when the SDSers side with the Arabs, there are always some people—quite often their parents—who demand to know how a Jew can feel that way.

PART THREE

LOOKING BACKWARD, LOOKING FORWARD

CHAPTER TWELVE

SDS AND THE THREE R'S

The New Left never really existed as an ideology. It just thought it did. SDS was formed from the vestiges of several very much Old Left groups. It had no real politics of its own other than a fresh, youthful idealism aimed at solving the nagging problems of redistributing wealth and power throughout society. SDS' history has been a reluctant but inexorable rediscovery of the Old Left's doctrine. The journey back toward its ideological beginnings has dragged SDS through a tortuous reliving of the historic conflicts that have wracked the Old Left. But those now in the organization are deeply convinced the trip had to be made. They are un-ashamed that their ideas now sound a bit old. There are some basic truths, they insist, that remain pertinent today no matter when they were conceived. The three R's for SDS began with reform, led to resistance, and have unofficially ended at revolution.

Upton Sinclair was one of the forebears of SDS. Back in 1905, at the origins of Students for a Democratic Society, Sinclair was the Ralph Nader of his day—though he was a good deal more radical. As Nader was to do again some sixty-four years later, Sinclair investigated the meat industry. In his graphic book, *The Jungle*, Sinclair revealed that Chicago meat packers were building up a monstrous industry. They were producing incrediby filthy products in the most gruesome and dangerous factories imagin-able. Their barely paid workers were being brutally exploited and often maimed in the tumultuous plants where men literally ended up being ground into sausages. The people who consumed the meat products were being poisoned. And all the while the uncaring men who owned the factories were growing richer and richer.

The book brought about the passage of the Pure Food and Drug Law, a statute Nader is still trying to have enforced properly. But Sinclair didn't have Nader's faith in legislation or the American system. He was a socialist, and while he may not have been much of a revolutionary by today's standards, he was convinced that effective change could come only through the abolition of the capitalist system which encouraged such greed in the first place. Sinclair teamed up with another writer, Jack London, one of the original American Bohemians, who had himself railed from soapboxes about the crushing of the population in the headlong capitalist rush to industrialization. And with a third partner, one James Graham Phelps, the somewhat wayward son of a millionaire financier, they founded the Intercollegiate Socialist Society. Unlike its descendant, SDS, the ISS had a primarily intellectual or "armchair" approach. Its members wrote and debated. Once in a while they gave speeches. There was little real organizing in the contemporary sense of bringing people together to fight for a particular goal. The society published a magazine called *The Student Outlook* which coined the phrase *industrial democracy* to describe the goal of socialism. And in 1921, the society emerged in slightly recast form as the League for Industrial Democracy (LID). Sinclair later said industrial democracy meant "production for use and not for profit," which amounts to a euphemism for socialism.

LID attracted some prominent leaders. Norman Thomas became its executive director. John Dewey, the famous philosopher and educator, was its vice president. Heywood Broun was on the board of directors. The group was apparently close to the somewhat utopian-oriented Fabian Society of England which George Bernard Shaw and Beatrice and Sidney Webb helped build. But while socialist in its support for labor causes, LID was passionately anti-communist. In the early 1930's, LID formed a student wing, the Student League for Industrial Democracy (SLID). And in 1935, that was merged with a competing group to form the American Student Union, one of the first really large and militant student groups in the country. By 1939 the ASU reportedly had a paid membership list of 12,000. In 1936, the group staged a national peace strike to emphasize its pacifist, non-interventionist program. The ASU vehemently opposed ROTC, still the scourge of student radicals, saying that it was an attempt to "militarize" students.

SLID re-emerged as a separate entity after World War II. It functioned on quietly through the Fifties (all Left groups grew very quiet during those hard times), but as the civil rights movement was born and the Left began to reawaken, the League for Industrial Democracy decided it needed a new look. Among other revitalization measures taken in 1959, it renamed its youth group Students for a Democratic Society.

A student from the University of Michigan named Al Haber became SDS' first leader. He organized a conference at the school in the spring of 1960 with former SLID national secretary James Farmer who had attached himself to the Congress of Racial Equality. The conference held a series of discussions about the civil rights sit-ins in Greensboro and Nashville. And the group began to settle on what was to become an early SDS focus: organizing white Northern communities in support of the civil rights movement. A month later the first of a stormy series of SDS conventions was held. SDS conventions have defined the politics of the group, and because SDS has been the most prominent student organization in the past decade, the meetings were to set the direction for the radical student Left in the country as a whole. But with only two chapters represented, one from Michigan and the "John Dewey Discussion Club of Yale," the first gathering was by far the tamest.

That summer students in Berkeley began organizing protests against the House Un-American Activities Committee. Tom Hayden, a University of Michigan student, went to the Coast to join them—his first exposure to real organizing. He then came back to work with University of Michigan students in SDS. The next summer he hit the road again, traveling south with a great many other young white radicals to work in the civil rights movement. He was beaten by a racist white mob and later wrote a pamphlet for SDS called "The Revolution in Mississippi." It was Hayden's debut as a polemicist, and while it had nothing to do with real revolution, student activists found it an intensely inspiring document.

SDS leaders were already feeling driven to put themselves into action to fight against the social evils that more theoretical Leftists had traditionally only bothered to describe. That sense of a new commitment was bolstered by an open "Letter to the New Left," which C. Wright Mills published in the British *New Left Review*. The "letter" and the British journal itself were the chief popularizers of the term "New Left" in this country. Students were in "moral upsurge" all over the world, Mills said. He urged New Left youth in the United States to test its creativity and see if it could go beyond Marxist tradition to make itself the force for radical change in society. His underlying concept that there could be a *revolutionary youth movement* that would end the socialist reliance on workers was to re-emerge eight years later as the ideological question that broke SDS in half.

Impressed with his pamphlet on the struggle in the South and badly in need of a manifesto if they were to become the vanguard of a new movement, the SDS leaders commissioned Tom Hayden to outline what direction the new student activism could take. Six months later, in June, 1962, he presented the SDS convention at the AFL-CIO camp in Port Huron, Michigan, with a sixty-one-page document he and Al Haber had written. It was known as the *Port Huron Statement* and it launched SDS as a national movement. More than 100,000 copies of the statement were eventually printed and distributed by SDS, which suddenly burgeoned under its philosophy. Yet the organization was to outgrow the simple faith and acceptance of Hayden's manifesto in only a few years. By 1968, two SDS veterans, writing in *New Left Notes,* looked back on the *Port Huron Statement* and decided it was "a quaint and interesting document." The problem with Hayden's manifesto, people later noted, was that it didn't clearly define who the foe was.

The introduction, an "Agenda for a Generation," began: "We are people of this generation, bred in at least modest comfort, housed now in universities, looking uncomfortably to the world we inherit." With that, Hayden began a rambling dissertation on the dehumanizing forces of our industrial lives. Some of what followed was an almost religious description of how life should be. And in that, the young theoretician postulated SDS' first real political orientation: "participatory democracy."

> We regard men as infinitely precious and possessed
> of unfulfilled capacities for reason, freedom, and love.
> In affirming these principles we are aware of countering
> perhaps the dominant conceptions of man in the twenti-

eth century: that he is a thing to be manipulated, and that he is inherently incapable of directing his own affairs. We oppose the depersonalization that reduces human beings to the status of things—if anything, the brutalities of the twentieth century teach that means and ends are intimately related, that vague appeals to 'posterity' cannot justify the mutilations of the present. . .

We would replace power rooted in possession, privilege, or circumstance, by power and uniqueness rooted in love, reflectiveness, reason, and creativity. As a social system we seek the establishment of a democracy of individual participation, governed by two central aims: that the individual share in those social decisions determining the quality and direction of his life; that society be organized to encourage independence in men and provide the media for their common participation.

All of this vision, people were later to point out, is formalized in the idea of socialism, but socialism spells out how it would be attained and Hayden didn't. He went on instead to describe what he called the "root principles" of participatory democracy:

> #That decision-making of basic social consequence be carried on by public groupings;
>
> #That politics be seen positively, as the art of collectively creating an acceptable pattern of social relations;
>
> #That politics has the function of bringing people out of isolation and into community. . .
>
> #That the political order should . . . provide outlets for the expression of personal grievance and aspiration; opposing views should be organized so as to illuminate choices and facilitate the attainment of goals; channels should be commonly available to relate men to knowledge and to power so that private problems—from bad recreation facilities to personal alienation—are formulated as general issues.

Work, he said, should be based on incentives "worthier than money or survival." It should be educative, creative, self-directed and encourage independence along with a respect for others' dignity and social responsibility.

Then there were a few items that SDS quite vehemently disagreed with a few years later. "We find violence to be abhorrent because it requires generally the transformation of the target, be it a human being or a community of people, into a depersonalized object of hate."

Communism was also abhorrent to the old SDS. "As democrats we are in basic opposition to the communist system," Hayden stated. ". . .The communist movement has failed, in every sense, to achieve its stated intentions of leading a worldwide movement for human emancipation."

He ended with a call for a great alliance of liberal forces to build student power and make the universities more relevant: an absolutely dead-end approach, SDS currently believes. Students and faculty, he said, "must wrest control of the educational process from the administrative bureaucracy. . . They must import major public issues into the curriculum. . .As students for a democratic society, we are committed to stimulating this kind of social movement, this kind of vision and program in campus and community across the country. If we appear to seek the unattainable, as it has been said, then let it be known that we do so to avoid the unimaginable."

The *Port Huron Statement* was straight out of the old populist tradition. The vision of making society somehow more responsive to its individual members brought with it the idea of breaking down the size of governing institutions so that the people could be heard better. But that's a vague vision that doesn't necessarily challenge the system at all. It could be a foreshadowing of socialism, or it could instead be the sort of rhetoric about listening to the silent, unheard majority which Richard Nixon recites so solicitously. SDS was still a long way from knowing which way to go. A year later in June, 1963, the organization convened again and the position it was to take as an alternative to the system began to clarify. Richard Flacks, who later became a sociology professor at the University of Chicago and suffered a brutal beating by a group of rightists, presented an essay called "America and the New Era." It attacked the hollow liberalism that was being pushed by John F. Kennedy's New Frontier. Flacks called it "corporate liberalism," aimed actually at sinking the roots of big business even deeper into society.

Flacks saw society clearly broken into two forces. The establishment, which was granting only token reforms to preserve the "existing power arrangement," and its opposition—"the new insurgents" who would fight for civil rights and organize on the community level to fight for less unemployment, peace, racial equality and more responsive universities and government. It was SDS' first gesture in rejecting the hope of liberals. While the organization, through LID, was still receiving financial support from the labor movement, the statement also attacked the leaders of many organized unions who, it said, had become part of the establishment and were now inclined to resist change as much as the corporate executives.

That summer the United Auto Workers gave SDS a grant of $5,000 to help SDS fight unemployment and continue its civil rights organizing. The grant has been a source of embarrassment to both SDS and the UAW in recent years. The union, by 1970, had become one of SDS' primary targets. In its new Worker-Student Alliance program, SDS concentrated a heavy effort on supporting the 1970 strike the UAW called against General Motors. But SDS' support was aimed at the rank and file workers. The union itself was attacked repeatedly as a sell-out operation which would put its workers back in the plants as soon as their militancy could be siphoned off on picket lines. And the UAW under Walter Reuther's successor, Leonard Woodcock, did in fact settle for a contract that didn't even earn back the wages lost during the time of the strike.

But the $5,000 got SDS started on a long, hard venture into community organizing. It also began an internal conflict that is still going on in SDS and the student movement as a whole over whether the young radicals should concentrate their efforts on campus or try to go out and merge with other elements of the population in a broader attack on the system. SDS' project, JOIN (Jobs or Income Now), got half of the UAW grant and made unemployment its major focus. (Unemployment was again a major SDS campaign in 1970-71 when it soared to new heights as a result of Nixon's economic policy.) SDSers and local union organizers in 1963 began handing out apples at the gates of plants to warn workers of the desperate pinch that could lie ahead for them, reminding them of the Depression when the unemployed were reduced to selling apples on street corners.

But JOIN soon took on much the same approach as SDS'

other new UAW financed undertaking, the Economic Research and Action Project (ERAP). Headed by Tom Hayden and his co-defendant-to-be in the Chicago Conspiracy Trial, Rennie Davis, ERAP was aimed at building the "New Insurgencies" called for in Richard Flacks' proposal. Following the pattern that was developing in civil rights organizing in the South, SDS sent teams to live in Northern black ghettos or poor white neighborhoods. The cadre tried to help their new neighbors pressure the establishment to relieve their most urgent needs. One of the first groups moved from Swarthmore College to nearby Chester, Pennsylvania, and polled the black community there to find out what it wanted most. It helped build demonstrations against overcrowded schools and later helped form block associations to pressure the city about housing and police brutality. Intellectuals began comparing SDSers with the Narodniks of Russia in the 1870's, students who went out into the rural areas to help organize peasants. Their slogan was go "to the people," to *Narod*. SDS paralleled the Narodniks further when it later split apart over the use of terrorist tactics.

The community organizing efforts almost always failed, but they taught SDS a lot about the intractability of the system and what comes from trying to work as "insurgents" from within rather than as rebels on the outside. Reforms were the stated goals in the beginning.

A major priority in deciding where SDS would locate its ERAP groups should be where there seemed potential for "the creation of short-term social reforms," Rennie Davis outlined. The SDS organizers began campaigning for better city services and the like and jokingly called their organization "GROIN," for Garbage Removal or Income Now. Tom Hayden's group located in Newark's Clinton Hill area, near where the great Newark rebellion eventually began. They spent years pressuring landlords to clean up apartments and fighting to get local residents onto the board of a War on Poverty agency. But their primary effort was concentrated on the tiny task of getting a traffic light installed at an intersection where several children had been run down. It failed.

By 1964 the SDSers had almost entirely given up their expectations of winning even the most nominal concessions from the system. The idea began to emerge of launching campaigns just for the sake of showing the people you are organizing exactly how bad the system is. SDS began moving to raise the population's "consciousness" even as its own awareness was just beginning to come clear. Rennie Davis advised ERAP organizers to make demands that are likely to be denied even though they are perfectly reasonable because that would "involve people in experiences which develop a new understanding of the society which denies them opportunities and rights and will open possibilities for more insurgent activity in the future."

ERAP went on for about four years. It took SDS through the rise of militant student activism at Berkeley in 1964 with the Free Speech Movement, through the great escalation of the war in Vietnam, and through the American invasion of the Dominican Republic which, seen by radicals already beginning to formulate an analysis of American imperialism, was the radicalizing clincher. ERAP was the last try SDS made to work with liberalism. "Those of us involved in ERAP have come a long way," wrote Richie Rothstein in 1967. They had come to see the liberal, organized labor approach "as no more than a manipulative fraud perpetrated upon the dignity and humane aspirations of the American people." That conclusion, Rothstein said, "we owe in large measure to four years of ERAP experience. In a healthy pragmatic style we tested an optimistic hypothesis about the limits of American pluralism," and began to conclude that what was needed instead was a movement to "revolutionize" America.

SDS leaders were photographed after the 1963 convention with their fists raised and clenched—the first time the organization displayed what was to become its trademark. In a few years, the symbol of militancy was being stenciled onto T-shirts and university walls and became the logo at the top of *New Left Notes*. When the editors accidentally left it off one issue, SDS was deluged with letters from irate readers who were afraid there had been a sudden setback in the organization's militancy. An SDS national planning meeting once discussed the idea of hiring a sky-writing airplane to draw a giant fist in the sky over a national demonstration, but nothing came of the idea.

The Free Speech Movement which hit Berkeley in the fall of 1964 marked the political reawakening of American college students. In fact, the long 1964 series of demonstrations and strikes and confrontations with the police at Berkeley was based directly on the right of collegians to carry on political activity at their schools. It caught SDS as much by surprise as it did the rest of the nation. But SDS was quick to learn from it. The Berkeley leaders came to an SDS national council meeting and were welcomed triumphantly. C. Clark Kissinger (no known relation to Nixon's Henry), SDS national secretary at the time, drew on the Berkeley experience to write an *Organizer's Handbook,* expounding on the virtues of what was coming to be known as "direct action." Demonstrations, picketing, leafleting, marching and many forms of civil disobedience not only get publicity but invigorate the protesters as well, he noted.

That school year, SDS emerged with several sizable actions and the organization began to establish its leadership on the newly aroused campuses. At its December national council meeting in New York, the membership endorsed a program of demonstrations to be taken against Chase Manhattan Bank and other corporations that were giving heavy financial support to the apartheid government in South Africa. It was the first time the SDS national body had singled out a program of action for chapters throughout the country. No one knew if it would "take," but to a limited extent the regions followed the lead. At least six different cities saw big SDS demonstrations against Chase, and in New York, at the bank's headquarters, SDS held a sit-in with more than 600 people, 40 of whom were arrested. Even more significantly, the 1964-65 year marked SDS' first major national demonstration.

Several leaders proposed at the December 1964 meeting that a "March on Washington" be held by SDS that spring to protest the increasingly ominous American involvement in Vietnam. Surprisingly, the membership rejected the idea at first. Many still thought that SDS should spend its time trying to build grass roots dissent over the entire American way of life. Vietnam was too much a "single-issue" thing which wouldn't lead on to overall reform, they said. Marches against the war, they said, would be ineffective, no matter how large they were. Many in SDS now think that position has proved to be true, but at the national council meeting the leadership was able to rally enough support around the idea to reverse the initial rejection and put out the call.

The government gave the organizing for the April 17 march quite a boost during February, 1965, when President Johnson ordered heavy bombing in North Vietnam and it became clear that thousands of American foot soldiers would be on their way to back up the "advisers" the U.S. already had in on the ground fighting. SDS was not in a coalition with other groups in sponsoring the march, but it made very clear that it would welcome participation by any organizations that also opposed the growing war. A whole spectrum of communist and socialist groups' endorsements poured in: The W.E.B. DuBois Clubs, youth group of the Communist Party; the May 2nd Movement, youth group of the Progressive Labor Party; the Young Socialist Alliance, the youth group of the Socialist Workers Party. And virtually every other Left organization decided to participate.

The still heavily anti-communist League for Industrial Democracy, which had continued to pay the SDS national secretary's salary and give the group other assistance, "went through the roof," Kissinger later recalled.

SDS began holding teach-ins on the war (the first was in March at the University of Michigan), at which it squeezed in mention of the up-coming march. But no one, especially the SDS organizers, expected a turn-out of much more than a few thousand people. Thirty thousand came. They filled an area near the Washington Monument and cheered when SDS President Paul Potter urged that a movement be built "that will not tolerate the escalation or prolongation of this war but will, if necessary, respond to the administration war effort with massive civil disobedience all over the country that will wrench the country into a confrontation with the issues of the war."

Suddenly SDS was a great power in the New Left. Two months later, when it held its convention, it had 125 chapters and 4,000 national members. A ban on communist participation in SDS, which had been written into its constitution when LID founded the organization, was voted out at the convention. SDS, the constitution had maintained, was opposed to any totalitarian form of government and any advocates or apologists for that kind of a system were ineligible for membership. This was changed to: "Membership is open to all who share the commitment of the organization to democracy as a means and as a social goal." Technically, neither provision really excluded communists, since they consider socialism anti-totalitarian—and the ultimate and really only true form of democracy anyway. But the writing of a new clause was a deliberate gesture obviously welcomed by two rival groups: the Communist Party, USA, and its opponent, the Progressive Labor Party. Both groups began functioning as somewhat isolated factions within SDS, with PL taking by far the greater interest. The CP still tried to keep its DuBois Club active and concentrated a lot more effort on that than on winning much of a standing within SDS. PL, on the other hand, totally dissolved its youth group, the May 2nd Movement, and suggested that its members join SDS.

LID had been increasingly edgy with SDS' growing enthusiasm for direct action politics—officially because it was afraid such an approach might disqualify it from tax exempt status as a non-profit and therefore acceptably docile organization. But the League, which is still functioning, was primarily worried about the communist company SDS was beginning to keep. It wanted out and SDS, though it was receiving financial support from LID, liked the idea of going its own way. In October, the student group formally voted for an "amicable severance" and on January 1, 1966, the umbilical cord was cut. SDS was ready to move on to the second R—Resistance.

Huge plane loads of American ground troops were pouring into Vietnam by mid-1965. When school opened the next fall, the draft had become a primary issue. SDS leadership tried once to commit the organization to a formal campaign of draft resistance, advising its chapters to try to get all students to register as conscientious objectors. But that caused an uproar with the still reform-minded membership. A referendum of SDS members rejected the whole proposal, with SDSers supposedly voting against the idea because they "opposed its illegality." So the national leadership softened its line a little, announcing instead that SDS would work for more peaceful forms of national service than the military draft. Paul Booth, the national secretary, announced in words that were soon to be openly satirized: "I want to build, not burn."

The backing and filling SDS had gone through to arrive at a suitable way to fight the draft had been a frustrating experience. After it, the SDS leaders decided the organization had better make a long, hard assessment of its political goals in the light of the changing situation in the country. They called a national membership conference for the winter of early 1966 which turned into the first intensive and chaotic political discussion SDS had ever had. A lot of things needed defining. Exactly what was "the establishment"—"the power structure" they'd all been referring to? Was it more appropriate for the organization to take a broader "anti-imperialist" stand than its present anti-war position? What were the fights around the world for national liberation really all about, and what was the threat or potential in the spread of communism? Finally, where was the most potential for organizing: among students, poor people, workers, or in ghettos?

A great many people had different answers to the questions and SDS as an organization didn't officially come up with any, but the old hostility to questions of ideology was gone. Members threw themselves heartily into the debates and established a "Radical Education Project" which was instructed to put out literature to be used by study groups in the chapters. It was the beginning of SDS' rediscovery of the old masters. The ideology was coming along—and so was the action.

SDS broke loose in the fall of 1966. Dozens of campuses were hit hard with protests, all of them a little different, and all of them led by suddenly swelling and militant SDS chapters. "Student Power" was being tested as a concept, and being put to work to chase all vestiges of the military off the campus. Robert McNamara, Johnson's Defense Secretary, ventured into a lion's den at Harvard after daring to decline a challenge by the SDS chapter to debate the propriety of the war. More than 800 demonstrators surrounded McNamara's car and wouldn't let the Secretary leave until a dean declared they were committing the serious crime of "taking physical charge" of another person. That sounded like kidnapping and the protesters, feeling they'd made their point, allowed McNamara to return to Washington. More than a dozen chapters began persistent campaigns to get their schools to refuse to provide class rankings to the Selective Service, which was making a practice of calling up all the students it found who were not in good standing academically.

Queens College SDSers in New York helped lead a sit-in against a marine corps recruiter. Campaigns which were to spread all over the country were launched against recruiters for the CIA and the Dow Chemical Company, which was unashamedly manufacturing napalm for bombing Vietnamese, saying it would do whatever else the country asked of it. At Columbia, the SDS chapter picketed CIA recruiters with several hundred students in

November. Then, when the agency renewed its head hunt at the university in February, 1967, the first sit-in at Columbia was held. That same month, SDS at the University of Wisconsin escalated the fight against Dow with a sit-in that resulted in several arrests and the banning of the organization from the campus. This was the first time SDS had been considered so threatening that college administrators actually acted to insulate their students from the radical leaders.

At the University of Pennsylvania, SDS demanded that the administration drop its research work on chemical and biological warfare devices. The faculty agreed with the radicals, but the university ignored both groups and renewed a $900,000 government contract for its "Institute of Cooperative Research." SDS responded with picket lines. At Berkeley, the navy set up recruiting tables and the SDS chapter set up its own tables alongside. The two got along as poorly as everyone expected they would. Arguments turned into fighting and after the university deans failed to quell the dispute, the police were called in. Mario Savio, who'd led the Free Speech Movement, and Jerry Rubin, who was later indicted with Hayden and Rennie Davis in the Chicago Conspiracy, were among the six students to be arrested.

The universities were under attack, and on the basis of that single objective fact, an ideology began developing to explain the trend. Although the protests were primarily centered around the war, they were exercises in student power that had never been felt before. Carl Davidson, who was emerging as SDS' latest polemicist, tried to rationalize the whole phenomenon in a pamphlet he wrote called "Toward a Student Syndicalist Movement." He drew greatly from old Upton Sinclair in defining the role of the universities. "Our educational institutions are corporations and knowledge factories providing the know-how that enables the corporate state to expand, to grow, to exploit more efficiently and extensively both in our own country and in the Third World," Davidson said. He said that student radicals should respond by taking control of the schools through the formation of student unions and campus political parties.

And he saw a whole arsenal of weapons that could be brought to bear against the existing university power structures: sit-ins in the administration buildings, harassment and disruption of student government meetings, class boycotts, organized violations of parietal rules regarding dormitories, such as "sleep-outs" for the coeds, racially integrated "freedom parties" in segregated apartments, the seizure of the schools' IBM data banks, and disruption of oversized classes. He recommended long-term campaigns to win students the right to participate in planning the curriculums, in abolishing all grades, to reduce class size and to make the students' dormitories self-governing.

The radicals shudder now to contemplate how the fierce attack SDS had going against the war was threatened when Davidson and his followers started thinking about minor issues like class size. Davidson's whole program now seems like a diversion away from attacking the system and into trivial applications of power in the students' limited self-interests. And while student power raged on for several years, somehow the more political goals of SDS survived along with it.

In the winter of 1966-67, SDS met again in a national council meeting at Berkeley and this time, after a nineteen-hour debate, the delegates voted to endorse a militant draft resistance program which was proposed as a major concentration of effort for the organization. It was openly acknowledged that the step was a major one for SDS. The proposal itself was entitled "SDS and the Draft: From Protest to Resistance." SDS leadership urged the chapters around the country (which had already been showing a startling independence in determining their own programs and resisting national mandates) to call on everyone to resist the draft. Get college youths to leave their schools and go out to organize draft resistance in the working class communities, and help men already in the armed forces resist, even by directly aiding deserters.

With the formal arrival of SDS at the resistance stage, several of the most active leaders began talking somewhat vaguely in terms of the next step: *revolution.* Carl Davidson about that time called himself a "revolutionary" in *New Left Notes*, setting himself off from the majority in the organization which he said favored "sweeping reform" or "radical social change." He said that since the U.S. was not yet in a revolutionary situation, SDS should try to help bring the country toward that stage by stimulating the "radical or revolutionary consciousness" of the rest of the population." The new national secretary, Greg Calvert, agreed with that analysis. Draft resistance, he said, would involve radicals in actions and groups would eventually emerge as "revolutionary cadres."

They weren't openly quoting them very much at this point, but a number of SDSers had started reading Marx and Lenin and Mao and Che. They were also reading Herbert Marcuse's *One Dimensional Man*, and embracing his "neo-Marxist" theory that the highly mechanized society we live in has produced a "New Working Class" which would replace Marx's industrial workers as the force for revolution. That new class, Marcuse postulated, is made up of technocrats and teachers and social workers and professionals—the kinds of people college students were on their way to becoming. Greg Calvert told a conference at Princeton that the student power struggles SDS was getting involved in would lead on to revolutionary battles when the students got out of school and made the same kinds of demands on the economic institutions of society.

A head-on ideological clash had to come in SDS when this concept was extended to say that the industrial workers in the country not only would not be a revolutionary force but would, in fact, be the backbone of resistance to revolution. The Old Left types were gaining strength in SDS and still believed in the factory workers. Ignoring them in favor of social workers and technicians was a "petty bourgeois anti-working class" approach that would totally sell out the movement, they said.

With SDS on the move in almost every city, the organization was growing far more rapidly than its casual staff could keep up with. The national leaders toured the country in early 1967, and later reported that they had discovered chapters functioning in places that the national office hadn't even known existed. They estimated that at least 30,000 students were working with SDS chapters and said 6,000 students had actually signed up as national members.

The organization was beginning to arrive at much of the political view it now has of the struggle for power in the world. The war in Vietnam, a resolution stated at the national convention in June of 1967, was not the "mistake of an essentially good government," as liberal politicians and protesters seemed to be-lieve. It was instead "the logical result of a government which oppresses people in the U.S. and throughout the world." The organization demanded nothing short of immediate and total withdrawal of American forces from Southeast Asia. Any negotiated settlement was seen as inherently unjust since the U.S. had no right to negotiate anything about the fate of the Vietnamese. The war, SDS declared, was flatly imperialist and must be stopped by intense resistance. In only half an hour's discussion, the more than 300 delegates to the convention voted resoundingly to offer aid to servicemen who wanted to go "underground" rather than fight the war.

SDS also put itself on record as supporting the rebellions of ghettos all over the country. The organization endorsed a program of support for the rebellions, committing organizers to try to make it clear in white working class neighborhoods that the uprisings were not racist riots against all whites but were instead rebellions against the same power structure that was destroying the whites' lives as well. ERAP and JOIN workers went out to build an understanding of the ghetto rebellions in poor white neighborhoods of mostly Southern workers who had moved north to Chicago, Cincinnati and other cities. Many SDSers who are still fighting for an interracial alliance of working people agree with the JOIN organizers who wrote in 1967: "White radicals who refuse to undertake serious organizing efforts in the poor white ghettos of America's cities . . . are helping to kill the potential for a radical movement in America. And they may be helping to make more real the genocide of black people."

For several years college administrators had been attacking SDS for its supposedly "destructive" attitude toward American institutions. "Why don't you guys really try to do some good like the National Student Association," they gibed at the radicals. SDSers would come back with the vague accusation that the NSA was a "CIA front group." It had long been obvious that the liberal NSA must have been getting a lot of extra money from somewhere. And its officers strangely were being given draft exemptions for their work with the group. But it wasn't until the spring of 1967 that the news actually broke. It was admitted that the NSA had in fact been on the CIA dole. It served as an exhilarating reaffirmation of the radicals' refusal to be co-opted.

By sheer coincidence I was visiting Tom Hayden's community organizing project in Newark the morning the *New York Times* printed the CIA-NSA admissions. Tom just kept reading the embarrassed official acknowledgments and chortling. I remember him shaking his head and saying: "We've been saying for years that those NSA guys were bought off but everyone kept telling us we were paranoid." Jeff Jones of the SDS New York regional office, and a Weatherman-to-be, said SDS had to destroy all the liberal institutions that the NSA stood to protect. "Build not. Burn!" he wrote, parodying SDS' earlier line on organizing.

Progressive Labor had won a sizable following on many campuses and those chapters began displaying PL's concern for allying with the workers. At Queens College, SDSers joined the picket lines of New York's striking transit workers. And chapters in the West and Midwest began organizing students to support the struggles of steel and copper workers; some helped in the organizing of migrant farm workers. A number of chapters went in for student power struggles that seemed meek and even silly by comparison. At least two schools saw SDS leading the fight for beer sales on campus. And at Pennsylvania State College, SDS launched a campaign to have the price of football tickets rolled back. At some schools SDS even spent its efforts in civic service. The State University of New York at Binghamton, which now has an extremely militant SDS chapter, held an SDS-led fast to raise money so that the International Red Cross could give some Thanksgiving dinners "to the children of North and South Vietnam."

Through most of the 1967-68 school year SDS chapters kept growing stronger. A very militant demonstration against Dow Chemical recruiters at the University of Wisconsin ended in a rock throwing battle with police—proving the administrators who had "banned" SDS weren't exaggerating its threat as others had claimed. And Progressive Labor members of the chapter at Brooklyn College led a strike of about 8,000 students after several radicals had been arrested for flouting navy recruiters in their campus enlistment efforts. SDS at Harvard held a massive sit-in against Dow. Princeton SDS led a blockading of the Institute for Defense Analysis. At Stanford the group had a well-publicized demonstration and sit-in against the CIA. At Berkeley the SDS chapter was hitting on all fronts: a massive campaign to bar ROTC was underway, and both Dow and the CIA came recruiting and got demonstrations instead of applicants. It was beginning to seem like every prestigious school in the country was being hit. Ed Connelly remembers one of the lower level deans at Columbia actually telling him it wasn't looking very good for Columbia, which had a reputation for being an "active campus," not to be experiencing its own sizable display of insurgency. Little did he know what was coming.

Columbia started heating up by mid-year. The chapter was badly divided but the factionalism was producing an added stimulus for members to push that much harder on their pet projects. The Progressive Labor people were most concerned with halting the expansion of the university and its consequent destruction of poor people's homes. While the university's attempt to build a gymnasium in the Harlem park was the issue that finally brought Columbia down, at first only PL's followers on the SDS "expansion committee" cared much about it. Months later in an appearance at Harvard, Mark Rudd was to boast: "The gym issue was nothing. We manufactured it. I'd never even seen the gym site before we marched there." Others in the Columbia chapter, however, had been organizing around the gym issue for months.

Columbia SDS began its spring offensive early the year of the great rebellion. In February, SDS openly defied a new rule banning "in-door demonstrations." It sat in with about one hundred people to prevent recruiting by one of Dow's ubiquitous representatives. Then, in the last week of the month, two big demonstrations were held at the gym site. Twelve people, including six Columbia students, were arrested at the first demonstration, and thirteen people, twelve of them students, were arrested at the second.

On March 27, SDS marched on the administration again, this time to demand that the university cut its connection with the Institute for Defense Analysis. For that, six students were placed on disciplinary probation. Then on April 9, Mark Rudd beat university Vice President David Truman to the lectern during a memorial service for Martin Luther King who had been assassinated five days before. "Dr. Truman and President Kirk are commiting a moral outrage against the memory of Dr. King," the hefty SDSer called out. "Columbia's administration is morally corrupt, unjust and racist. How can the leaders of the university eulogize a man who died trying to unionize sanitation workers, when they themselves fight the unionizing of their own black and Puerto Rican workers? How can these administrators praise a man who fought for human dignity when they have stolen land from the people of Harlem? How can they praise a man who preached non-violent disobedience while disciplining their own students for peaceful protest? If we really want to honor this man's memory then we ought to stand together against this racist gym."

On April 23, there were about a thousand people waiting in Low Plaza to watch SDS make good its vow to invade Low Library and demand an end to IDA and the gym. Many, it might be added, were also there to watch a group of conservative students make good on their vow to trounce SDS. Still many more were there to take part, on one side or the other, in the action. The administration was frightened. One dean delivered a letter to Mark Rudd offering a meeting between SDS and the administration in a university auditorium. Dean Erwin Glikes, the man who had felt left out when the other prestigious schools were having more protest action than Columbia, tugged at Rudd's sleeve, begging him to stop the march when SDS moved out for Low.

The drawbridges were up—the administration had used the now standard ploy of locking all the entrances to the building. Rudd, somewhat befuddled, didn't know what to do next and he lost control of the group when someone from the anti-expansion faction howled: "To the gym! Let's go to the gym site!" Three hundred students poured off campus and into the park. Rudd, confused because there was still a fairly large crowd left at Low, didn't know which way to head. He finally opted for the action and scampered off to find the gymnasium excavation. When he got there the students were already hauling down the long barrier of fencing and wrestling with the police who were guarding the site. More police swarmed down on them, caught one student, lost him to the crowd, then caught him again and handcuffed him.

Everyone swarmed around Rudd, telling him what should be done. He wanted to seize and occupy the gym site until the arrested student was freed. Others said they should regroup back on campus with the rest to "get our shit together." That argument won out. The radicals were furious with Rudd. He'd let things come apart. A big demonstration had been bumbled and fragmented, someone was arrested, and the big SDS threat now looked silly. Mixed in with all the advocacy he was getting from his followers was the demand that Rudd, who'd only recently taken the leadership of the chapter, *do something*. Back on campus, he finally acted.

He climbed up on the Low Plaza sundial and announced: "We want IDA to go. We want the people under discipline to get off. We want this guy who got busted today to get the charges dropped—to get unbusted. We want them to stop the fucking gym over there. So I think there's really only one thing to do—we'll start by holding a hostage. If we can't get into Low Library . . . we'll have to hit the undergraduate administration instead. We're going to hold whoever we can. Let's go!" "SEIZE HAMILTON HALL!" a student cried from the crowd as it headed out for the undergraduate deans' offices.

They got their hostage in an acting dean named Henry Coleman. They announced to him that he couldn't leave the building until their demands were granted, so he holed up in his office where he was to spend the night. As word spread of the action, black militants from Harlem and around New York poured into Hamilton Hall. Their grievances against the university were far greater than the students', and so was their militancy. They wanted to barricade the building and prepare to fight to keep it. But Rudd didn't buy the idea of an Alamo-style stand. At about 5:00 the next morning, it was agreed that the whites would leave Hamilton to be defended as the black leaders wished. So the white radicals, many feeling rebuffed and frustrated, filtered out of Hamilton Hall and onto the dreary campus. Without much talk they sort of meandered up the steps of Low again and gathered, about two hundred strong, in front of the southeast entrance to the university administration building.

Several students in the front picked up a plank and twice made for the glass-paned door with it, then stopped. Then, almost in an act of disgust, they launched it through. They poured in, silently, and rushed up the stairs to the president's office. Another battering ram was improvised from a signpost and the Columbia University chapter of Students for a Democratic Society began its history-making occupation of the inner-sanctum of the university's power structure. Five buildings were eventually seized by the radicals. The police finally poured in early in the morning of the sixth day of the occupation. They were brutal. Dozens of heads were broken. Anyone on the campus the next morning who couldn't at least display a bruise was presumed to have been absent when the police arrived. The official count of injured was 148, but many more went uncounted by the local hospitals because they bandaged their own scalps. The police arrested 712. The entire student body was horrified, along with the faculty and even a few outspoken low level administrators. Columbia was hit with a strike which closed down the university for the rest of the school year.

And SDS put out the call to the rest of its chapters:
"CREATE TWO, THREE, MANY COLUMBIAS."

CHAPTER THIRTEEN

SCHISM

The old pros knew it could never last. Back in the naive formative years, before SDS had done much thinking about ideology, it had an almost doctrinaire tolerance for political differences. No one much cared about a member's specific ideas on how change could be brought about, or even on what had to be changed. SDS was wide open. Anyone who wanted to try to fight against the many evils of society, it was declared, would find plenty to keep him working in SDS. But there was no room for such tolerance once SDS was aiming for revolution.

The Left's whole approach to analyzing society and bringing about change is based on a concept of opposites in conflict. Marx and Engels called it "dialectical materialism." Mao Tse-tung calls it "contradiction." The world is made up of two groups, they say: the forces that rule and the forces that are oppressed and must fight for liberation. Any significant force in the world works either in the interest of one group or the other, they say. The problem is that sometimes it's hard to tell which way a strategy will function. So there's always the danger of setting out to help liberate the oppressed, but playing into the hands of the rulers instead.

History is a long chain of mostly ineffective and sometimes even destructive attempts to overthrow the rulers, the Left ideologues say. It hurts every time such a revolutionary movement fails because people become that much more convinced that there is no hope at all. So serious revolutionaries feel bound to analyze exactly what must be done, and then to make sure no other group with a different analysis gets in their way. Real fights result when conflicting programs crop up within the same organization.

The old-timers saw two very distinct ideologies developing in SDS—an "internal contradiction"—which they recognized very clearly as paralleling Left history and which they knew would have to be fought out. By the time of the Columbia rebellion, the internal struggle was already raging. Progressive Labor and its adherents were adamant that students alone would accomplish nothing in the long run. Battles just for student power were not only wastes of energy, they said, but would alienate others in society who deplore such rampages. Then any college radicals who tried with PL to unite with the outside community would be rebuffed. The action freaks would have given all students the reputation of being crazy and reckless.

Who were the SDSers to fight for? PL said it had to be for the factory workers, black and white, who even in this prosperous society can hardly make ends meet and must work under intolerable conditions. Students could shut down the schools and throw off ROTC, but only the workers could stop the production of weapons and so snuff out the war. Without their support, no revolution would ever succeed. The workers aren't fascists, or even rigidly conservative, PL maintained. The few who do vote for men like George Wallace do it because Wallace says he's going to fight the big government and give power back to the little guy. PL sees the duty of revolutionaries to go out and show those workers that they should take control themselves.

Others in SDS simply didn't buy the idea. They said it was too old hat; it hadn't worked yet and it certainly had no relevance to a highly technologized country like the U.S. The industrial workers are bought off here, they said. They will never make waves. Hope, they said, lies with the youth of the nation who are rejecting the materialism and alienation that comes with capitalist society. You have to ally with workers, they agreed, but they said everyone except those capitalists who actually own the corporations are workers. And working people should be reached with a broader program than the better wages that Progressive Labor had been concentrating on in its strike support work. The meaninglessness of work, the great pressure in this society to consume more goods, the fragmentation of society by automation—it all had to be fought as part of capitalism.

The anti-PL forces didn't have a clearly conceived strategy they preferred to PL's Worker-Student Alliance plan. They were constantly being pressured to refine their own ideas to combat PL's. It was a great incentive to force SDS to confront vital political questions, but tension was building greatly within the organization. It broke into the open for the first time when SDS met in East Lansing, Michigan, for its annual convention about six weeks after the Columbia bust. PL organizers had worked very hard to get a big showing at the convention, encouraging everyone who agreed with the Party to come so that SDS could be wrested from the hands of the existing national leadership which PL considered anti-working class. The PL-Worker-Student Alliance caucus at the convention numbered about eighty people, many of them having won five-vote proxies in their chapters. While it was still a minority in the crowd of more than 800, the caucus was strong enough to direct a great deal of the debate to what it felt were primary questions. As the debate droned on for seven days (the convention had been scheduled to take only five days but the conflicts weren't that easily resolved), the factionalism grew sharper and sharper. Some people started calling it "PL paranoia." PL called it "anti-communism," which itself was subject to some debate.

The anti-PL faction couldn't stand to see all of the Worker-Student Alliance people voting as a bloc all the time, though it should have been no surprise that a caucus would represent a united political force. Tom Bell, a former upstate New York regional traveler for SDS who'd become a teamster, rose at one point to condemn PL for its persistent and united opposition to a proposal he and several others had made. They wanted SDS to concentrate more on building urban chapters than campus organizations. A PL member answered by charging that Bell was "red-baiting." And that really got Bell: "Red-baiting?! I'm the real communist here, not you guys from Progressive Labor." With that, hundreds of anti-PLers stood and started chanting "PL OUT! PL OUT! PL OUT!" Newcomers to SDS were confounded. They could barely grasp the distinctions between each faction's political position, let alone decide who the *real* communists were.

A few specific arguments did emerge. Many SDSers were incensed at PL's condemnation of the North Vietnamese leadership for accepting aid from the USSR, which PL with its then pro-China stand found "revisionist." They argued (as many in SDS still argue) that when thousands of people like the Vietnamese rise up in a country to fight back against American imperialism, it is arrogant to condemn their efforts because they aren't as pure in their communism as they might be. Many SDSers found Progressive Labor's perennial concern with strike support far too limited. Using Lenin's term to critize the trade union orientation of the Bolshevik's rivals, they called PL "economist." Revolutionaries have the obligation of bringing concepts to the workers that go beyond their self-interest in higher wages, argued Mike Spiegel of the anti-PL faction at Harvard. "We have to organize not around self-interest but class interest. We must address ourselves to the values of capitalism as they are expressed on all levels of social life, not just the economic level."

And finally the most classical Left conflict of all emerged at the convention: the rivalry between anarchism and communism. A group of hippies from the Lower East Side of New York City had joined together to form an SDS chapter they named "Up Against the Wall, Motherfuckers." They came brandishing the black flag of anarchism and they kept preaching "Do it! Do anything!" To them all the rhetoric was "bullshit." For several days during the convention, the anarchist black flags, and the red flags the communists brought in to respond, flew together over the hall. But the old-timers said those two flags never stay together for long. They predicted again that SDS would split.

The 1968-69 school year continued the long string of SDS demonstrations against ROTC and all sorts of military and industrial recruiting. It also escalated the internal conflict at a series of three SDS national meetings. The Motherfuckers, as the Lower East Side group was known for short, were helping to bring out the "contradiction" in SDS over the question of drugs. Progressive Labor was deeply concerned that the great drug explosion on the campuses would totally defuse the growing revolutionary spirit. At the SDS national council meeting held in Boulder, Colorado, in October, PL introduced a proposal urging SDS to condemn drugs as "selfish escapism." PL pointed out that Castro had outlawed drugs in his revolution because he was certain they were being sent in by the CIA. That was hitting the Motherfuckers where they hurt.

"LSD has burned more fucking people out of the system than PL leaflets will ever do," Tom Neuman of the Mothers, as they were known for extra-short, kept insisting. PL made the usual charges that others were red-baiting, and the Mothers came back and accused PL of "drug-baiting."

SDS reaffirmed its position that weekend that the up-coming national election was a fraud that would only foster the illusion of democracy. The organization echoed the complaint of many non-radical voters that a choice between Humphrey and Nixon was no choice at all. SDS called again for the immediate, total withdrawal of U.S. troops from Vietnam and voted its support for "the People's war in Vietnam." Ghetto rebellions were endorsed again as attacks on the ruling class and SDS picked up a line from the Black Panthers in saying black people had the right to liberate themselves "by any means necessary."

SDS gathered again for a huge internal confrontation just after Christmas in 1968. There had been lots of rumors about the existing leadership, the so-called national office faction, purging Progressive Labor. And there were equally unfounded counter-rumors that PL was going to try to organize enough of a showing to actually take control of SDS. The clash developed over the political programs that each faction proposed SDS take on for the future. A clear indication that the 1,200 "delegates" at the convention didn't yet understand what the political conflict was all about is that *each* faction's program was approved. Part of the problem was that both proposals sounded strong and the political differences between them were attached, to a great extent, to some of the most esoteric questions the Left debates.

The "national question" was one of the biggest bones of contention. The great hope of all socialists is that workers in not just one country but all the "workers of the world" will rise up together and seize power. The purists maintain that socialism as a system can only exist successfully on a worldwide basis. In line with this, Progressive Labor and many other groups actually disparage any form of nationalism because it fragments the workers with patriotism and gets in the way of that vital international union of workers. PL criticizes the black nationalism of the Panthers, and the nationalism of groups like the National Liberation Front of South Vietnam. Other ideologues agree that eventually international socialism is a necessity, but they quote Mao and other theoreticians who maintain that the fights that are raging around the world for "national liberation" are a very positive intermediate stage in the establishment of worldwide socialism. The imperialists have to be thrown out of countries like Vietnam, they say, before the workers can establish their own power.

The anti-PL forces at the December meeting in Ann Arbor said SDS should view the fight against racism in the U.S. as an "anti-colonial" struggle. Blacks in the ghettos were being oppressed as a colony, they said. Every aspect of their lives was being dominated by white racism. Racism wasn't just a question of inferior wages as PL maintained, but it was instead the total subjugation of blacks "as people, not just as workers." And the opposition to PL had finally worked out a political program of its own.

PL argued against the Marcusean proposal submitted by national secretary Mike Klonsky, called "Towards a Revolutionary Youth Movement" (RYM). The proposal specifically denied that it was looking at youth "as a class," but that is how PL interpreted its real effect. The proposal laid out a program for action which SDS, under PL's leadership, has since almost entirely undertaken. But the Progressive Labor faction distrusted what it felt lay beneath the RYM proposal.

SDS should try to organize working class colleges, community colleges and trade schools, not just the well-to-do universities it was then concentrating on, Klonsky proposed. In addition, it should attack the universities as the arms of the corporations that exploit workers and encourage imperialism. SDS should build "alliances with non-academic employes on the campus," the RYM proposal said (a program which was to emerge as the Campus Worker-Student Alliance under PL). SDSers should move into the factories and working class communities to "eradicate prejudices against workers." They should fight university centers of counterinsurgency research and racist sociology and education schools.

The RYM proposal was generally interpreted as something that PL's unstinting education campaign in SDS had brought about. But the proposal also called for the encouraging of "dropped-out and forced-out youth" to join SDS' movement, and for campaigns for open-college admissions for all black and brown students. PL feared that the welcoming of hippies would lose SDS to "youth culture," with all its apolitical hedonism. And the Party rigidly opposed open admissions demands because they encouraged viewing blacks as a separate group and because PL felt working class kids shouldn't be encouraged to go to colleges that would "just try to make them bourgeois."

Jeff Gordon, the student organizer of PL, had attacked the RYM program in an article in the Party's magazine. "Their theory is far from revolutionary," he maintained. "It boils down to counter-institutions under capitalism, hippy dropout communities and pop-art protest." But finding little, if any, of that sort of thing in Klonsky's proposal as it was presented to the national council, Gordon admitted he agreed with a lot of what RYM postulated. But he said the proposal was peculiarly different to the "practice" of its supporters in recent months. He described several "wild-in-the-streets" rampages and weird drug sessions the national leadership had been involved in. That's what was really behind the "youth movement" that was being proposed, Gordon said. Since that would in fact be an assault on working people and form a barrier to reaching them, PL opposed the RYM program.

Klonsky responded that he wasn't virulently in opposition to Progressive Labor. "Don't think for a minute that when the Man comes down on PL, we won't stand beside them," he said. "I even agree with the idea of a worker-student alliance—in principle. But I think PL's dead wrong about how to go about building it. We ally with workers by waging struggle against a common enemy and not by subjugating our movement patronizingly to every trade union battle." The RYM proposal was adopted with a narrow majority. The RYMers were euphoric. The PLers were despondent. Then, when the PL proposal on fighting racism (which attacked the RYM idea of viewing blacks as a colony) came to a vote, that too squeaked by.

Neither side had really won. The two factions sparred for a while with chants; Klonsky's group gibing at PL's anti-NLF posture by chanting "Ho. Ho. Ho Chi Minh." And PL came back: "Mao. Mao. Mao Tse-tung." When a group tried to smooth over some of the bitter differences at the end of the conference by singing "Solidarity Forever," the anthem of the American labor movement, others brought the grim reality of SDS' condition home by chanting: "Defeat false unity." It didn't look like SDS could come through another meeting like that in one piece.

Mark Rudd was having a hard time keeping up with his image. In fact, from the time the news media settled on him to satisfy its hunger for personalities and spokesmen, the pressure must have been incredible for him. Rudd's indecision during the Columbia rebellion was well known to everyone around the campus, but Mark was presented matter of factly in the news as a striking figure of revolutionary bravado—which he had fallen far short of portraying convincingly in person. The Columbia uprising had launched SDS into new heights of conflict. The organization wasn't quite sure how it had happened, but members generally agreed it was something to be replicated and intensified around the country. Mark apparently felt people were looking to him to show how that could be done. "I *am* a press-created leader," he later admitted in a campaign speech for the national secretary's post. "The media made me a symbol of the New Left. While I don't approve, the movement needs leadership and symbols. My name exists as a symbol and at this time I think that's a good thing."

Besides having to grapple with complex questions of ideology, SDS also had to resolve the difficult tactical question of how to continue escalating the attack on the power structure. Rudd and almost everyone else in SDS had been shocked with how powerful a threat the student radicals had posed once the militant working people of the black community had come to join the white radicals in a coalition against Columbia. The coalition was something the PL-oriented expansion committee had predicted. But the phenomenon, once it actually came to life, had to be formularized into a specific strategy. While some SDS theoreticians concluded that it was vital to ally students' campus campaigns with the interests of the oppressed people in the outside world, Mark and others saw the experience chiefly in terms of action. It had happened, they said, because SDS had moved. With its building seizures, SDS had quickly inspired others.

Wild in the streets was just how Mark and his followers thought SDS should be. In the midst of all the heavy theoretical discussion at Ann Arbor, they proposed that SDS show up at President Nixon's inauguration the following month and make "a strong, militant presence felt." People were pouring into SDS because of the glory that had come with the Columbia rebellion, supporters of the Rudd proposal argued, and SDS would have to continue to show that it was a "fighting movement" to keep them. Significantly, Rudd's proposal for Inauguration Day demonstrations at the South Vietnamese Embassy and the offices of the International Police Institute were rejected by the group. The "Action Faction" was too given to "exemplary actions" by tiny groups of provocateurs. "That kind of confrontation is just going to bring down more repression on us and turn off the people we're trying to reach in the factories and ghettos," one opponent charged. "That shit has nothing at all to do with organizing."

It was clear at the Ann Arbor meeting that most of SDS still believed very strongly in the concept of *mass actions* which might not necessarily be so violent but would involve many times more people and pose a longer-term threat. Rudd and others disagreed. They had read Che and believed that a daring daylight attack on the law and order of the system would inspire others to come out and do the same.

The whole strategy of terrorism is somewhat akin to a ploy the good guys always used in the old westerns when they'd found themselves terribly outnumbered in a gunfight. Skipping around behind the big rocks, they laid down a cloud of fire that made the bad guys think *they* were way outnumbered and didn't have a chance. While the terrorists never actually expect the government to give up, they do hope to make things look a lot shakier than they really are, and to prompt an overly repressive reaction that will bring out even more support. This was the assumption that Mark's Weathermen were to labor under for many months and then finally recant as a mistake. But in early 1969 they were just beginning to try out the idea.

Even without the support of SDS nationally, a small group of "action freaks" from SDS and elsewhere made a showing on Inauguration Day along the route of the Presidential motorcade. They burned American flags, waved NLF flags, and finally charged through the downtown area, heaving trash at cars and stoning every cop in sight. About a hundred of them were arrested. Attorney General John Mitchell vowed a get-tough policy on radicals in response to Nixon's wrath, and the PL predictions that millions of Americans would be turned off by such episodes was borne out completely.

The national council met in Austin for one last sparring match before the big fight. Most of the patience had dissolved on both sides by the March meeting and fist fights kept breaking out. It struck unaffiliated radicals as a crazy affair, with one faction or another suddenly breaking out copies of Mao's *Little Red Book* of sayings and waving them in rhythm like China's Red Guard. The national question took up most of the meeting. The anti-PL faction, representing the existing SDS leadership, had prepared two resolutions which directly attacked Progressive Labor for its criticisms of the NLF and the Black Panther Party. The Panthers were called the vanguard of the fight against American capitalism. And the North Vietnamese under Ho Chi Minh were praised for waging the sharpest attack in the world to liberate people from American imperialism. Both resolutions passed with easy majorities.

"Hot Town: summer in the city," a RYM proposal, hardened SDS' revolutionary line, calling for the eventual overthrow of the ruling class by the working class through armed revolution. It called on SDSers to mass in the major cities that summer to build urban cadres of white radicals who would be available to support the fight for black liberation in the country.

A PL-supported resolution was barely passed condemning student power struggles which were still being waged by some SDS chapters over faculty hirings and firings, the establishing of dormitory regulations, abolishment of grades, etc. Efforts to gain influence in institutions that inherently serve the interests of the capitalists, the resolution said, are at best wastes of time and will invariably weaken truly revolutionary efforts.

After ten years, SDS had emerged as a self-declared "revolutionary" organization. The split couldn't be held off any longer.

Almost everyone knew there would be a split at the annual convention in June. The big questions were how it would come, which group would do the splitting, and which group would remain in control of SDS. Belligerently cynical Jerry Rubin declared: "Whoever wins loses." Progressive Labor had been prodding SDS to refine its ideology and to direct its efforts to a pro-working class strategy that would lead on toward revolution. SDS accepted a great deal of what the Party was teaching it, but in the end much of the membership dug in, adopted some ideological answers which were in classical opposition to Progressive Labor's, and insisted on defining their own "youth" movement. PL didn't like drugs and long hair and Ho Chi Minh and the Black Panthers. For some that seemed like plenty of reason not to like PL.

By June, 1969, there was hardly a college in the country that was willing to host a national meeting of SDS. The state schools were blocked from granting the SDSers space by their politically minded governing boards. The private schools didn't want to risk antagonizing their corporate endowers. Space at sixty different colleges was solicited by the SDS national office in Chicago and all eventually said no. Many administrators openly agreed with a Cornell officer who admitted his school had its hands full with just one SDS chapter. It wasn't about to welcome the entire national organization. SDS finally ended up gathering in a converted skating rink at the ramshackle Chicago Coliseum, whose management didn't care where its money was coming from. Demand for the dingy space was all too rare to be fussy. At $400 a day, they'd have housed a convention of arsonists—which in a way is what they were doing anyway.

Fifteen hundred SDSers rambled into the big hall under the watchful eye of a zoom-lens movie camera the police were using from a third floor window in an old stone schoolhouse across the street. And just in case they missed catching anyone with that, they had two more photographers shooting full face and profile stills of the radicals as they came through the entrance. "It's a free country," a Chicago cop told the press. "We can take anyone's picture we want." And the atmosphere didn't change inside the Coliseum either. SDS guards appointed by the national office staff searched everyone's identification and then frisked them, ostensibly to find weapons. After two days of some overly lingering frisking, Jeff Gordon of PL charged that the "security" force was feeling up the SDS women. So the national office assigned women to frisk the women.

The tests of power came early. First was a proposal by the

RYM-aligned Liberation News Service that newsmen (unless they were from the *New York Times*) be admitted to the convention if they agreed to pay $25 admission and would sign an oath not to testify against SDS on the basis of anything they saw or heard. PL objected to the idea resoundingly. "We have our own press. We don't need the capitalist pig press which isn't going to print the truth. Bar them all," demanded Ed Clark of New Orleans. And the convention voted to do just that—by a three-to-one margin. Then there was the agenda. It was traditional for big SDS meetings to spend most of the time broken up into workshops so that more people will be able to get in on the discussion. But PL had brought a massive following to the convention—easily 600 people were sporting buttons for the Worker-Student Alliance caucus. The national leadership under Mike Klonsky didn't want to let those caucus members loose with their opposition politics. Workshops, he warned, were "PL's hunting ground for naive young people." But the delegates weren't so afraid and voted for the workshops anyway.

RYM was already on the run. It was apparent that after three years of indefatigable organizing, political persuasion, and leadership in SDS' biggest battles at Columbia, Harvard and San Francisco State, Progressive Labor had brought a majority faction to an SDS convention. Mark Rudd, Mike Klonsky, Bernadine Dohrn and others from the RYM group presently in power could see quite clearly that they were about to lose control of SDS. On the second day of the convention they caucused upstairs with groups from California and the Midwest and forged a RYM alliance based primarily on the idea of heading off PL. Some called themselves Weathermen, from a line in a Bob Dylan song (ironically Dylan himself is said to have once been very close to Progressive Labor) which says: "You don't need a weatherman to know which way the wind blows."

Bernardine Dohrn, the lawyer from the University of Chicago who was one of the three existing SDS national secretaries, Rudd, and a few others had recently published a Weatherman manifesto which took up about five pages of fine print in *New Left Notes*. But the most anyone could get out of it was that SDS should form a youth movement to support the anti-imperialist fights that were going on around the world for national liberation. Klonsky argued with it. A writer for *Ramparts* was so totally boggled by the document that he noted: "You didn't need a weatherman, but you needed superhuman stamina to read through the ten thousand words of Left cliché prose, and you still wouldn't know which way the wind was blowing unless you left the Coliseum to check. Then you'd have to stand in line to be searched on your way back in."

A lot of convention discussion was spent on how to fight male chauvinism, both inside the movement and in society at large. Too much sexist shit had been going on in the movement, it was agreed. A group of SDS women from New York decried a leaflet that had been distributed by the RYMish Revolutionary Student Union at Berkeley during the fight over a patch of land the RSU wanted to convert into a "People's Park." For some unexplained reason all the leaflet had on it was a picture of a half-nude girl peeling off her sweater and the caption, "Today we relax." Women had to be given an equal place in the movement and treated with dignity, not lechery, they said.

By the third day, things had gotten around to the national question again. PL was maintaining that it supported the liberation fights of people around the world, but that nationalism by itself was a reactionary tendency. "Cultural nationalism" as it was being pushed by the Black Panthers, without giving due attention to the real "class" oppression of blacks, was a destructive diversion, PL speakers maintained.

A contingent of Panthers at the convention saw the threat of their rivals in Progressive Labor taking over SDS and snuffing out the warm support the Panthers had been receiving from the white radical group. So they moved to snuff out PL. Chaka Walls, one of the leaders of the Panthers in Illinois, took the microphone and began a rapid-fire, no-more-bullshit rap that is the oratorical style of the Panthers:

"I'm gonna tell you motherfuckers something, now. Blacks have the right to self-determination. You motherfuckers have got to get it straight that they have the right to choose." The RYM faction was cheering wildly. PL was getting it from the Panthers, and once that happened the unaffiliated delegates would have to side with RYM or be lumped in with the "racists." Either SDS had to come out in support of black nationalism, or it would be

written off as "counter-revolutionary." "Those PLs do more damage to the revolution than the pigs do," Walls said. And he warned
that in Chicago, the Panthers don't go lightly on such types.
"You'd best not forget it." RYM was riding high. And Chaka,
digging it himself, hung in there.

"Now about this male chauvinism thing . . . my view on that
is I'm for *pussy power* myself." Some of the RYMers tried to
laugh, but that one hung heavy after each side had just spent a day
vying to see which would most effectively champion the cause of
women. "Now, the way I see it," Walls went on, apparently
oblivious of his sin, "there's a lot revolutionary women can contribute. I'm glad to see all these women here—enough for the
revolution. The way women can contribute is by getting laid." The
WSA people in the back of the hall took up a chant, fainter than
most of their earlier chants, but it kept building: "Fight Male
Chauvinism! Fight Male Chauvinism! Fight Male Chauvinism!"
The Panther got off onto Superman, somehow. "He was a punk,"
he said. "He never even tried to fuck Lois Lane."

The chant was booming then and Walls couldn't make anything heard. "FIGHT MALE CHAUVINISM! FIGHT MALE
CHAUVINISM!" The RYM faction was silent, not wanting to
attack their ally but not daring to defend the rampant attack on
women the Panther was sending down. Finally another Panther
leader, Jul Cook, came to the microphone. He attacked PL and the
Worker-Student Alliance for talking big at the convention but not
accomplishing much on the campuses. "What have you been
organizing, moles?" Several PL leaders who'd just led the campaign that had shut down Harvard jeered "BULLSHIT!" But then
Cook got a little confidential and said: "You know, I'm with the
brother, though. I'm for pussy power myself." "FIGHT MALE
CHAUVINISM. FIGHT MALE CHAUVINISM." And over the
chant, Cook roared the capper: "The position for a woman in the
movement is prone!"

The next day was spent discussing how racism is manifested
in the U.S. and how it should be fought. Mike Klonsky from the
RYM group was adamant in insisting that blacks had the right idea
in talking about secession from the oppressive "mother country"
to set up their own state. PL and a great many others said that was
just running away from the problem. What really had to happen is

that black and white workers had to be brought together to fight against the corporation owners and the oppressive government. Klonsky kept insisting that by taking that position, the PL supporters were "denying black people the right to self-determination," picking up the line that the Panthers had used the night before. And standing in the way of blacks like that, he kept saying, was racist.

But it was obvious to everyone that PL was going to be able to have its "Smash Racism" program adopted by the convention. The RYM faction didn't even have a specific anti-racism proposal to present. So when the time came for RYM to argue against the PL-WSA proposal, Jul Cook of the Panthers came forward again. This time he had a prepared text. The Black Panther Party, along with the Young Lords Party (for Puerto Rican liberation) and the Brown Berets, a Mexican-American militant group, had gotten together, Cook announced, and had decided that the PL-WSA people are "acting like pigs. You're holding back the black and brown peoples' struggle for self-determination. Take down your pictures of Mao; take down your pictures of Che [PL actually never put Che's picture up since they considered him far too given to individual and unproductive acts of adventurism]. If you can't relate to Huey P. Newton, you aren't revolutionaries at all. All you are is revolutionary talkers. You haven't shot anything more than rubber bands; haven't busted nothing more than jelly beans."

He went on for about forty-five minutes. No one tried to interrupt him. He got into some heavy threatening: "Immediately after this convention, chicken-shit PL is going to change its position, because they are chicken-shit. They act like cops. They act like counter-revolutionaries. They are the reincarnation of Leon Trotsky [the symbol of ideological degeneracy to hard-line Marxist-Lenininsts, including PLers]. Chairman Mao supports liberation for all oppressed people," he said.

And that finally brought on the response. Quoting from Mao is like quoting from the Bible. You can lift a passage and have it support you and then someone else can lift another passage and have that contradict you. The WSA caucus started chanting "READ MAO. READ MAO. READ MAO." Cook wound up: "PL is counter-revolutionary." And the caucus started bellowing "BULL-SHIT. BULLSHIT. BULLSHIT."

It was RYM's last offensive before retreating. They started a booming chant, melodically and soulfully, the way the Panthers do it: "POW-ER TO THE PEE-PAL. POW-ER TO THE PEE-PAL." And the WSA slipped into its more specific version of that, not missing a beat: "POW-ER TO THE *WORKERS*. POW-ER TO THE *WORKERS*". It went on and on in the vibrating hall—fifteen hundred people trying to resolve a weighty ideological question by making their own chant dominate. A group of Panthers rose and began walking ominously to a table over near the side of the hall where PL was selling its literature. They were met by a PL defense squad and the groups stood glowering at one another.

Klonsky tried to take the microphone but the WSA group was howling for the right to rebuttal and Jeff Gordon with a dozen supporters came forward to answer the attack. However bizarre and irrelevant the debate may seem, it had the entire hall incensed and panicked. SDS was clearly on the breaking point. The esoteric political distinctions were only the vehicles for the intense, virulent disgust and resentment each side had for the other. Gordon spoke calmly. He obviously wanted things to calm down. "The Progressive Labor Party will not be intimidated out of SDS," he began, to cheers from his caucus. The Party supports the Panthers on many things, he said, but on many others it offers criticism "in a constructive and comradely fashion." PL is in support of the people of the world who are fighting against imperialism and for self-determination. But he said those fights would only succeed if they ended up in establishing socialism.
He attacked the existing SDS leadership, the RYM faction, which he said had found itself and its ideas obviously defeated and so, in desperation, had used the racist ploy of hiding behind the Black Panthers to cover RYM's own bankrupt position.

The hall began rocking to the bellowing WSA chant of "Fight Racism." Up near the podium the desperate RYM leadership gathered to find a way out. Finally Mark Rudd came forward. He spoke almost meekly. "This isn't getting anywhere, and if we keep going we're just going to have fights—we won't be resolving anything politically. I suggest we recess for an hour." He paused and decided he wasn't telling everyone as much as they were already figuring. "And frankly I'm not just saying this to cool it. We have to caucus to figure out what we want to do." But it was obvious that the rest of the RYM leadership didn't think that resolving things was as desirable a goal as Rudd was making it seem. Bernardine Dohrn kept arguing with Mike Klonsky who was physically trying to hold her back. She suddenly broke away from him and came shouting onto the P.A. system:

"Some of us are going to have to decide whether our political principles allow us to remain in the same organization as people who hate the Black Panthers and deny the right of self-determination to the oppressed. Anyone who wants to discuss that, follow me." And she wheeled and marched out of the hall into an adjacent room. She was clearly calling for a split in SDS. Rudd had no trouble deciding which side he was on and fell right in behind her. Klonsky, looking very troubled with the whole business, followed Bernardine too. And then from around the room those who were casting their lots with Dohrn, Rudd and Klonsky rose slowly and joined the exodus.

It was a crucial moment. The Worker-Student Alliance people wanted their politics to lead in SDS, but they didn't want a badly broken organization to be their inheritance if they could help it. Many started calling out: "NO SPLIT! NO SPLIT! SIT DOWN! STAY AND STRUGGLE!" In the end, two-thirds of the convention stayed while about five hundred opted to join the breakaway RYMers.

All the next day the convention proceeded with almost eerie calmness, discussing racism more, and the war, and women's liberation. But everyone was wondering when, and if, the others would come back. For a long time the people in the other room didn't know what was going to happen either. They didn't agree politically on a lot of things and as soon as the one unifying factor—fighting off PL—had disappeared, their own differences came to the fore. They couldn't even decide if it was best to attack PL on the basis of what the Party had been doing on the campuses, or on the basis of its highly refined ideological positions.

After hours of discussion, three alternatives became clear: they could leave SDS formally, indicting PL for its politics, and establish a new group—someone suggested calling it Radicals for a Democratic Society. Or they could stay in SDS and try somehow to fight beyond the convention to have PL expelled. Or finally they could march back into the convention and just declare that they were the "real" SDS and that anyone in PL or in agreement with PL was expelled.

Jared Israel, a PL leader from Harvard, conferred that night with Mike Klonsky and came back into the main convention to announce that RYM was coming back. He cautioned everyone to be disciplined. He implied that the WSA people should avoid a provocation that would split SDS, and he said if there was a lot of hissing and chanting a fight might break out and "the Chicago pigs will come in here and bust us all." Soon the processional started. It must have taken quite a while to choreograph the whole thing. First a line of RYM women, arms folded, came marching into the main hall, up to the platform and surrounded it shoulder to shoulder. Then, while they stood in a weird silent vigil, a line of men came marching along the same path and circled the women who were circling the podium. Then, with the Black Panthers in the lead, followed two long columns of RYM men who marched into the main hall, a few wearing T-shirts stenciled with "*Shit on PL*" across the chest. In perfect drill formation they split in the middle of the hall to send a column down along both sides and then met in the middle of the back. They were chanting, "Two, three, many Vietnams," a saying of Che's. The WSA was totally surrounded and didn't know if it was going to be attacked physically or just verbally.

Hulking Klonsky led Rudd and Dohrn in once the troops were in position. Mike leaned over the microphone and stated: "It's been agreed there will be no fights. I'm sure there won't be." He said it threateningly. Then Bernardine came forward.

"We've been in the next room for the past twenty-four hours discussing our political principles," she cried out. "We support the national liberation struggles of the Vietnamese, American blacks and all other colonials. We support anyone who takes up the gun against American imperialism. We support the governments of China, Albania, North Vietnam and North Korea. We support women's liberation. We declare that all members of the Progressive Labor Party, the WSA, and anyone else who does not support these principles, are objectively racist and counter-revolutionary. *WE DECLARE THAT THEY ARE NO LONGER MEMBERS OF SDS!*"

The convention couldn't believe it at first. People started

laughing. The defeated RYM faction had come back to declare that it, the minority, was ousting the majority. But then it began coming clear. There were going to be two SDS's. On every campus there was going to have to be a power struggle to see which faction would be able to keep the name, and they'd be bound to spend all their time fighting one another instead of the common enemy. They started screaming, "SHAME! SHAME! SHAME!" and pointing up at the podium. But Bernardine and Mark and Mike and five hundred members of "the other SDS" were already walking out into the night. The WSA people didn't know it at the time, but the splitters were in kind of a hurry. They wanted to get downtown to the SDS national office to lay claim to the valuable membership and subscription lists, the files and bank accounts, and the $80,000 printing press.

The great "internal contradiction" in SDS had been resolved.

"We've just taken over the most important organization in America," Jeff Gordon of PL-WSA announced once the RYMers were safely out of the hall. But there was very serious question whether divided as it now was, SDS could sustain that importance.

The press started writing SDS' obituary. The *New York Times* was almost ecstatic in an editorial which wistfully boded "the decline of the SDS." "Least of all would [the decline] . . . be a loss to the campuses of the nation," the *Times* noted. "On the contrary, it would clear the way for legitimate dissenters on campuses from Cambridge to California who share many of the SDS ideals but reject its arrogant and coercive ways."

For a few months the RYM people actually did try to fight to establish themselves as the "real" SDS. People in the movement made another pitiful play on Che's saying: "Two, three, many SDS's." At New York University the month after the split, the two SDS's met head-on. Mark Rudd had come back to town and called an "SDS regional meeting." The WSA SDSers who'd won control of the organization through normal political channels at the convention weren't about to have their victory erode in the field. They came to the meeting in force. Rudd had all the doors to the meeting room locked except one, and behind that was a whole goon squad of musclemen frisking people, giving them lengthy interrogations ("Are you now or were you ever a member of PL?"), and making them swear loyalty oaths to the Albanians, the NLF, the Black Panther Party, etc. And when the sergeants-at-arms found the first pro-PLer and tried to eject him, the fight was on.

Someone from way inside the door started flailing a long, hooked window pole up and down trying to brain a WSAer or two at the door. More RYMers charged forward hurling potted palms, chairs, lamps. The WSA people kept rallying and coming back for more. With a hearty fist fight underway and the WSA stalwarts winning out, the resourceful RYMers broke out a high-pressure fire hose and turned it on the opposition. NYU's Loeb Student Center looked like the ruins of Pompeii. The police finally emerged with drawn pistols. After indicting the RYMers for having to ally with "the pigs" to save their skins, the WSA left to hold a rally outside.

The ritual was repeated a few weeks later at Harvard, with the WSA gaining entrance that time and the RYMers suffering numerous casualties. In Chicago, the factions clashed for week after week, with RYM winning most of the initial encounters but the WSA finally mobilizing a massive force and beating the RYMers to a pulp.

A regional traveler for WSA-SDS in Ohio was captured by a group of RYMers, including Terry Robbins from Kent State. "We're going to kick the shit out of you, you jiveass, honkey, racist, counter-revolutionary, revisionist PL pig." They held him captive for about an hour, discussing whether or not they should "stomp him." He warned them that there were 300 people in Boston who were sworn to protect the WSA organizers and would swarm down on Ohio like the Red Guard to obliterate RYM. In the end they let the WSAer go. (About eight months later a bomb exploded in the Greenwich Village townhouse where it was being manufactured by a group of Weathermen. The police found two bodies that were identifiable, but a third remained unnamed for almost three more months until the Weathermen issued a "Declaration of a State of War" which identified the third body as Kent State's Terry Robbins.)

The RYMers were apparently enjoying the intermural clashes. Mark Rudd, who was elected RYM's national secretary at a rump session outside the convention, went around displaying bruises in various stages of healing from the beatings he'd taken in different cities. "We sometimes beat them up and they sometimes beat us up," he told a newspaper reporter. "We usually beat them up when we find them." But by mid-fall both groups were forgetting one another to go their own ways. And as the PL people had warned, the road for RYM led to the underground and terrorist attacks against the people.

Before the breakaway RYM group could even get out of Chicago to begin its organizing, it split in half. It was getting to seem like the uncontrolled division of cells in cancer. RYM I, which used its label "Weatherman" increasingly often as the months passed, included Mark Rudd, Bernardine Dohrn and a big group from the Midwest. They were committed to the wild-in-the-streets approach, egged on by a very deliberate aversion to any more intellectualizing.

But Mike Klonsky and his followers, while they had some esoteric political differences with PL and a stylistic aversion to its discipline, agreed that PL was right in asserting that the working class was the key to a revolution. The terrorism and vandalism that Rudd and Dohrn were talking about would just turn the workers off, they said. So they split off and established themselves as "RYM II," the fragment of a fragment.

And even RYM II had within it a number of "contradictions" over the definition of its role as a revolutionary cadre, a mass organization, or something in between. So not long after RYM II was formed, it fractured into three more fragments.

Meanwhile RYM I gave up trying to call itself SDS at all. It had put out a few issues of its own version of *New Left Notes* and then gave up on that too. By its leaders' own admissions later, the group was going crazy. The only way to inspire the disenfranchised youth of the country to follow them, they had reasoned, was to show they had nerve. No more sissy shit theory. They'd go out and punch in a few faces. That way they figured they'd become the first *revolutionary* street gang that ever existed. They studied karate and went around wearing motorcycle helmets and carrying Viet Cong flags. In Detroit and Chicago during the summer they marched onto beaches, railed at the people there, got themselves attacked, beat up and often arrested. They started calling all whites racists and telling them to give up their "white skin privilege." That got them beat up some more.

They scheduled a "mass action" for Chicago in mid-October, supposedly to protest the war and to intimidate the city which was about to put the Chicago Conspiracy and some Black Panthers on trial. Their slogan was "Bring the War Home," which they did their best to do.

For most of the fall the Weathermen lived communally, swapping women on demand and taking a lot of drugs. They were convinced they had to purge their "petty bourgeois" mentalities, so spent lengthy sessions in "self-criticism," attacking one another's supposed weaknesses and apparently generally playing chicken as urban guerrillas. You couldn't go soft and be allowed to stay around.

The Weathermen tried to organize high school students and put out a lot of leaflets, but soon gave up on that technique in favor of Che's "exemplary action" approach. Throughout the Midwest, they'd charge into high schools screaming, "JAIL BREAK! JAIL BREAK!" They began talking about themselves as "the Red Army." They followed the policies and directives that came from their leadership, Rudd, Dohrn and a few others, who were known as the "Weather Bureau." Just after school opened in Pittsburgh, about two dozen Weatherwomen dashed through South Hills High School chanting "HO LIVES" and hoisting up their shirts to show that avoiding nudity was just another bourgeois idea they had no use for. They were all arrested.

They mobbed a house party a woman was giving in Columbus to try to sell pots and pans. In Detroit, they burst into a community college class while it was taking a final exam, barricaded the door, beat up two guys, and gave a long speech on what was happening in the world.

The worst thing about the Weathermen, as far as what was left of SDS was concerned, was that those crazy vandals were being called "the militant faction of SDS" all the time in the press. And the hostility people might have had toward SDS before the Weathermen broke loose in the streets was warmth compared to how they felt once the rampages started (to say nothing of the fear and resentment when the Weathermen escalated to bombings). It never came across to the rest of the population, but the most virulent criticisms of RYM during this period (and even now) came from the remains of SDS.

"The owners of this country and their government and press love to paint SDS as a bunch of vicious rich kids, out for kicks, fanatics, fascists-on-the-left, ready to kill anyone who won't mouth insane slogans," *New Left Notes* said early in the fall. "By attacking the people, RYM is trying to live up to that lie. The government can smear SDS with RYM's actions." The long indictment was entitled: "WARNING—RYM MAY BE HAZARDOUS TO THE PEOPLE." It wasn't just a factional hostility that brought on the criticism. SDS was struggling for existence. With membership and subscription lists and printing facilities and money all taken over by the RYMers, the people who won control of SDS in Chicago almost had to start from scratch. And while they were making their hardest effort to bring what they felt was a rational and constructive perspective to the famous student organization, the Weathermen were serving as the last straw in convincing the country that student radicals in general were nuts.

The Weathermen held their "Days of Rage" in Chicago on schedule. Under the new slogan, "Smash the Glass of the Ruling Class," they featured several mad dashes through main streets, smashing in car windshields and beating people—not rich people or police or store owners, but just anyone, with clubs. Then in December they held what was billed as a "War Council" in Flint, Michigan. Rudd and Dohrn told of the thrill of fighting in the streets. Mark added that street fighting was probably kid stuff compared to the exhilaration that a person must feel "from killing a pig or blowing up a building." Mark's old friend from Columbia, John Jacobs, known as "JJ," postulated: "We're against everything that's good and decent." And to prove it, Bernardine Dohrn astounded everyone by trying to make revolutionary heroes out of Charles Manson and the rest of the "Tate Eight," who were on trial for killing actress Sharon Tate and several others in Los Angeles.

"Dig it," says Bernardine. "First they killed those pigs; then they ate dinner in the same room with them; then they even shoved a fork into a victim's stomach! Wild!"

For a great many of the 400 people who attended that War Council, what the Weathermen were outlining sounded terribly like facism. Someone dared tell that to Ted Gold, another of Rudd's friends from the Weather Bureau and Columbia. "Well," Ted shrugged, "if it will take facism, we'll have to have facism." He too died when the anti-personnel bomb of dynamite wrapped with nails and other shrapnel went off by accident in the Greenwich Village townhouse bomb-factory about two months later.

The Weathermen went underground and into bombings about a week after the War Council. At the most, about two hundred people went under with them. "Guns and grass are united in the youth underground," Bernardine wrote in her first communique via the radical press. "Freaks are revolutionaries and revolutionaries are freaks. If you want to find us, this is where we are: In every tribe, commune, dormitory, farmhouse, barracks and townhouse where kids are making love, smoking dope and loading guns—fugitives from Amerikan justice are free to go."

But less than six months later, after a long series of "exemplary" bombings which scared people off instead of bringing them out, Bernardine announced "A Change in the Weather." She talked in her "New Morning" statement about the tortuous life underground where the Weathermen "believed and acted as if only those who die are proven revolutionaries. Many people had been argued into doing something they did not believe in, many had not slept for days. Personal relationships were full of guilt and fear. The group had spent so much time willing themselves to act that they had not dealt with the basic technological considerations of [bomb] safety.

"The townhouse accident forever destroyed our belief that armed struggle is the only really revolutionary struggle. It is time for the movement to go out into the air, to organize, to risk calling rallies and demonstrations, to convince that mass actions against the war and in support of rebellions do make a difference . . . a group of outlaws who are isolated from the youth community do not have a sense of what is going on, can not develop strategies that grow to include large numbers of people. . . . People become revolutionaries in the schools, in the army, in communes, and on the streets. Not in an underground cell."

History had been upheld again. Like every other terrorist group before them, the Weathermen had discovered you can't accomplish anything without tremendous support from the people. It's what the "pigs" back in SDS had been trying to tell Bernardine and the others all along. But if the Weathermen do come out in the open to campaign politically again, they'll find their bombings created a society that's a lot more reluctant to listen to them than before they went under.

CHAPTER FOURTEEN

"ALLY WITH WORKERS!"

Worker-Student Alliance: It sounds like an inherently impossible combination. The two elements just aren't supposed to mix. It's like trying to blend fire and water. People hear SDSers eagerly talking about the potential of the alliance and come away saying it's the most fantastic hallucination the Left's ever had. Hard-nosed, hard-pressed workers will never ally with students to do anything, people keep telling SDS, let along launch a joint attack on the system. Workers hate students, they say, and workers respect the system.

The cynics have an easy time making their point. They recall the days during the Cambodia-Kent State crisis when construction workers in New York City swarmed down on student peace protesters, splitting their long-haired heads open and waving the star-spangled banner. They talk about the movie *Joe*, and the auto worker in Detroit who took it so seriously he relived it by murdering his young daughter and the hippies she'd taken up with. If you get workers and students together at all, they say, it will be as foes in a pitched battle against one another—certainly not as allies in a fight against the system.

The intensely committed SDSers can't help but be well aware of the prejudices that separate workers and students. In trying to forge the alliance, the radicals constantly face hostilities from both sides. Neither half of the alliance is coming in easily. For many students, the radicals' reverence for the workers seems bizarre.

They believe that there are few workers left in this country outside of the middle class, and they think most workers are dirty, dumb, happy, beer-swizzling television addicts who are super-patriots to boot.

If there were an easier way to bring about the change SDS thinks is necessary in this country, the organization probably would never have taken on the alliance effort. But the young radicals are absolutely convinced there isn't another way. So they are proceeding on the conviction that the need for both groups to get together and the potential once they do are so great that the prejudices must and can be overcome.

It's clear to SDS that students alone have almost no power. They can launch an electoral crusade like the McCarthy campaign and maybe even have it win. But all that becomes irrelevant once you've decided it doesn't matter who's running the system as long as it's keeping a few people very rich and most people relatively poor. SDS has generally concluded that the workers must control the means of production in this country and keep the fruits of that production. For that to happen, the small cluster of wealthy people who are now in charge will have to be overthrown. Since they won't go willingly, it's going to take a fight. And for the fight to win, it's going to require the might of the workers along with whatever assistance the students can offer them.

The Worker-Student Alliance idea was an utterly logical program for Progressive Labor to bring to SDS. The Party's primary conviction is that the revolution will only come from a victorious fight by the workers against "the bosses." The obvious program then for PL's student arm is to have it ally with the workers. PL first recommended its program in the form of a "Student Labor Action Project" (SLAP) at the turbulent SDS convention in East Lansing in June, 1968. The Party couldn't have chosen a more opportune time. France had just come within a hair's breadth of revolution a month earlier, and it had happened because the workers and students had decided to fight together.

A lengthy reconstruction of the "May Revolt" is impossible here. In essence, what began as some fairly frivolous campus protests against anti-sex dorm rules grew into a national university rebellion. Students occupied buildings and were brutally busted by the police. Soon they began battling in the streets. The fight kept escalating until many parts of France, especially the Latin Quarter in Paris, became scenes of street warfare complete with barricades. The country's workers, who had been ground into increasing poverty by inflation of prices far ahead of their own wage gains, seized the time to move themselves.

With the government already failing in its efforts to stifle the students' rebellion, the workers moved to shut down the country with a general strike. And following the tactics the students had set at the Sorbonne and other campuses, the workers began "occupying" their factories. In Nantes, the workers took over an airplane plant and held the manager prisoner in his office. Then workers in Renault factories all around France took control of their plants. Workers joined the students behind the barricades in Paris. It looked like a complete victory had been won when the De Gaulle government ordered in the army and the soldiers refused to fight their "brothers."

In the end De Gaulle's lieutenant, George Pompidou (De Gaulle himself strangely rushed out of the country on a vaguely described mission as soon as the rebellion began to snowball) broke the general strike through an agreement with the big French labor unions that gave a massive across the board wage increase to all the workers. The gains were almost immediately erased with price hikes and the workers ended up little better off than when they had begun. But that was chalked up on the Left as another revolutionary lesson. Next time around the workers wouldn't trust the unions, they said. And the revolt itself, which came at the same time as the Columbia rebellion, brought inspiration to the student movement here and fear to the power structure. Don't be too quick to write off this threat here, one newspaper columnist cautioned his readers. "Remember, no one thought it could happen in France either."

Most middle class Americans are certainly wrong to believe that the U.S. has somehow become so prosperous and automated that we no longer have a working class. There are about 78 million people presently working in civilian jobs in the U.S., according to the government's Bureau of Labor Statistics. Just under 20 million of them are middle class, in professional and managerial positions. The remaining 58 million, almost three times as many, are very clearly in the working class. About 28 million are blue collar workers, more than two-thirds of them generally considered only "semi-skilled" or "unskilled." Another 20 million are waiters, cleaning women, night watchmen, etc., lumped under the category of "service workers." About 4 million are farm workers, and 18 million are clerical and sales workers under the general "white collar" category.

It's also a surprisingly inaccurate assumption that wages in America have raised the workers out of their once lowly status and assimilated them into the middle class. In fact, according to the government, the average production worker in the U.S. in 1970 was earning only $6,088 a year. His "spendable" income, after taxes and other deductions, was only $5,096. And all the while, the Bureau of Labor Statistics says, the average family of four in metropolitan areas needs $10,933 a year to maintain a "moderate" standard of living. The industrial workers get only a little more than half of what they need for comfort.

And there's every indication that SDS is right in saying that, far from being contented, American workers are becoming extremely bitter and restive. The whole idea that they're happy is as specious, the radicals say, as the claims of Southerners that their "niggers are happy," or the Old South's plantation concept of "carefree slaves." Far from growing increasingly prosperous as the economy "expands," the government figures show that workers' "real wages"—their relative buying power—has been stagnant or actually declining over the past six years. In response, they are striking more than they have every done in this country. When the union leaderships try to hold them back, they wildcat. More than a third of last year's 5,700 major work stoppages occurred while union contracts were still in effect. And the workers are now actually sending their leaders back to the negotiating tables by rejecting one out of every seven contract offers that are put up to them for acceptance.

"The U.S. workers who are the targets of the SDS effort aren't an exploited proletariat. Rather, most are quite middle-class in both income and outlook," the *Wall Street Journal* claimed in a long editorial which labeled the SDS alliance idea as "patently silly." If the *Journal* knew the actual figures, as it must, it was ignoring them. Six thousand dollars a year isn't middle class by anyone's standards—and certainly not by Wall Street's.

It's a bewildering thing when the third of the population that has been lucky enough to have "made it" can forget that the other two-thirds exists at all. It's certainly true that society has become segregated on a wealth or "class" basis as well as on a racial one. Prosperous suburbanites rarely have poor factory workers living on their blocks or even going to school with their kids. And the factories themselves are set off in isolated areas which are quite out of the way of middle class people as they play and shop and work.

To a great extent, middle class people deliberately avoid exposure to the working class, particularly the black working class—except when they need service. They move out to the suburbs. In New York, they go to very great expense to send their kids to private schools rather than immerse them in the "savage" public schools. But there's more to ignorance of the existence of the millions of people who manufacture the goods of middle class existence than lack of contact.

Many middle class people now look back in their own lives to the times when they were still poor immigrant families, or just after that, to when they were nearly starving in the Depression. They've risen out of that hardship now and are proud of it. They consider themselves "self-made men." And somehow they firmly believe that anyone who hasn't risen up with them just wasn't motivated enough because "the opportunities are there." If they did it, why can't everyone else? When you ask them then who's going to sew the clothes and wire the televisions and sweep the floors once everyone's selling stock and practicing law, they don't really know. It's an objective truth that someone has to do that kind of work, in fact that most of the people have to, and that in our system those people aren't paid much more than half what the others make. But it's a fact we very quickly seem to forget.

Even if the workers are there after all, and are poor and militant, as SDS claims, they aren't suddenly full-blown revolutionaries who immediately open their arms to the overtures of the young radicals. SDS knows that. Many workers *are* openly hostile to long hair, so SDSers don't usually let their hair grow long—or grow beards, or even dress much like hippies. They're more likely to wear jeans and work shirts and work boots. SDSers dress, like most other people, in a way that emulates the people they respect the most.

While the Worker-Student Alliance effort has only been underway for about three years now, SDS has had a number of experiences that it has found very encouraging. At San Francisco State, when a strike led by SDS and a black student group shut down the school for months, the students crossed the Bay to picket with a group of refinery workers on wildcat against Standard Oil in Richmond. Then the refinery workers came over to San Francisco State to join the students' picket lines. The two groups fought the police both at the refinery and the college. When a scab-driven truck almost ran down one of the SDSers who was picketing at the refinery, the strikers hauled the driver out of his cab and nearly beat him to death.

In Chicago, a wildcat by Railway Express Agency workers was being broken by a court injunction which prevented the workers from picketing. SDS offered its help and was readily welcomed. The next day thirty students arrived at the REA offices as they'd promised and the workers who were gathered across the street, unable to picket themselves, cheered them while SDS threw up its own picket line. They kept it up for several days and badly hurt the company's operations until the strike was settled.

During the nationwide General Electric strike, chapters all over the country pitched in, raising money and collecting food to bring to the men on the picket lines. Assembly-line workers were asked to come to campus to explain to the other students what the strike was all about and what they could do to help. Beyond the usual desire to lend whatever direct assistance they could to the strikers, the SDSers hoped to build ties. Through their display of support for the strikers they hoped to show that students weren't all so bad. And they also hoped to make friends in the factories who might later on become a network of potentially revolutionary leaders.

In the most successful cases, the SDSers really did make close friendships with groups of workers. After the REA strike in Chicago, SDS invited the freight drivers to visit them the next weekend and see an inspiring film about how a community of zinc miners beat off the courts, the government and their company in a successful strike. Eight of the drivers came and several brought their wives. Everyone wanted to have a good time, but they were all clearly conscious of the great differences in their lives.

The film obviously moved everyone, but when the student "host" asked for comments about it afterward, everyone was understandably timid. There was a long, awkward silence. And then one of the black workers spoke up. He talked about how in the film the races had gotten together to beat the mining company, just as black and white drivers had united against REA. He talked about how the government and the courts were on the sides of the mining company in the film and REA in his own experience. And he said that the only way to overcome all the "allies" the corporations have is to get some of your own. "All this goes to show that if people just stick together, we can turn the whole world over if we want to," he concluded.

Everyone was elated with the speech. There was long applause and the workers began articulating a lot of the feelings they'd had on the job about racism. Black and white drivers said the united strike had made it clear that racist feelings among the workers were just weakening their chances of really fighting the company. They talked about earlier tensions amongst them that had been made to seem foolish when they had wildcatted together. (The strike had been started by blacks who went out first, then waited and hoped while the whites moved slowly—almost reluctantly—across the street and joined the wildcat.) Eventually one of the workers turned toward the students and asked them to explain just who the hell they were and why they had decided to come out and support the REA wildcat.

One of the SDSers explained that the students had read in the paper about the injunction and figured the statement that the strike would be over because of it was a lie. So they decided to come out to REA and see if they could help. He told how SDS had tried for a long time to go it alone in fighting against the war and had come to realize that students alone didn't have any power. And he explained how the war was hurting the workers too, by drafting their sons and using their money just to gain control over a whole new group of workers in Southeast Asia who'd be a cheap replacement for U.S. labor. A lot of the workers readily agreed to that. Finally the student noted that the same group of men who were the directors of the corporations were trustees of the universities. In all probability one or two REA chiefs were also helping to run the big schools in Chicago, he said. "Since we've got the same enemy, we might as well fight him together."

The group broke up well after midnight. They'd all come

with a lot of fear about the whole thing, not really knowing how it was going to go and worrying that there simply wouldn't be any way to communicate over the cultural gap. But when the barriers had fallen away, it had been exhilarating for everyone.

After several years of SDS' reliable strike supporting, workers are now actually summoning the aid of the students—and union leaders have on occasion taken to blaming their memberships' insurgency on radical rabble-rousing. In Los Angeles just after the Cambodia crisis, at about the same time construction workers were being bused to Wall Street to pummel the peace protesters, teamsters came to the college campuses to leaflet for support. Some weeks before they had gone on a wildcat and unofficially accepted SDS' offer of assistance. At first a number of the drivers baited the young radicals and told them they could do fine without any "Commie" help. Other drivers welcomed the students, but SDS soon decided if the support it was trying to give was just going to divide the workers, it wasn't worth it. Then a court injunction was handed down barring the teamsters from picketing. Scab trucks started pouring through to the truck docks; it was clear the strike was going to be broken.

So the teamsters went on a "lit blitz" of L.A. campuses, handing out thousands of leaflets calling for student support. And the leaflet echoed SDS' own idea of alliance: "We need each other's solidarity and support." For many days SDS and hundreds of not-so-radical students formed car pools, gathered on the lonely campuses at 5 A.M. and headed for freight terminals all around the city. The students would form revolving picket lines at the terminal gates while the teamsters stood at the sides and helped shout at incoming scab trucks. The alliance held up for three weeks. The strikers kept saying they'd have been defeated almost immediately if it hadn't been for the students' support.

When the police started roughing up the students' picket lines to get scab trucks through, and harassed the strikers themselves mercilessly, the workers began joining with the students in calling them "pigs." The cops work for the rich guys, most of them decided. If the student picket lines weren't strong enough at one terminal on a particular day, strikers would drive off to freight docks in other parts of the area to ask any extra students there to re-deploy themselves.

"It was an inspiring time," Don Ford of UCLA SDS recalls. "The union leaders—make that *mis*leaders—kept hassling SDS and PL about giving out literature. But the workers kept telling them, 'What's the matter? You scared we're gonna find out you guys are selling us out?' And when the goons made it impossible for us to get literature out on the lines, the drivers would stop us way down the road in our cars and buy papers like mad. In the end an awful lot of those workers saw their interests were on the same side as the students', and lots of those students who'd never seen a worker before kept saying how we were right—that those guys are really 'right on.' "

Much socialist doctrine is based on the assumption that capitalism is inherently doomed and that eventually it will collapse of its own inadequacies. It has to keep expanding, depends on inflation and the continual stretching of a worker's yield. And periodically it reaches a point where it can't go any further and begins to tumble. Recessions are encouraging periods where capitalism displays those weaknesses, the radicals say. And depressions are the times of collapse where the workers, if they know where to go, will move to prevent the capitalists from getting themselves back together to rebuild. Some purely theoretical ideologues—the activists disdainfully label them "armchair socialists"—say there's nothing to do but wait for the inevitable economic collapse to occur. SDS, PL and a great many other groups say you have to go out and educate all the time or the workers won't necessarily seize the time and the system.

But both approaches constantly try to read the economic indicators, just as the capitalists do, to take the system's temperature. Sometimes the radicals are prophetically accurate. Progressive Labor saw the unemployment crisis that gripped the country in 1970-71 coming far before the government's experts admitted a lot of people would be losing their jobs. And while the nationwide wildcat of mail workers which stalled the economy in March, 1970, seemed to come out of nowhere, SDS had been warned it was brewing fully a year earlier.

The Labor Committee, which was run out of SDS in 1969 for supporting what most of the radicals thought was a racist strike by New York City schoolteachers, had poured over charts and tables and interviewed mail workers. They arrived at a New York Regional SDS meeting and announced: "The post offices are going to blow. All the objective factors for a really fantastic and militant assault on the system are there, and SDS has to get ready to join it. The post office is running on the labor of a tremendous black and Latin work force concentrated in the urban areas. The workers are young and they're getting the worst wages imaginable. They have no hope because their unions are total sell-outs. They've been promised wage increases that never come and they're militant as hell. If they go out, everything stops: the stock markets, the banks—everything. This could be really big." Most of the SDSers just needled the analysts for being "economistic" and for their "civil service mentality." SDS didn't do anything.

Then the post office blew and James Rademacher, the president of the mailcarrier's union, blamed the whole thing on SDS anyway. He said the workers had been incited by SDSers who penetrated the postal system the summer before. "Their objectives are to disrupt, and they have been successful up to this point. Those members of the union who are striking aren't members of the SDS troops, but they are undoubtedly being encouraged in some areas by the disruptive tactics of the SDS," he charged.

Apprehension spread throughout the establishment when SDS escalated its program of reaching the workers by launching a "Summer Work-in." The whole idea was to encourage college students, both in and out of SDS, to take more industrial jobs during the summers than they might otherwise, even if it meant making a lot less money, so they could see firsthand what it's like to be a worker. And at the same time, they could make close contact with workers on a much more intimate basis than sporadic strike support efforts allow.

As SDS made very clear in all its promotional literature for the Work-in, the goal was not to arrive at the factories and try to shut them down. It was mostly a learning experience. If a few workers could be attracted to joining the long-range effort, that was great. But time and again the SDS organizers cautioned the Work-in participants not to just shoot their mouths off. The most important thing was to listen and make friends. When questions about the war or racism or women's liberation came up, the student radicals should try quietly to explain how the war was hurting the workers and how they would have to overcome both sexist and racist prejudices to make themselves stronger. But even that had to be done quietly—almost intimately. "No speeches," was an absolute rule.

Although the students were cautioned that they might have to lie about their backgrounds to get jobs, once they were in the plants working they should be open about being student radicals and try to explain what all that turmoil on the campuses was really all about. J. Edgar Hoover and others interpreted all this as an insidious plan SDS had come up with to "infiltrate" the nation's industry and sabotage it. The FBI provided chambers of commerce around the country with copies of the Work-in manual and advised them to reproduce it and mail it out to every big firm in their area. The radicals had to be combed out and headed off.

"The SDS and its followers have left a bitter wake of arson, vandalism, bombings and destruction across the Nation," the FBI director wrote in a machinists' union newspaper. "And you as [machinists] may soon be meeting these fanatic, anarchist revolutionaries." And he went on to hypnotically deputize the workers to help the FBI in its efforts to protect the nation. "You . . . can be alert to the machinations of these youthful extremists. You will not be fooled by their diabolical double talk, their attempts to paint a distorted picture of this country. You will be able to identify them if they come into your plant. You will be able to counter their false and incorrect arguments. You will let them know that you don't accept their revolutionary concepts. The International Assn. of Machinists and Aerospace Workers has played a valiant role in making America the great country which she is today. By helping defeat this SDS offensive this summer, you, as readers of *The Machinist*, will be rendering your Nation a great service."

James M. Collins, a freshman Congressman from Texas, escalated the level of industrial panic even further by issuing in June, 1969, what he falsely claimed was a list of the major defense plants in the South and Southwest that SDS had "targeted for student violence." He went on to list every big defense contractor in five states and claimed SDS had "formulated a most ingenious plan to transfer chaos from the college campus to the industrial assembly lines."

In New York, word leaked out to the newspapers about a

conference that had been held for 250 big businessmen concerned about the Work-in. SDS thought the panel pretty well represented the power structure in microcosm: in addition to the executives, it had an assistant FBI director, the New York police commissioner, a high echelon man from the Pentagon, a university chancellor and a labor leader—all advising on how to cope with the threat or as someone put it, how to "look out for the work-in." And all the while this was going on, executives kept insisting that they weren't at all worried. The businessmen said their workers would never be "taken in" by SDS ideas. But many of them put on extra plant guards following the conference and in some cases they reportedly actually "infiltrated" the production lines with their own men to comb out the students.

None of this had much effect on the SDSers themselves. They had no intention of sabotaging or even direct organizing and didn't see themselves as the threat the government and executives apparently felt they were. Most interpreted the scare wave as an attempt to make the workers too afraid to talk to them once they were "inside." But that didn't happen very often. Several times workers would ask Work-in participants, "Are you one of those radicals?" And when the students admitted they were, and explained why they were, they were almost always received in a friendly way. I know of no cases where the workers actually did, as Hoover seemed to be suggesting, turn in the students to management.

A PL member from City College in New York got an all-night job loading trucks at a freight terminal and made the mistake of being too dogmatic the third night he was on the job. One of the other stevedores started asking him about student rebellions. The radical defended the uprisings somewhat emotionally. It happened during the 4 to 5 A.M. "lunch break," and workers all down the long table stopped eating and playing cards to listen in. Pretty soon the questions got around to Vietnam and the radical spouted statistics about imperialism and how the U.S. was profiting by the war. Suddenly the worker who'd started asking the questions leaped up and shouted: "Listen! When push comes to shove, are you for us or are you for the communists?"

The young radical felt everyone in the room staring at him. He noticed one of the stevedores fingering the handle of his loading hook. "All I could hear was the hum of the air conditioner and my heart beating." Figuring that since he'd gotten himself in that far, there was no principled way out, he answered it straight: "I'm a communist." No one said anything. After a while the other workers started munching again and resumed their card game.

For several nights the Work-iner was frankly afraid of being jumped. He knew one of the workers was a radical Right terrorist—a "Minuteman." Many times he noticed other workers talking amongst themselves and pointing his way. He heard several say, "That's the communist." Then he'd go over to them and say, "That's right," and explain what he thought it meant to be a communist. He worked on that way for the rest of the summer. He talked to almost all the workers, faced almost no hostility, and he was never turned in by his fellow workers.

Exhausted from the unaccustomed strain of manual work, the Work-iners still try to keep up their schedule of evening meetings. And at least once a week during the summer, the Work-in people gather in small study groups of about ten participants to discuss their experiences on the job. Much of the time is spent passing along the things the workers have said which seem to validate the political assumptions the students had previously made on the basis of sheer theory. Sometimes the Work-iners hear things so close to SDS' own rhetoric it's almost unbelievable. Mike Sobel, a really friendly, articulate Harvard student who was working in a lower Manhattan hardware supply house told the study group I was attending last summer about a black co-worker who turned to him one day and said:

"Do you know the capitalist pig who owns this place is exploiting you and your labor?" Mike started to grin and chuckle at the ironic emergence of revolutionary rhetoric from a fellow he wouldn't have presumed to speak to the same way.

"Don't laugh, it's true," the worker said, beginning an explanation.

"I know it's true," Mike finally got out. "What can we do about it?" Then his co-worker just shrugged. For most of the radicals, that was the biggest frustration of the Work-in. They came to the work, not with the arrogance Hoover and others accused them of, but with an almost tender timidity and deep respect for the workers. They grew really fond of them and found their plight was worse than they had expected. But they could do relatively little in the immediate sense to help them. Some felt the frustration more than others. Sharon Levine, a very intense Boston University student who was working in a nearly all black garment district sweatshop, felt it most of all in our group.

"We keep saying how brutally bad it is where we work. Man, I know how bad it is. Those women are taking home about $60 dollars a week and that hardly buys food for some of their families. Everything in that shop is absolutely hopeless, and we can't do anything to help. That's the limitation of this Work-in. What the hell am I supposed to do? What's the logical conclusion of all this?" The logical conclusion was that eventually Sharon's shop and every other shop would finally grind to a halt. The workers would recognize their own power and would shut them down. She could try to help them see that, everyone told her, and tell them that the students will do what they can to help. It was like the old freedom song: "Keep your mind on the prize—hold on." In the end Sharon felt good about the Work-in. "I used to try to tell people what it's like for the workers and they'd say, 'How do you know?' Now I can say I've worked with them."

There were plenty of frustrations along with the inspirations. Mike Sobel was unpacking cases of pliers that had been imported from Japan. He and another worker would unwrap the newspaper the pliers came in, then pack them into shipments with new newspaper. "Wow, it's kind of strange to think of guys way over in Japan wrapping this stuff up in newspaper just like we do," Mike said. "They work for a lot less over there," the man responded. Mike picked him up on it.

"Yeah. That's why this guy brings the stuff in instead of using American stuff. He's after cheap labor. They call that imperialism." And with that word the conversation suddenly died.

Even some inspirations turn out to be frustrations. A while back two Work-in SDSers managed to get jobs in the same factory without knowing the other was there. The second day on the job one of them saw the slogan "POWER TO THE WORKERS" scrawled on the bathroom wall. He was amazed and went on with his work convinced that at least one of the other guys out there was a revolutionary. The next day he met his friend and told him about the writing on the wall. "I know," the other said. "I put it there."

But the students could, on occasion, accomplish minor victories. They could break the unwritten rule of not telling your co-workers how much you're making. Jim Fisher, the Harvard minister who confronted David Rockefeller, was working in a pipe factory in Boston during one Work-in summer. He'd been hired at $2.50 an hour and he knew that the boss was paying most of the Puerto Ricans in the shop only $1.80. It cost him his job, but he told his co-workers how much he was getting. The other workers got together to pressure the boss to pay them as much as he'd paid the white college guy who worked no better or harder than they did.

For most of the school year that followed the split in SDS, chapters concentrated their efforts in building an alliance with the workers right on the campuses. At Harvard, SDS held a dean captive in his office trying to pressure the university to stop paying experienced black painters "apprentice" wages. At Yale, SDS came to the support of a black dining hall waitress who'd been repeatedly harassed by her boss until she finally threw cranberry juice in his face and was fired. The radicals held four university officials captive for several hours to press the demand; the university struck back by suspending forty-seven students.

Very similar campaigns were carried on at almost every school in the country where there was an SDS chapter. Soon almost every radical group was at least trying to seem concerned with the workers.

But such struggles weren't what many SDSers and nearly all the rest of the country's college students expected from the famous radical student organization. Only Berkeley SDS, which deliberately looked beyond the narrow concept of the campus Worker-Student Alliance, managed to launch a tremendous battle in the old SDS tradition in 1969-70. And when SDS generally failed to win a leadership role in the short-lived national student strike in May, 1970, a number of SDSers began to recognize they had a problem.

"When they moved without us this spring it was clear we had lost control of the student movement," Jerry Harris of the University of Chicago told an SDS planning meeting that summer. "We've got to get that lead back."

Part of the problem was that Progressive Labor, with its narrow and highly advanced concept for what really makes revolution, had moved from a position of leadership of a *sect* of SDS to running the *whole* organization. And in the process it hadn't broadened or even adapted its original program to make it more applicable to the massive organization as a whole. Internal problems began growing up in the organization again, exacerbated by the frustrations the chapters had suffered in trying to organize great crowds of students around the grievances of the campus workers. A few bitter chapters, particularly the big ones at Columbia and the University of Chicago, broke with Progressive Labor by the time SDS met in December, 1970, for its first convention since the 1969 split. And all of a sudden the old-timers began predicting that another split was brewing in SDS.

CHAPTER FIFTEEN

AMERICAN REVOLUTION: A SECOND COMING

As long as it is organizing students, SDS will keep up its attacks on the universities. But in the three years since the Columbia rebellion, it has become more and more obvious within SDS that there's no way to eradicate the evils that the universities perpetuate without going off-campus after the forces that fostered those evils in the first place. And so SDS is getting ready for the all-out assault directly on Mother Society. The battles on the campuses will probably soon become only staging actions for the great stuggle that's got to go on outside.

The universities have hardly been sanitized. They're still terrible employers and they're still in every way the servants of the government and the corporations. When the cereal industry comes under question for peddling "empty calories," rival corporations get together and defend themselves through the mouth of a Harvard nutrition "expert." And when the CIA comes up with a plan to regain control of Indonesia, it gathers up a team of economic and military advisers from Berkeley, MIT, Cornell and Harvard to engineer the deposing of Sukarno and the slaughter of more than 300,000 civilians presumed to be "pro-Communist."

"Every week we are told by some 'courageous' administrator that the university system must not allow itself to become 'politicized' by radical students," said an editorial in *Ramparts*, which reconstructed the Indonesian massacre. "But it is clear that institutions like the Ford Foundation and the Pentagon politicized it long ago. The 'scientific' intellectual doctrines it promotes as objective and neutral are in fact the political dogmas with which U.S. agencies and interests dominate people in the Third World. And behind the facade of its abstract models lie the techniques and personnel for the management of a modern empire."

But the universities have learned a lot in the years they've had to contend with the radicals. They've hidden, or will lose, the most flagrant evidences of how they serve the system. ROTC is already gone from many campuses and will in all likelihood be eradicated althogether in a few years. War research has either been abolished or camouflaged under inscrutable academic titles, or farmed out to off-campus institutes which the universities can claim they have nothing to do with. The CIA and the military don't come recruiting at all on a number of campuses and do so at many schools only under heavy cloaking. So many of the prominent "issues" the radicals used to be able to rely on are now gone. SDS chapters now spend long hours searching for issues that will dramatize evils well enough to mobilize the masses of usually sessile students. And when the radicals do find an issue, the chances are the administrations will find a way to co-opt it.

The Columbia administration was intransigent in going ahead in 1968 with its plan to build the new gymnasium in Morningside Park. The more students and community people protested, the more emphatic the university was that it would not be "bullied." Its only gesture towards co-optation, the eleventh-hour offer of a minuscule swimming pool for the community, was so feeble it only incited even greater resentment.

But Columbia has learned a lot. When students and the community started getting together again in 1970 to force the university to open up several hundred vacant apartments to poor people in desperate need of housing, the university slipped right through the radicals' fingers. Columbia negotiated a deal with the city. In return for quite a tidy annual revenue to be paid by the city, it would allow welfare recipients to occupy some apartments (as they were preparing to do by force anyway). But only on a temporary basis. When Columbia decided to take the housing back, the city would clear the tenants out. The radicals lost their issue and Columbia kept its development plans unobstructed while turning a neat profit at the same time.

SDS' work on the campuses is going to have to concentrate

on the more basic role of the universities. "These desperate searches for issues aren't the way anymore," says Ed Connelly, the "veteran" who helped lead the SDS tour of Columbia. "What's wrong with this university isn't secret. It's how it is openly propping up the corruption and brutality of society as a whole." Operating on that assumption, the targets on campus become plentiful indeed. Every aspect of the universities that serves as a stepping stone to bourgeois life becomes fair game.

All the courses aimed at preparing the students for "careers": all the professional schools, especially business and law, which turn out the functionaries of capitalism (medicine might be spared with only massive reforms since presumably there will still be some health problems after the revolution); all research for the government and corporations, and a lot of it that's supposed to be "pure"; and virtually all recruiting, not just by the CIA and Dow Chemical, but by anyone other than the representative of a revolutionary organization—it will all have to go. People will still come to learn at the universities, but they'll learn what they're curious about—not what will prepare them for careers. And the way many radicals envision it, the bulk of the curriculum will be taken up with revolutionary theory and history.

But fighting for all of this will not build a revolution. It will merely provide a program for campus radicals and prepare them for the broader struggle. "You can't have a revolution on campus, but you can have revolutionaries," an SDS leader from Boston explains.

The period of transition to this concept of the student movement will put radical activity into something of a dormant state. On many of the campuses where tremendous uprisings have occurred already and there's a dearth of other issues, educating is already underway for a broader attack. At other schools the lessons of rebellions elsewhere are being digested and a serious attempt by SDS chapters is being made to avoid a repetition of others' mistakes. Everywhere there is a tactical gap between terrorism which hurts instead of helps, and mass actions like building occupations which are now coped with quite easily by the wiser administrations. But this hardly means the movement is dead.

The press, especially the news magazines, seem to make an annual habit of writing off student radicalism as an extinct phenomenon during the slow winter months and then describing it "coming out of nowhere" when the spring thaw brings on an even greater level of struggle. Now a spring, or several springs, may be coming on when most campuses actually will be relatively quiet. The media are bound to repeat the assertions even more confidently that it's all over for the student Left. But that will reflect a failure to understand what the student rebellions were all about. Since nothing major has changed in society, the forces that brought on those years of battle are still very much in play. If there's no visible result for a while, that ought to bode even more peril for the establishment. The rebellion's just getting itself together. It will emerge with a much more basic threat—and probably a lot stronger.

However outlandish the radical rhetoric may seem, the United States may well be on the way to revolution. I don't think any society believed it was going to have one until it was actually underway. Marie Antoinette was confident enough in her power to utter, "Let them eat cake," when she should have been having nightmares about the guillotine. It doesn't make much sense to argue that a country like this one, because of its advanced state of industrialization, can't have a revolution. The same claims could have been made before America, France, Russia or China rose up. Thomas Jefferson said the country should have a revolution every twenty years to keep it headed straight. By that standard we've fallen behind by nine revolutions, with the tenth to come due five years from now.

Revolutions occur when a sizable part of the population (not necessarily even the majority) becomes convinced that its problems are unsolvable within the existing system. And judging from the discontent that is now seething in every corner of American society, there's every reason to believe a sizable part of our population has already concluded the system does not have the capacity to heal itself. It's neither a coincidence nor a fad that there is open rebellion going on not just on the campuses but in the ghettos and in the streets at the same time as the workers are rebelling against both their employers and the unions. There is so much crime people wonder if society itself is falling apart. It well may be. As Yeats described, in *The Second Coming:* "Things fall apart; the centre cannot hold; / Mere anarchy is loosed upon the

world, / the blood-dimned tide is loosed, and everywhere / The
ceremony of innocence is drowned." Fourteen million Americans
are on welfare and five and a half million are unemployed. High
schools are now prisons. The armed forces are now increasingly
beset with desertion, sabotage, subversion and open refusal to
obey orders—an outbreak of rebellion that could literally leave the
establishment defenseless. Policemen, always the force for breaking wildcat strikes, are wildcatting themselves. The Catholic
Church gives us the Berrigans and a "Priests' Plot," and even Dr.
Spock becomes a public enemy. Apparently no one is safely loyal
enough to the government not to have J. Edgar Hoover tap his
phone—save J. Edgar himself, of course.

At a press conference during the Cambodian crisis last year,
a reporter actually asked President Nixon in all seriousness
whether or not he thought the country was on the brink of
revolution. And the President found it pertinent enough to give a
long and somber answer. Of course he said that he didn't think it
was. But a year before, every reporter in the country would have
laughed at the very suggestion of asking the President such a thing.
It was an astounding moment that no one gave much notice. I
mentioned it to a friend who's a Washington journalist and he later
astonished me even more by suggesting that the President himself
had *planted* the question so he'd have a chance to talk the idea
down!

There is so much rebellious force in the country now that the
police worry every time a big crowd is gathered—for any reason.
And they are right to worry. A rock festival turned into a huge
rebellion recently in Chicago. And one major college actually
called off a football game recently because the administrators were
afraid to let that many students come together in one uncontain-
able crowd. Conductors on the Long Island Railroad wouldn't
work in 1970 until armed guards were put on the trains to protect
them from the commuters who were being tortured by the constant deterioration of train service and had to take it out on
someone. Housewives have taken to the streets over inflation. And
there's increasing plausibility in talk of a "taxpayer's rebellion."
Even the businessmen who've supposedly made it in the system
take as many drugs and seem as miserable as their children.

About a year ago, newspapers ran a two-paragraph item off
the UPI wires, reporting that a group of the biggest corporations

were getting together to spend several million dollars on the construction of a fortified underground complex where vital business data and documents could be stored and where top executives could take refuge in times of extreme social instability. But if the revolution does come, the millionaires are bound to find that going underground will do them no more good than it did the Weathermen.

Politicians keep decrying the senseless lack of order in the country. But they seem to be talking about more and more rebels while fewer and fewer people listen to them. The Left hopes to unify these forces of rebelliousness into a revolution. And the continued deterioration of the economy is helping to bring the disparate rebels together. Certainly SDS doesn't need the President to know which way the wind blows.

Several SDSers were walking across the Columbia campus not long ago when one of them pointed out the names engraved over the entrance to the university library: Homer, Herodotus, Sophocles, Plato, Aristotle, Demosthenes, Cicero, and Virgil.

"Someday soon those guys' names are going to come down and be replaced with revolutionaries," he said.

"Leave Plato," someone said. "He was all right."

"What names do you think will go up there instead?" another SDSer asked the one who'd had the vision.

"Oh, certainly Marx, Lenin and Mao. . . ." He was bewildered at not having any more candidates—then broke into a wide grin. "And maybe one of us."